KENT COOPER and The Associated Press

AN AUTOBIOGRAPHY

COOPER, Kent, newspaperman; b. Columbus, Ind., Mar. 22, 1880; s. George William and Sina (Green) C.; student Ind. U., 1898-1899; hon. LL.D., Drake U., 1932, Ind. Univ., 1941, Clark Univ., 1945, Northwestern Univ., 1947; Litt. D., New York Univ., 1948; LL.D., Univ. Western Ontario, 1951, St. Lawrence Univ., 1951; m. Daisy McBride, 1905 (died 1920); 1 dau., Jane (Mrs. George L. Seeger); married Sarah A. Gibbs, 1942. Began writing for newspapers, 1891, reporter Indianapolis papers, 1899-1903; bureau mgr. Scripps-McRae Press Assn., Indianapolis 1903-07; traveling rep. United Press, 1907-10, in connection with delivery of news by telephone, idea of which he conceived; apptd. traveling insp. Associated Press, 1910, chief of traffic dept., 1912, asst. gen. mgr., 1920-25, gen. mgr., 1925-48, and exec. dir., 1943-51, in charge news service and personnel of The Associated Press and its subsidiaries; est. Associated Press (now La Prensa Asociada) in South America in 1918; conceived, 1926, and est., 1935, The Asso. Press system of Wirephoto, a wire method of news photo delivery, the first method of that kind; est. Asso. Press world news service, 1938; chairman Board La Prensa Asociada, 1940-51; est. Associated Press of Great Britain, 1931, pres., 1931-38, chmn. 1938-51; est. Asso. Press of Germany, pres. 1931-38, chairman of board, 1938-51; pres. Press Assn., Inc., 1940-51; pres. Wide World, Inc., 1941-51; pres. New York City News Assn., Inc., 1942-51. Mem. adv. bd. Pulitzer School of Journalism, Columbia Univ., 1929-56; advocate of world-wide freedom of press, aided in bringing about resolution passed by Congress, Sept. 1944. Fellow Sigma Delta Chi (journalistic fraternity), 1954; Designated "Significant Sig of Sigma Chi" (college fraternity), 1952; Designated "Outstanding Hoosier of 1944" by Indiana Society of New York. Clubs: Dutch Treat, University, Silurians (N. Y. City); Everglades, Bath and Tennis, Four Arts (Palm Beach, Fla.); Member American Society Composers, Authors and Publishers; "Distinguished Service Member" American Society of Newspaper Editors; "Honorary Member" National Association of Science Writers, Inc. Author: *Barriers Down,* 1942; *Anna Zenger, Mother of Freedom,* 1946; Foreword to *In Our Image,* ed. by Houston Harte; *The Right to Know,* 1956. Composer and lyricist: *About the Girl* (operetta), 1943, and numerous songs and marches. Address: 50 Rockefeller Plaza, New York 20, N. Y.

KENT
COOPER
and The
Associated Press

AN AUTOBIOGRAPHY

RANDOM HOUSE   NEW YORK

070.92
C78 K
37822
july 59

CONTENTS

ILLUSTRATIONS

KENT COOPER and The Associated Press

AN AUTOBIOGRAPHY

1

WHO PROMPTED

THIS WRITING?

AT A LARGE DINNER in honor of a renowned New York surgeon, a newlywed, I happened to be seated next to the charming bride. At once she started to shower me with unending praise of her "marvelous, wonderful" husband. While I was politely giving her my undivided attention, the soup course was served. In crescendo she continued to praise her great surgeon. The soup was taken away untouched. The fish course was brought. Still she talked. The fish was removed untouched. By the time the entrée arrived, she suddenly became interested in food but asked: "And what do you do?"

"Did you ever hear of The Associated Press?" I asked.

Balancing a forkful, she exclaimed: "Oh, yes, certainly! My husband takes it. He takes all the newspapers."

The lady was just one of millions who could have given no better answer.

Yet there is no other organization on earth whose product touches the daily lives of so many people as does that of The Associated Press. In this country alone a total of perhaps 150,000,000 people see its news dispatches and news photos identified daily by its initials (AP), or its logotype (AP), or its full name in each copy of 50,000,000 newspapers printed and circulated daily. Many more millions hear it similarly identified in radio and video broadcasts.

Any other name so widely connected with its product and thus identified for more than 150,000,000 people surely would be known for what it is and what it does. This is not so with The Associated Press, "the most complicated and delicately balanced piece of intangible machinery ever conceived by mortal man."

Simply stated, The Associated Press is a mutual nonprofit, co-operative membership association that collects and delivers news in words and pictures instantaneously for publication throughout the free world by several thousand newspapers, radio and television stations. Its members represent all shades of political, social, economic and religious thought. They require that its news be as accurate and unbiased as human endeavor can make it. The membership elects a board of eighteen directors from among its number, all of whom serve without remuneration, including the president of The Associated Press, who is elected by the Board from among its members. The Board also appoints the chief executive of The Associated Press. To him it delegates complete control of the news service and personnel. It was this position which I held for more than a quarter of a century.

Until 1893, the news in all sections of this country was almost exclusively provincial. It was made so by a number of local news agencies, all co-operatives, all interested primarily in vicinage news, and all having the words "Associated Press" in their names. The largest were the following:

The New England newspapers, excluding Connecticut, isolated themselves and their readers with the formation of the New England Associated Press, with stress upon New England news.

The Connecticut newspapers organized the Connecticut Associated Press and localized the news for their readers. For them, too, the rest of the country had little interest.

The New York City newspapers co-operated under the name of the New York Associated Press. The oldest of all the groups that used the name, it was organized in 1848.

The upstate New York publishers organized the New York State Associated Press, with prime interest in state news, mostly from Albany, the state capital.

In the South was the Southern Associated Press. Some of its newspapers were still soothing the wounds of defeat inflicted by the "damn Yankees." Others were trying to make their readers forget by arousing in them a longing for acceptance into a newly integrated national life with all sections of the country.

In the group of central states the loosely knit organization was given the misnomer of the Western Associated Press, though the territory west of its membership was larger than that east of it. Its news service, like all the others, was strictly provincial.

The twin cities of Minneapolis-St. Paul were the center of the group that called itself the Northwestern Associated Press, equally a misnomer because it had no members west or north of Minnesota and the eastern Dakotas. Its headquarters were in St. Paul. If it took its eyes off local occurrences, it raised them toward the Northwest to sponsor a northwestern empire that would reach to the Pacific Coast.

Another organization was the California Associated Press, which in haphazard fashion served newspapers in the mountain states and the truly northwestern states of Oregon and Washington.

With all eight of these groups stressing vicinage news, there was no cohesive relationship whatever between them and no national concept.

Then, in 1893, The Associated Press came into being as the first national press association. Through use of the telegraph, Associated Press employees diffused information country-wide so that the same news of national and international importance was read the same day in the same words in every state in the union.

The change was so marked that it seemed as if a magic wand had been waved to create the free flow of information from and to the North, the East, the West and South into a national news report. With the simultaneous, country-wide reading of the same news, America experienced the most potent unifying agent imaginable. A consciousness of country-wide togetherness was awakened. With the news leading the way, it and other contributing factors developed a national spirit that made America what it is.

That The Associated Press played the most important role in this development has never received adequate recognition in American history.

The idea of a national organization was conceived first in the western group, with headquarters in Chicago, solely because of the rapacious demands imposed upon it by the privately owned United Press of New York, which had the exclusive right to sell in America the news of the European cartel headed by Reuters.

The doom of that United Press was sealed in 1893 when the western group incorporated The Associated Press as a national co-operative to replace all the various provincial groups. The new organization planned to take into its membership every existing newspaper in the country. When word of this reached London it sounded ominous to Reuters, whose contract with the United Press was expiring.

Preferring to deal directly with a national association of newspapers, the Reuter agency offered the exclusive cartel contract to the newly formed Associated Press. It was promptly accepted. From that moment the new agency went forward to success.

It is emphasized, however, that there was then no patriotic motive for establishing a truly united nation. This unity developed without the members of the new association ever having thought of it. What they wanted to do was to kill the privately owned United Press, and they did. It succumbed in 1897.

In return for their allegiance to the national Associated Press, nearly all newspapers which took membership in it were guaranteed that no newspaper that might later be established in their respective cities would be permitted to join the national Associated Press without the consent of The Associated Press members in those cities. This promise of exclusivity was considered by all members to be a "franchise" and that is what they called it. Thus, besides killing the United Press, creation of a monopoly to protect existing papers against future competitors, instead of a patriotic desire to establish a united nation, was the motive. But regardless of the motive, the organization effectively disseminated national intelligence nationally and created that unity.

Of all the members in the new association, the owners of southern newspapers hailed the new development most enthusiastically and with gratitude. For them entrance into the membership of the first national press association meant that Civil War hatreds finally had been forgotten. They were welcomed in full brotherhood by the publishers of the North, the East and West. H. H. Cabiness, of the Atlanta *Journal,* eloquently expressed the South's appreciation of this in a speech at a banquet of members of the new national Associated Press in Chicago in 1895:

"I consider this the most fortunate day of southern journalism when I am permitted to come and be one of you in the great work of building up this national news association. I have felt all along when I was not a member of this association that when I did become one, I would be like the old woman who said, in the exuberance of her joy, that if she ever did get to heaven, she never would let the Lord hear the last of it. Now I feel that way. I not only appreciate, but I re-echo the kind, brotherly sentiments of the chairman of this meeting, in welcoming the South back to be one of you. Long ago, many years ago, we came back into the Union, but it took years and years of desolation, years of suffering, to bring us into the cordial feelings which I believe we are experiencing tonight. I want to say to you that the breezes which come from the Gulf are not more redolent of the perfume of those flowers of the South than southern hearts are filled with loyalty to this good Union.

"I realize that time is limited. I would like to talk to you about the bonds of sympathy which are being linked between the North and the South, and which are growing stronger day by day.

"We have passed through our darkest hours. In the morn, after the storm has passed away, and in the brightness of the sun, you see all nature robed in the most luscious gifts she can bestow. So it is with us. We have passed through, and are passing through, desolation and hard times and privations, but the time is coming when all these troubles will be gone and we will bask in the sunlight of a kind and smiling Providence."

If the exigencies of the newspapers in the nineties had not been as critical as they were, and monopoly against future competitors had not appeared so attractive, the cohesive national news agency so feelingly welcomed by the South might have come at a later time. But it did come then, and as it functioned, loyalty and devotion to it inspired its workers to deliver truthful and unbiased news, the ideal that rules its existence. Those that competed with it in later years followed that same ideal to the great good fortune of the American people.

The employees of The Associated Press, upon whom rests its success, have built a noble edifice. Not only the newspaper owners who financed The Associated Press but all the people of this country of ours are the beneficiaries of their work.

While references to the beginnings of this national development reach back into the nineties, this is the story of how one of its employees in the second quarter of the twentieth century radically changed the work of the great news agency so as:

First, to enlarge the scope of its news coverage to include information, pictures and news features that interest everybody and thus tremendously widen the circle of newspaper readers;

Second, having done so, to make the product lift that enlarged circle of American readers out of their isolation into an awareness of how large the world is and acquaint them with human activities and aspirations everywhere;

Third, to make it the world's greatest news and news photo agency with its news, pictures and news features available through The Associated Press, not alone to the people of the United States, but to as many in every country in the whole world as could be reached, hopeful that the truth would contribute to mutual international understanding.

With gratitude I attest to the fact that I succeeded in accomplishing those three changes because of the confidence in me by The Associated Press Board of Directors and the co-operation of The Associated Press employees. The names of the directors are listed in each of the association's annual reports. I wish I could name each employee who ardently accepted and helped to advance my militant plans to enlarge the mission of this great agency which was the first to set and has been the longest to maintain the highest of unbiased reportorial news standards.

For many years I have been asked by my wife to write an autobiography that would put into permanent form an account of these accomplishments. I also have been asked to do so by individual Associated Press members and book publishers.

Undertaking it, however, was delayed until some years after my retirement so that I could gain perspective and therefore be able to write from a detached viewpoint that would produce a story free of a mass of detail, even then mentioning only a few developments that have had and may yet have deep significance.

In 1958, the Board of Directors of The Associated Press formally requested that this autobiography be written. Because my wife was first to suggest and urge that it be done and because of her help through the years, I dedicate it to her.

"I dedicate it to her."

2

A NEW CENTURY

DAWNS

THE TWENTIETH CENTURY made its bow. A successful Boston publisher decided it was time for him to absent himself in order to test the ability of his sons by letting them take over the management of his newspaper. Upon his departure, he told them that the future of the newspaper was entirely in their hands and that he would not be available for advice. He wished them luck. Returning after what to him seemed a score of years, he went to the office. There were changes, many of them. The tempo of the place seemed to have quickened into startling activity and efficiency. New faces were everywhere. Wandering about, he entered a newly painted room filled with filing cases. A bespectacled young lady was in charge. They were strangers to each other.

"Can I help you, sir?" she asked.

"Yes, tell me what you do here."

"This," the young lady said, "is the morgue. I am in charge of it. We have here information on everybody of importance in New England—useful information for publication upon death. We call them 'obits' for short."

"Have you got one on General Taylor, the retired owner of this paper?"

"That old fellow? From what I hear about him around here he must have been years behind the times." She pulled out a drawer, lifted a bulky file, and said: "Here's his obit."

"That's very efficient," said the publisher. Then, with a twinkle in his eye, he asked: "Can you tell me when you are going to print it?"

"No," she replied, "but I'll find out."

"Never mind," he said. "I really don't want to know!"

That is the story General Taylor, of the Boston *Globe,* once told me about himself. Morgues in many newspaper offices were then new. They were steps toward modernization. A new generation was taking charge in many places.

At the same time, the news content of a few newspapers was being refashioned. News with wide human appeal, both interesting and important, was included. Without it the great day-by-day news panorama of American life had been incomplete—so woefully incomplete as to leave the picture starkly unreal.

For more than two decades of the new century, however, the work of the world's largest press association was unaffected by this new, all inclusive concept of what constitutes news. Indeed, not until 1925, when I became general manager, was a change reflected in the news report of The Associated Press. In other words, The Associated Press then began to make its contribution toward modern news presentation through its country-wide wire facilities. By so doing, it changed the newspaper-reading appetite of the nation. This it did by originating its own changes and adopting those of its member newspapers. Though a little late in starting to give the whole picture, it became and remains a restless, energetic, complete recorder of the story of human life in the twentieth century.

In the intricate task of collecting, writing, photographing and transmitting AP news in words and pictures, thousands have labored. Through the years they came from here, there and everywhere in the news vineyards. A record of how and what each individual and each newspaper staff contributed to Associated Press work in its first century would fill volumes. But it all was done year after year in harmony with a code which I once defined as "true and unbiased news—the highest original moral concept ever developed in America and given the world."

I got my first "smell of printer's ink" in 1891, at eleven years of age, while folding four-page newspapers for the delivery route I carried in Columbus, Indiana, then a town of four thousand people. During summer vacations in my high school days and after one year at Indiana University, I worked as a reporter for Columbus papers.

In 1899, my dying father wrote the last letter of his distinguished lifetime. It was a request addressed to his friend John H. Holliday, who, with Major Richards, had just announced the forthcoming estab-

lishment of a newspaper competitor of the Indianapolis *News*. My father wanted me to have a job on the new paper. A month later, before I was out of my teens, my father died, and I was a full-fledged reporter on the big, newly established Indianapolis *Press* at $12 a week. I was assigned to the court-house "run."

Getting my first big story was a lucky break even though I had to share it with Ray Long, a reporter of the opposition paper, the In-

Indianapolis Press *Local Staff (1899)—Gavin Payne, city editor, seated* (center), *holding glasses; his nineteen-year-old $12-a-week reporter standing at extreme right wearing Sigma Chi fraternity pin.*

dianapolis *News*. Ray afterward went to New York and became editor of Hearst's *Cosmopolitan* magazine. The story was about a development in Indianapolis in connection with the seething political campaign in Kentucky in 1899 which resulted in the election of William Goebel, a Democrat, to the governorship of the state, and his murder. It made Goebel's Republican opponent, William S. Taylor, an unwilling resident of Indianapolis as a fugitive.

Taylor was suspected of having knowledge of the crime. Governor Durbin of Indiana, a Republican, refused to extradite Taylor to Kentucky, but the refugee willingly agreed to give a deposition for use in the prosecution of Caleb Powers, who had been jailed in the Kentucky capital for the murder.

Taylor visited the official court stenographer in the court house in Indianapolis one day in 1900. They were closeted together for nearly two hours. Both refused to tell me more than that Taylor had dictated and sworn to a deposition for use in the Powers trial. Hoping to get the Kentuckian to talk, I walked along with him to the post office two blocks away and saw him mail a large envelope. Returning alone to the court stenographer's unlocked office, which was unoccupied, I sat down by a typewriter table and accidentally smudged my hand by laying it on a sheet of carbon paper. I picked up the sheet, held it to the light and was reading it when Ray Long came in.

"I'll bet you've got the Taylor deposition right on that sheet of carbon," Long declared. He looked down into the wastebasket and spied some discarded carbon sheets. We held all of the carbons to the light. One sheet had been used only twice and the lines did not overrun. Others were used more than that, but some of the wording could be deciphered. Working together, we extracted enough sentences to make a fairly complete transcript.

The Indianapolis *Press* thought the story hot enough to get out an extra edition, a copy of which Taylor bought. It brought the Kentuckian posthaste to the *Press* with a violently worded demand that he be told where the paper got the text. The city editor turned Taylor over to me.

"Who do you think disclosed it?" I asked.

"Not the court stenographer," said Taylor. "I watched him type the document and took the original and the only other copy with me. You saw me take the original and mail it. The other is in my pocket now. No one has seen it."

"Then who did disclose it?" I asked, feigning innocence.

"I know," Taylor said. "Someone in the post office saw me mail it in the plain envelope I used, opened it and copied it. That's how you got it, isn't it?"

"No one in the post office would dare do that!" I exclaimed.

"Why not?" Taylor asked. "I know now that it's being done all the time. I've suspected it but had no proof before. My mail is being opened in the post office. I'll see to it that the federal authorities make you tell who it was in the post office that gave it to you."

He was angry and determined, but did not realize he had disclosed a good second-day news story. I kept on asking questions and gaining answers until I had ample quotes on the charge that the United States mails were being rifled to get copies of everything Taylor had sent by post.

The next morning I told the postmaster about Taylor's charge. The postmaster said it could not be true but he would investigate. My second day's story quoting Taylor's charge against the post office was exclusive. Since no one else was present while he was talking with me, Taylor could have denied it in the Indianapolis morning papers of the next day. However, still angry and venting his spleen on the postal authorities, he repeated the charge to reporters of both papers.

With good first-page stories two days in succession, I wrote a little feature story the third day telling how the quotes really were obtained. Did I get any compliments from my city editor? Not at all! So I asked if I had done the three stories all right. The city editor coolly answered: "That's what you're expected to do!"

In Louisville, Kentucky, there was then an evening newspaper called the *Post*. Irvin S. Cobb, out of Paducah, had been a recent addition to the staff. His first out-of-town assignment came after the *Post* printed the story of the Taylor deposition. Cobb was sent to Indianapolis to interview Taylor. He got there the day the little feature story was printed telling how the deposition was obtained from discarded carbon sheets.

Cobb sought me out, and I introduced him to Long. Years later, Long bought many of Cobb's humorous stories for *Cosmopolitan*. The friendship of the three of us endured until the death of Long and Cobb some forty years afterward. My last outing with Long, however, was thirty years later, on a 60,000-acre hunter's paradise at Sea Island, Georgia. Cobb could not be there but other congenial friends were, including two former reporters originally from Indianapolis—Roy W. Howard and T. R. Shipp.

*Nimrods—Sea Island, Ga. (1928)—*Left to right: *K.C.;*
Roy W. Howard; Ben Ames Williams; Robert H. (Bob) Davis;
John N. Wheeler; John Oliver LaGorce; Ray Long; Thomas R. Shipp.

When my paper was put to press each afternoon, there were extra chores to be done. In 1900, the *Press,* like the New England paper referred to, had no morgue. When a prominent citizen died, data on his life hastily had to be collected and an obit written. I thought those I had seen were dreary reading. I wanted to enliven the stories about the dead by making them humanly interesting. One day I was assigned to do an obit of a businessman who, though successful, had been an introvert. Little was known about him. To me that was a challenge to make an unknown man well known after he was dead!

I knew the man's friends would read anything printed about him, no matter how dull. But one of my ambitions as a reporter was that any story I wrote about anything should be made sufficiently interesting to make good reading for everybody. So I resolved to find out three things about the late citizen which would interest others who, like myself, had never known the man:

First, I set out to get something the deceased had said or done that was amusing; second, I sought something he had said or done that was of sentimental value; and third, something he had said or done that was constructive. I got in touch with some of the man's associates and produced a story that brought a recommendation from Gavin L. Payne, my city editor, for a raise. The benighted managing editor of the *Press* vetoed the raise and gave Payne "hell."

"If you had given that story to me," he said, "it could have been entwined in an editorial as a beautiful tribute. Then it would have done some good. His firm is a big advertiser in the other papers. If we had worked that story into an editorial, it would have been the paper speaking of him officially, and we might have gotten a good advertising account. As it is, what an unknown reporter wrote won't help at all."

Nevertheless, it did help. The advertising manager of the *Press* had a bright idea on his own account. After the funeral, he personally presented a dozen marked copies of the paper to the dead man's son. He told him he could have more if he wished. Not only did he ask for and get more, but a few days later the firm's advertisement appeared in the *Press* for the first time. It was a big display. I, however, never got the raise. That was the reward for an endeavor to write an interesting obit in 1900!

Eighteen months later I was out of a job when the Indianapolis *Press* discontinued publication. Because I had been thrilled by the melodies of Victor Herbert's operettas, I wrote Herbert, who was then the conductor of the Pittsburgh Orchestra, asking for an opportunity to manage a tour for a dozen concerts in as many Indiana cities.

The tour was arranged. I was to get one-half of anything over $500 taken in at each of the concerts. Since the audiences were small, I never got a cent out of it. But I did get acquainted with Victor Herbert and was with him when he wrote down the first four bars of his greatest waltz. It happened this way:

We traveled from town to town in a day coach. Herbert always took the front seat so that he could put his feet up on the vacant seat that faced him. I sat opposite, adoring my idol. Herbert was humming and tra-la-ing as the train rolled along. Suddenly, between Indianapolis and Anderson, Indiana, he reached into his pocket for a pencil and paper. He had the pencil but no paper, so he just pulled out his stiffly laundered reversible cuff, which well-dressed men wore in those days, made a staff of five lines on it and jotted down some notes.

That afternoon I asked him what he wrote on his cuff on the train. Herbert said it was four bars of a melody. I asked for a copy of those four bars because I had seen him write them. He went to his hotel room and made the copy. Having been an amateur musician and composer in my boyhood, I took the four bars home, improvised twenty-eight additional bars and made a complete waltz of thirty-two measures.

Several years later I happened to see Herbert in Chicago. He said: "I'm back in the theatre. As Klaw and Erlanger refused to give me 3 percent of the gross receipts on each performance of my operettas, I quit composing. Now Charles Dillingham is paying my terms and I have an opening here tonight for a thing called 'Mlle. Modiste.' I'd like for you to hear it." He took out his card, wrote on it "Studebaker Theatre—Admit 1" and signed it.

I took the card to the theatre and luckily got a seat in the third row left, for that night's performance. Fritzi Scheff was the star. Her entrance song was, "If I Were on the Stage." Its refrain is, "Kiss Me Again" and begins with the first four bars of the waltz that Herbert had written on his cuff as we rode along that day on the train.

I saw Herbert several years afterward at the Lotos Club in New York. We enjoyed recounting the Indiana trip. Herbert remembered writing the four bars on his cuff. I sat down at the piano and played those four bars plus the twenty-eight measures I had added. Herbert listened intently and then, with the skill of the great musician that he was, he sat down and played my melody, note for note, but with a masterful arrangement of chords and shadings. He said that he had a trunk full of starting melodies to which he turned when given lyrics and that he must have done that with "Kiss Me Again."

Having failed as an impresario, there was nothing for me to do but try to get another newspaper job. Fortunately for me my work on the Indianapolis *Press* did not go unnoticed by the editor of the Indianapolis *Sun,* another evening paper. When I applied there, I saw

Fred L. Purdy, its editor, who said: "I'd like to have you on the paper here but we can't afford a good man like you. We don't pay enough."

"Thank you," I said, and asked: "How much can you pay?"

"Not enough," was the answer. "You must have been well paid at the *Press*."

"How much can you pay?"

"No use talking about it," Purdy answered.

Not expecting to get at the *Sun* the munificent $12 a week I received at the *Press,* I started to negotiate with a minimum of $9 a week in mind. "Will you pay me $10 a week?" I asked.

"Oh, of course we would pay you more than that. Of course we would. Why, yes!" Then, his enthusiasm rising, Purdy added: "It would make me happy to do better than that. If you will leave it to me I will make it all right with you, and you can start Monday."

That was Saturday. At work all the next week I was wondering if I would get as much as $18 a week, the going rate for top, middle-aged men in the Indianapolis newspaper field of that day. Maybe, I thought, from the exuberant way Purdy talked about it being more

Kent Cooper (1901)—
An impresario at twenty-one.

Victor Herbert (1910)—In 1901 he
wrote music on his reversible cuff.

than $10 it would be even $20; surely it would, at a minimum, be $15. After finishing work late on Saturday afternoon, I got my pay. It *was* more than $10—it was $11!

The *Sun,* then a one-cent newspaper of six to eight pages, is now the Indianapolis *Times,* successfully published as a Scripps-Howard newspaper. The *Sun* thrived upon ridicule. It snapped and snipped at people if they were not advertising in the *Sun.* Politicians called it an "upstart sheet." Tom Taggart, mayor of Indianapolis, defined it as a "Mary-lit-the-fire-with-kerosene-phut" kind of paper. Those who expressed wonderment that I would cast a shadow on my reputation by working on a paper like the *Sun* were told that either they didn't understand that only the editorial columns spoke their prejudices with vitriol or—they had never been hungry. I could write facts. I could not express my own opinions. The editorial columns did that aplenty! And that could be said by all reporters who work for newspapers not held in esteem by their friends.

On the *Sun,* I was given the police "run." I also had to do the "theatrical" reviews of the burlesque shows at the Empire Theatre each Monday night. Not far from my typewriter in the "local" room, there was a telegraph operator receiving news on a leased wire from all over the world. Offices in big cities—Chicago, Cleveland, Cincinnati, St. Louis, Kansas City, Detroit and many others—were sending news into that Indianapolis newspaper office. The wire was operated by the Scripps-McRae Press Association. It had no Indianapolis correspondent. One day late in 1903 I asked the operator, Jack Coleman, if he would like to send a one-hundred-word news story.

"You'll have to schedule it," he said. "Write a schedule."

"Which is what?" I asked.

"Tell 'em in ten words or less what it's about," was the reply.

The schedule was written and sent. The Chicago control office where Max Balthaser was in charge ordered the story. The operator ticked it off. All over that part of the country it went, perhaps by relay from coast to coast. Back came a message from Balthaser to the operator:

"Good story. What's name of our Indianapolis correspondent?"

Coleman tapped out the name on his telegraph key:

"Kent Cooper."

3

SAM BLYTHE'S
SYNONYM

IT GAVE ME a singular feeling when I realized I was to write news stories regularly, not for one paper in Indianapolis, but for newspapers all over the country—maybe the whole world. I was a press association correspondent! My horizons were lifted. I went back to my police "run" with a will to find news good enough, not alone for one local paper, but for "the wire." Stories were being sent. Newspapers in many cities and their readers were learning that there was love, humor, happiness, misery, mystery, murder, political and commercial news in Indianapolis the same as elsewhere. When one of my stories was full of '"human interest," Balthaser would send a message of commendation. Obviously "human interest" was preferred. On the police run it was not difficult to find it.

Had prosperity come to this $11-per-week police reporter? It had indeed! For at the end of the month an SMPA (Scripps-McRae Press Association) check came, signed by Lillian Price, cashier at headquarters in Cleveland. It was countersigned "Robert F. Paine, General Manager." The amount?—$2.50.

Some way had to be found to get acquainted with that general manager. There were some small, county-seat daily newspapers in Indiana that received no telegraph news. It occurred to me that perhaps the general manager would like them as SMPA "pony" clients. A letter promising that ten could be gotten to receive a telegraph "pony" service of 500 words a day at not more than $10 per week each, brought General Manager Paine to Indianapolis to get acquainted.

After a talk about prospects, I gave him a list of towns. He said he would "bone" the Western Union for rates, that if the rates were right and the facilities available, SMPA would pay me $10 a week to file its Indianapolis pony circuit of ten clients.

"We've already got one in Elkhart and one in Madison, Indiana, both of which we serve from Chicago and can transfer to an Indianapolis circuit," Paine said. "That means you've got to get eight more."

By the time the slow-moving Western Union came through with its quotation three weeks later, I had gotten the eight clients and arranged with my city editor to divide the $10 weekly. For his half, he sent part of the 500-word telegraph report while I was on my police run.

In another six months I had gotten enough clients to earn me $15 a week, and I gave up the police run to become a press association employee exclusively. Not having to pay half of my check to the city editor was enough to make me appreciate the change. Besides, I was also correspondent for Hearst's Chicago *American,* and Paine had said I could keep that connection because the *American* was a client of SMPA.

But there was still another reason for satisfaction. No longer would I have to suffer the frustration and chagrin that many a reporter writing local stories was experiencing at that time. Perhaps they still are, but I hope not. A part of my job was to get a feature story each afternoon after the paper had gone to press. As people always interested me, my stories were about people—about individuals, prominent or not, who would tell me of humanly interesting incidents in their lives.

If what I wrote made them glow in self-admiration, they undoubtedly were delighted to see it in print. On the other hand, if my queries brought out the slightest uncomplimentary fact and I said I would use it because it was newsworthy, a telephone call to my editor saying that "your young man was here and I didn't like one or two things he said he was going to write about me" would stop the story, sometimes even before it was written.

There was the instance of a new arrival in town. At the end of the last century, Widener-Elkins, a Philadelphia syndicate, bought and began rejuvenating the Indianapolis electric street railway. They wanted the benevolent co-operation of the city's political administration. To get it, a former Kansas City streetcar driver with a brusque but jovial way with politicians was brought to Indianapolis and made president of the company. It was quite a step up from streetcar driver in one city to president in another. His swaggering ways showed he realized it. His name was Hugh McGowan. When I called on him to get a feature story, he was curious and apprehensive as I began:

"I was outside Mayor Taggart's office today while you were closeted with him. Apparently one of you was telling the other a funny story, for I heard you both laughing. What was the story? I'm sure it's funny enough to print."

McGowan's face reddened in anger as he stared at me. "What's it your business, young man? Is that what you came here for?" he shouted.

The story must have been unprintable and he must have thought I was going to say so in what I wrote, else why his anger? Though his mien was menacing, I shouted back at him: "You are the head of our street railway, a stranger to Indianapolis people. You need their good will. If I can quote you pleasantly, what you tell me might arouse a favorable public opinion of you which indirectly might be an asset for your company, and you should be glad of it."

Plainly he did not comprehend nor want to. "I never let you in here for that purpose and you can get the hell out!" he roared.

While passing him on my way out, I noticed a large scar on one side of his forehead. I quickly recalled that in earlier days Missouri mules, not horses, were said to have pulled Kansas City's streetcars. McGowan had not been nice to me. As I reached the door I said: "That scar on your head . . . did a streetcar mule kick—"

That was as far as I got. He had already buzzed for a man who stood outside the door ready to act as bouncer. That may not have been his title, but in the story I wrote I said he looked like one. Anyway, the big fellow took my arm and pushed me to the elevator on the top floor of the Claypool Building, which housed the streetcar company's office.

"You made the boss mad. Don't come around here again!" he said.

"I wouldn't come back if McGowan begged me to," I replied as the elevator started down.

The feature story I wrote told just what happened and what was said, but I improved it by first going to Mayor Taggart, the always affable politician. I told him what had happened in McGowan's office. He told me the story that had brought the laughter, and I cleaned it up for publication. However, nothing I wrote of the visit to Mc-Gowan's office ever got in the paper. Fred Purdy, my editor, saw me at my typewriter.

"Hugh McGowan called me up and apologized," he began. "He said he was sorry he treated you like a dog."

"I'll put that in my story," I interrupted.

"Don't write anything on McGowan," Purdy said, raising his voice. "I told you he apologized!"

"Not to me, he didn't!" I replied.

He turned away and that was that—a second good reason why I was glad shortly afterward when I found a new boss.

Like many heads of great corporations at the time, McGowan later assumed the "public be damned" attitude. J. P. Morgan's minion, George F. Baer, president of the anthracite-carrying Reading Railway, during the big strike of anthracite coal miners in 1902, publicly intimated that the strikers could starve because, to use his phrase, they were "denying the Divine right of the mine owners" to operate the mines as they chose.

John Mitchell (1902)—
"It's the mine workers
who have a divine right!"

John Mitchell, predecessor of John L. Lewis, was then president
of the United Mine Workers' Union, which had ordered its men on
strike. His offices were in the Stevenson Building in Indianapolis,
national headquarters of the union. I went over to show him Baer's
statement and to ask for comment. I thought what Baer had said
would anger Mitchell. It didn't at all. He read it, reread it, and handed
it back to me, apparently pleased but saying nothing. Again I asked
for comment.

"I have none to make," he said, "but if all of the newspapers in the
country will print this 'Divine right' of the operators statement of Mr.
Baer, the strike will soon be over. The American public will be thinking that perhaps it's the anthracite miners who have a 'Divine right'—
the right to obtain shorter hours so that they can see the daylight before they go down and the daylight after they come up. Their lives
no longer will be spent perpetually in total darkness."

Derisive editorial comment on Baer's "Divine right" statement was
widely printed. It and the latter part of Mitchell's statement to me
may have had some effect in bringing about the settlement of the
strike.

In January, 1905, I wrote General Manager Paine asking for a
raise. An answer came saying that Paine had taken a year's leave of
absence and refusing the raise. It was signed "Ed. S. Wright, Acting
General Manager." I had never heard of Wright. I didn't like him.
Two months later I left SMPA and promptly incorporated my own
agency. It's full corporate name was "The United Press News Association." I called it the United Press, or just UP. All of the eighteen
SMPA newspapers I had been serving came with me. I had only state
news to give them but that was what they wanted.

One year thereafter, General Manager Paine had returned from
his sabbatical. He promptly ordered Wright to negotiate the purchase of all fifty shares of stock of the United Press of Indiana, which
I valued at $1 each; also my return to the Scripps-McRae Press Asso-
ciation at $35 a week!

Paine's remarkable career spread over parts of two centuries. He
was the editor of the Cleveland *Press* for twenty-five years and made
the paper tremendously successful. He also was the founder and first
general manager of the SMPA, the Newspaper Enterprise Association,
an illustrated feature service, and Acme News Photos, all owned by

E. W. Scripps. Later, as had Scripps, he moved to the Pacific Coast and became editor, then editor-emeritus of Scripps' San Francisco *News*. E. W. Scripps named his favorite son, who was his chief heir and successor, Robert Paine Scripps.

In 1924, at a meeting of editors of Scripps-Howard Newspapers, Paine heard the United Press extolled as excellent compared with the "old Scripps-McRae Press Association," which Paine founded. Recalling the early struggles of SMPA with its meager news sources compared to the prosperous UP of sixteen years later, Paine could stand the belittling of his beloved Scripps-McRae Press Association no longer. He arose and said: "I don't know why you are damning the SMPA and praising the UP. I'd have you know SMPA wasn't so bad.

Robert F. Paine (1900)—
In 1940, at eighty-five,
he longed for letters.

As a matter of fact, SMPA had all the news The Associated Press collected and a little bit it picked up on its own account." In 1925, Edward T. Leech, of the Birmingham *Post,* a Scripps-Howard newspaper, regaled the Alabama Associated Press members with this anecdote at a luncheon in Birmingham in my honor.

Before he left for California in 1906, Paine sent me his future address with a note saying that if I ever needed him I should write him at once. No letter went until thirty-four years afterward. By that time he was eighty-five years old and was affectionately called "Uncle Bob" by his associates. My letter and his reply follow:

July 12, 1940

Mr. R. F. Paine,
San Francisco *News,*
San Francisco, Cal.

Dear "Uncle Bob":

I have just read in *Editor and Publisher* that you are ill and that "impatient over enforced idleness, Mr. Paine is eager for messages from friends."

That expressed eagerness of yours gives me the first peg on which to hang an excuse to write you after thirty-four years. You have long been a shining star in my galaxy of great newspaper personages. And why not? In February, 1906, you wrote me from Cincinnati to see you at the Grand Hotel one Sunday morning, and you said that if you were not awake, for me to rout you out without the least formality. You also had written to me in 1905 that you had a high opinion of my ability. That was after Ed Wright must have thought I would do better outside of the Scripps-McRae Press Association than in it. So I organized the United Press of Indiana, which you ordered Wright to buy from me a year later, after I had taken all of the pony business in Indiana away from SMPA. Well, I remember it all. You don't, naturally. You were big and I was little. You are still big, and I am still little, at least in the ways of growing old graciously and righteously.

Some time I hope to have a chance to see you and tell you what great things you did for me when I was a lad.

Meanwhile, with affectionate regards, I am

Sincerely,
Kent

July 20, 1940

Dear Nephew Kent:

I have your letter of July 12th and never before have received a communication that gave me more delight.

It has done me more good than the barrels of Standard Oil Nujol and other discouragements that they have been pumping into me.

Believe it or not, I have always been interested in your career. Each step you have taken to lift The AP out of its laziness I have observed quite as closely as I have the doings of Karl Bickel and Hugh Baillie.

I certainly do recall that time when your United Press of Indiana made Ed. Wright swallow his cud of importance.

It pleases me to feel that I was of some little help to you when you were a lad, for you are one of the very big ones of the profession.

I am most grateful for your letter.

You have my sincerest wishes for more and more successes in your work for The AP.

Affectionately,
Uncle Bob

Thirty days after writing me this letter, Robert F. Paine died. He was the first to encourage me in the press association business which became my life work. Indeed, if it had not been for him, I might never have spent my life in the news agency field.

From the moment that my first little news story was sent on SMPA leased wires throughout the country in 1903, press association work had intrigued my interest. It became the basis of my ambition, which finally led me to a career in The Associated Press. Serving newspapers throughout the land, press association work already had opened a vista of opportunity.

Unlike local reporting, state, national and international contacts may be made in press association work. Its news collection field has no geographical boundaries. With world-wide communication facilities available, there is no important point to which an inquiry can be addressed without assurance of an answer.

How true this is was once dramatically revealed by Bob Davis, traveling correspondent for the New York *Sun*. His column in the issue of the New York *Sun* of December 24, 1932, written at Shepheard's Hotel, Cairo, Egypt, began:

Scene I. Cairo.

Seven years ago on the afternoon of December 22, while on a tour of the world in the agreeable company of Samuel G. Blythe, I found myself in a wicker chair under a potted palm tree here on Shepheard's veranda.

Bob Davis (1925)—
He took the hurdle
at Shepheard's
Hotel, Cairo, Egypt.

Scene II. Headquarters Associated Press. New York office of General Manager Kent Cooper.

Phone rings.

"This is Mr. Cooper."

"Dewart of the New York *Sun* speaking. I want to find Bob Davis, footloose somewhere in the Eastern Hemisphere. Last advice he had left Weltervraden, Java. Can The AP locate him?"

"Probably. I'll flash all points."

Scene III. Shepheard's veranda. Forty-five minutes later, New York time.

Enter messenger boy: "Message for Mr. R. H. Davis. Message for Mr. R. H. D-a-a-vis."

"Beware!" said Sam, lifting a warning finger; "some New Yorker has got wind of your arrival and wants to take you for a dash down the line. We're not supposed to be here—yet. Have a care."

I let the messenger go by, wondering what might be in the wind. Presently the boy returned and repeated the insistent call, which had an ominous echo. Sam shrugged his shoulders. "Take it or leave it," he said, observing that I had ceased to be indifferent. "Suit yourself."

I took the hurdle, grabbed the message, and read this: "Robert H. Davis: Frank A. Munsey died this morning six-thirty communicate with Dewart."

I returned to the shade of the palm tree, and sent for steamer lists. "This means back to Manhattan, Sam, at least for me. After twenty-five years with F. A. M. I'm sorry to have been absent when he passed on."

"How did The Associated Press know that you were in Cairo?"

"They didn't. Nobody knew."

"If that's the case, you've been paged and located by cable ten thousand miles from home. Service, boy—and not of the common kind."

With the world's great communication systems always at its command, Samuel G. Blythe, the renowned *Saturday Evening Post* writer of another day, gave a synonym for The Associated Press in that one word—*Service!*

4

MAJORING IN
TELEPHONY

A FULL STORY about the part the great communication systems of the world play and have played in news collection and distribution could be a saga of its own. Only a newsman in an isolated place far from means of communication, with a big story on his hands all written and ready to send, and no way to send it—only a newsman burning with the necessity of getting his story to his newspaper or press association office far or near with no available transmission facilities, ever could feel the martyrdom of frustration faced by having no telegraph, no cable, no telephone, no radio facilities.

The first electrical transmission of news was by telegraph. By means of it, news was collected and disseminated on land wires. Next it was the cable that did both. Then the telephone became an instrument of news collection, but not distribution. Later, news agencies used radio. But long before radio filled its dual role of collecting and disseminating news, I conceived the idea that the telephone should be used for distributing news as well as for collecting it. Of the four methods, the telephone became the best for small newspapers to start their upward climb to greater public service.

Not expensive, it became a means that lifted some hundreds of strictly local papers out of their provincialism. Graduating from telephone service to leased wires, they made their readers as familiar with national and international affairs as those in the great cities who read the metropolitan press.

In other words, it broadened the base of American interest in world affairs and, by widening the circle of synchronized reading of the news in the nation, to which I have referred, it contributed to the unity of spirit with which America faced the world wars.

This idea, which enlarged the scope of service to newspaper readers who never before enjoyed it, originated in Indianapolis. The testing ground was the whole state of Indiana, beginning in 1906, when the telephone first was used to distribute press association news. Small newspapers, which until then had been receiving 500 words of telegraphed news, or none at all, were the beneficiaries together with the Scripps-McRae Press Association, of which I was bureau manager in Indianapolis. Correction of another instance of the "public be damned" attitude which pervaded big corporations at the time served as the key to unlock the facilities of the great Bell Telephone System for news dissemination purposes.

The telephone company's subsidiary in Indiana was the Central Union Telephone Company. Its arbitrary manners and high rates had brought forth a newly established home-owned system with lower rates. The Central Union declined to meet the competition. It found itself with no good will and a lot of idle time on its telephone circuits. A new management, headed by Horace Hill, was sent out from New York to do something about it. Hill's arrival was news, and I went to interview him. Instead of talking for publication, he offered me a job as a press agent. He wanted me to create a more favorable public attitude toward the company. He didn't know it, but he offered me a salary twice what I was receiving as an employee of SMPA.

Not wanting to engage in corporation publicity, I declined the offer but suggested to him that so far as the good will of the newspapers of the state was concerned, the best thing he could do would be to make a low telephone press rate for news, something no telephone company in the country had ever done. The telegraph companies always had such a special rate. I also told him that if he could make the rate as low or lower than the telegraph rate, I would try to get my employer to change from telegraph to telephone in the delivery of the daily 500 words of news I was sending. Hill said he would make the experiment if I would help him.

I was confident the change from telegraph to telephone would result in better service for my small papers by increasing the daily word-age delivered to them. It did. But I did not foresee that this step ultimately would lead nearly every small newspaper in the country to take full leased wire service and thus end the "pony" class of press association members and clients. This it has done.

When I began telephone delivery of news in 1906, The Associated Press had no distribution of news from Indianapolis to small papers. It did not try to gain new members representing either large or small newspapers. That left an unlimited and always increasing field for opposition service growth. With the telephone method, the SMPA clientele was increased 50 percent in one year in Indiana alone, the number going from eighteen to twenty-seven. In 1907, SMPA was absorbed by the United Press, and I went to New York to meet my new boss, H. B. Clark, the new UP president. He had learned of my success with the telephone method and that I had gained new clients for the organization. I told him I was also taking some of them out of The Associated Press membership.

"Be cautious about that," said Clark. "The AP never has made a raid on our clientele but if we start it they may wake up over there and retaliate."

His remark was prophetic, but neither of us then had any idea that three years later I would be with The Associated Press doing exactly what he had predicted. During that first meeting, Clark asked me to become a traveling agent to extend the telephone method of UP delivery to small newspapers all over the country. In the next three years I went from Indiana to Ohio, Pennsylvania, West Virginia, Kentucky, Illinois, Wisconsin, Missouri, Iowa, Kansas and Oklahoma, "cautiously" weaning a lot of small papers away from The AP as Clark had suggested.

Also, I changed the method of news delivery for UP clients from telegraph to telephone, besides gaining scores of new UP customers among the small papers. Some metropolitan AP papers were added to the UP's full leased wire service as a supplement to their AP. As to the latter, Clark said I need not be "cautious" but for me "to make it clear the service is supplemental to The AP."

Eagerly rushing about the country as I did was a real test of physical endurance. When I first started to travel for the UP I had a healthy body and good digestion. I soon lost both by living at hotels where the rates were not more than $2 a day for room and meals. Many nights I had to drink quantities of strong coffee to keep awake in order to catch trains which seldom were on time and which, especially in icy winter, seemed always to leave after midnight from unheated stations where I had to wait, distance travel by any other means than rail not then being available.

Two years of this and I began worrying about my stomach. I wondered whether because of the success I had had I could get out of the two-dollar-a-day-for-hotel-and-meals class. Clark had made no criticism of my expense accounts, and I wanted none. So I wrote him

Hamilton B. Clark (1912)—
He wrote a charmer.

to ask if he would approve a more liberal expense allowance basis. His answer was a Clark charmer. It read:

Just remember that you are not on the road for 'the billion-dollar U. S. Steel Corporation but for an up-and-coming press association, your connection with which some day may make you rich.

His letter had not said to spend more. It had not said to spend less. It did have a vague promise about the distant future. I did not inch forward in expenditures very far. However, one more year of it was all I could take.

With my ill-treated stomach demanding a change, I conceived the idea of again going into business for myself by incorporating "The American Transmission Company," for which I wanted to make a contract for facilities with the American Telephone and Telegraph Company. My plan was for my transmission company to telephone all press association news reports—AP, UP, and INS—to the small paper clientele of each throughout the country. I went to New York to see A.T. & T. General Manager Charles H. Wilson about it. He was cordial but politely evasive in commenting upon my scheme, and then changed the subject.

"Twenty-five years ago," he began, "I was the construction engineer who built the pneumatic tubes under the streets of Chicago that connected the Western Union telegraph offices with all the newspapers. Through these tubes The Associated Press, located in the Western Union Building, sent copies of its reports to its members. Melville E. Stone was half owner of the Chicago *Daily News* at the time I met him. In 1893, he became general manager of The Associated Press, and I have continued friendly contact with him ever since. Over at The Associated Press, which has headquarters right across Dey Street, at 195 Broadway, Stone has worried about what you are doing with telephone transmission to United Press small paper clients. He told me so.

"He also is worried because the recently established Interstate Commerce Commission has been looking into the Western Union Telegraph Company's rates for favored customers, one of which is The Associated Press. He has some situations that are in open violation of the Commission's regulations. To correct them, the use of telegraph would price The Associated Press news report out of many newspapers. He has paid no attention to my suggestions that he try the telephone, like you are doing, over the country. Now I think you can sell him the telephone idea and Kent Cooper at the same time. Stone is an old man. You might succeed him one day."

I went to see Mr. Stone. As I walked across Dey Street to his office in the old brick Western Union Building at 195 Broadway, I realized I was going to meet one of the great journalists of the time. Yet I was wondering why, after three years, he had shown no reaction whatever to the UP's successful campaign for growth, which had taken away many of The AP's small newspaper members. I was thinking that he must not have cared, that The Associated Press was strong and great and would remain so.

The furnishings of the executive offices of The Associated Press at that time remained just as they were when first installed there in the old Jay Gould Western Union days. Perhaps they could be described as mid-Victorian. There was a red carpeted room about forty feet square which was used by the Board of Directors for its meetings. Mr. Stone's desk was in one corner of it.

I got into the anteroom of that office because Mr. Stone had a rule that he would see anybody who called upon him. But he also had a plan of making short shrift of anyone who did not promptly intrigue his interest. The then general manager of The Associated Press had a cute trick of letting the doorway frame him as he stood barring the entrance to his office. One whom he did not know simply had to furnish his own key to get in by a quick terse sentence.

Mr. Stone's old secretary, Philip H. Kerby, Mike Moran and Colonel Austin G. Durrie, eighty-eight-year-old brother-in-law of James W. Simonton, general manager of the New York Associated Press in 1866, were in that anteroom, which was nothing more than a cubicle outside of Mr. Stone's office. Except for young Moran, who had graduated from messenger boy to typist of Mr. Stone's letters (which Kerby would dictate to Moran at the typewriter), the place was not even pleasantly antique—it reeked with old age.

A question flashed through my mind as to why I was there. Was it necessary for my future that I be there? The satisfaction that I thought would be mine in meeting the justly renowned general manager of The Associated Press had not materialized. Each minute added to the depressed feeling aroused within me. Either I had to escape into Mr. Stone's office or leave the place quickly. The little room appalled me. I feared its atmosphere would suddenly age me. And I shuddered at the thought that if I went to work for The Associated Press, I might be assigned to the vacant side of a badly worn old double desk at one side of which old Durrie sat.

Suddenly Mr. Stone appeared at the door. Recovering from my thoughts with such mental agility as I could muster, I recalled that Wilson had said that Mr. Stone had no confidence in the telephone transmission of news because it would jeopardize accuracy. That was a challenge to something I thought I had amply demonstrated to the contrary. A little resentment toward the doubting Mr. Stone suddenly came to mind. Standing in the doorway, with somewhat pleasant brusqueness he asked me what I wanted.

I said: "News is transmitted by telephone with accuracy and I can prove it to you."

He noticed that I was looking around while awaiting his answer to my statement. Apparently he thought I wanted to talk to him confiden-

Melville E. Stone (1926)—Theodore N. Vail had not darkened his door.

tially. That was not in my mind. I merely was looking for a way out to end the visit, wanting to escape in any direction.

"Come in," he said, and removed himself as the bar to my entrance. He did not ask me to sit down, so I stood while he sat.

"You said news could be transmitted by telephone with accuracy. How?"

I replied: "The best answer to that is that Associated Press news is reputed to be accurate. Practically all the local news that The Associated Press gets from its member papers is telephoned in by the reporters of those papers, so that if there is inaccuracy in telephoning news, The Associated Press is guilty of inaccuracies by putting this local news on its wires. By using local news collected by telephone, The AP proves my statement, since you would be the last to challenge the accuracy of the organization."

"That might be as to local news," Mr. Stone said; "but it is collected by local telephones in the city where one can hear telephone conversations clearly. It is difficult to understand what anyone has to say on long-distance telephones."

"The best proof that you are wrong," I continued, still standing, "is that it works, and I can tell you where it works."

"All right," Mr. Stone said. "We will take an example: How would you get 2500 words a day by telephone to Burlington, Vermont, at a rate that the newspaper can afford to pay?"

Now it just so happened that in plans I had made to develop patronage for the UP in the more isolated places in New York State and New England, I had informed myself on how to serve Burlington. I was unaware of one thing: The Associated Press service to Burlington was one of those the Interstate Commerce Commission had said must be regularized, and this meant a greatly increased cost to the newspaper. I began:

"You cannot serve Burlington economically either by telephone or telegraph from your New England bureau in Boston. You can do it economically from Albany, where you have a bureau. The mileage from Albany is only 156, and the cost for sending about 2500 words daily divided into three ten-minute telephone periods from Albany would be $16 a week."

He turned, picked up a pencil and a copy of the *Official Railway Guide,* thumbed through it to the Rutland Railroad timetable, did a little arithmetic of mileage, and discovered the distance was exactly what I had given him—156 miles.

"Sit down," said Mr. Stone, and added: "Your figure is right. I want you to come to work for The Associated Press."

"Oh, no thank you," I said.

"Why not?"

"Because," I replied, "my observation as an employee of a competitor of The AP has convinced me you head a moribund press association."

Mr. Stone jerked back his shoulders, looked for an instant as if he had been offended, then with a smile somewhat tolerantly bestowed, said: "Wouldn't you hold out a helping hand to save a dying institution?"

"I guess I would if I were sure it was worth saving and showed some indication it didn't want to die."

The fact that he disregarded what he could not but construe as impudence on my part showed he really was interested. "How much do you get from the United Press?" he asked.

"Fifty dollars a week and a very modest expense allowance for traveling," was the reply.

"All right," said Mr. Stone in a tired manner, "I will give you $60." He pressed a button for his secretary, having turned away from me on the assumption that the deal was closed, for it was not habitual for young newsmen to turn down an offer of 20 percent more salary.

But I had no idea at that time of accepting $60 a week. Nor had I the slightest idea of wanting to work for The Associated Press, which my brusque conversation should have indicated to its general manager. Only a few hours before, I had delusions of at least a thousand dollars a week through the formation of the American Transmission Company. Old Kerby came in, and Mr. Stone started to dictate a note to the treasurer saying that I had been employed. Arising to hurry out of the place, I said: "Thank you, Mr. Stone. I am not interested."

He actually blushed. He laughingly told me several years later that such a thing never had happened to him before. Then, too, it had occurred in the presence of his elderly secretary, who, I noted, on hearing my remark, cleared his throat and with reddened face gulped down his astonishment. Mr. Stone dismissed him and turned to me: "Young man, you are making a great mistake."

Contemplating that I might be, I asked: "Would I work directly for you?"

"Yes," he replied. "I have been authorized to employ traveling inspectors, and I can engage you under that title, although the salary is higher than I had expected to pay for those positions." He plainly was nettled.

I repeated: "I will report to you directly?"

"Yes," he said.

"Where will my desk be?" I asked with mounting fear.

"Why, that's a double desk in that next room where Colonel Durrie works. You can have the other side of it."

That was an unhappy suggestion. My thoughts shot back to my first sight of that old desk. I recalled not only the scarred old desk, but the gentleman with gray sideburns who was leaning over the other side of it, and how I had smiled reassuringly to myself that I was in the wrong place; that if ever I had to go to work for The Associated Press I would surely wind up with gray sideburns and stooped shoulders in a cubicle used as an anteroom to somebody's office.

Recalling these reflections, I shrank at Mr. Stone's suggestion of that desk as one would with mild horror at being sucked into a vortex that could only end in quick senility. Realizing that I had not said I would work for The Associated Press, I tossed off the flippant remark: "I would make a poor twin for the old gentleman with sideburns."

Mr. Stone did not like the attempt at humor. By rising he dismissed me, saying: "Let me hear from you promptly. You have proved to me that I must meet the competition you are creating. If you won't do it, I will get someone who will."

5

THROUGH THE

BARRIERS

OF YESTERYEAR

THE PRELIMINARIES that led to my Associated Press connection have been recited because they depict what faced young men in those days; for Mr. Stone was not an exception. Giving employment was a condescending grant, only a step higher than doling out charity. The employee was supposed to think himself lucky to get a job. The employer had no thought of being lucky in giving one. He did not evaluate as such the talent that eager youth afforded. The age-old era of apprenticeship was giving way to an era of profitably recognizing the dignity of labor and the talent of earnest youth.

Mr. Stone's parting threat uttered as I left his office was not the reason for my almost discourteously abrupt departure. I just had a feeling that I had to get out of there. For one thing, I suddenly remembered that if I did not get a train to Indianapolis that afternoon I would not be back home for my 1910 Thanksgiving dinner the next day. I made it to Indianapolis all right. Then, but not because of the threat, I delayed until Tuesday of the following week to wire a decision to Mr. Stone.

During that delay I reminded myself that The Associated Press, being a mutual organization, did not provide for stock that could be bought and that, therefore, there was no way I could ever get any. I often had been promised United Press stock. The promises never had been fulfilled. Finally I decided that since there was no stock available to me at either place, I would be no worse off by making a change, that it would be an adventure worth trying if I could get Mr. Stone to raise his offer of $60 weekly.

Five days of reflection pictured a real opportunity in the biggest press association of all. I thought I might go further with it than I could at the United Press where there were several competent young men with high ambitions, including Roy Howard, then only twenty-seven years old. Some of them, like Howard, had even met Scripps, the owner. They had gotten personal inspiration and assurances from him. I had been there seven years and had not met him.

Moreover, in my travels for the UP, I had observed The Associated Press at work. Its men were elderly. I had seen few young AP men anywhere. At the UP I was in competition for advancement with men who were my own age or younger. Even Clark, its president, was young enough to be Melville Stone's son. I thought I might have less rivalry at The AP. The resolve I reached carried with it my decision to make a break with the United Press quickly. Two telegrams were economically squeezed into less than ten words each. The one to Clark, of the UP, prepaid, read:

REGRETFULLY RESIGNING CLOSE OF WEEK BETTER OPPORTUNITY. RE-GARDS.

The one to Mr. Stone was sent collect. Surely it would be worth the cost to The AP of a fifty-cent telegram for Mr. Stone to get an answer he had requested. It read:

YES FOR SEVENTY-FIVE IF WORK DIRECTLY FOR YOU.

Clark's reaction to my telegram was economical. He sent no reply at all. Mr. Stone's answer came the next day, prepaid:

SIXTY-FIVE DOLLARS WEEKLY IS ALL I CAN OFFER YOU NOW. WILL EX-PECT YOU HERE MONDAY.

The message had not met my figure and utterly disregarded my stipulation that I would work directly for the general manager. This latter undertaking was important to me. I had that relationship with the president of the UP. If I started with The Associated Press at the bottom, it would take a long, long time for advancement in what I had told its general manager was a moribund institution. Nevertheless, I wired my new employer that I would be there the following Monday, and left Indianapolis on Sunday in time to report the next morning at 195 Broadway. That was December 5, 1910.

Then, and as many times afterward until I got used to it, I expected Mr. Stone to be awaiting my arrival with interest. He was not! What did happen further reveals the employer attitude of that era. When I reached New York I went to the office, hoping to get there before Mr. Stone did. I waited impatiently more than two hours, then asked Kerby how much longer I would have to wait. He replied: "I don't know." I waited another hour, then inquired of Kerby again. "I doubt if he will be in today at all," he said. "He's leaving this afternoon for Chicago on the *Century.*"

Showing my annoyance I asked: "What's his telephone number? I want to call him up."

"Oh, no," said Kerby. "You can't call him up."

"Then what am I expected to do?"

He answered: "I'm sure I don't know."

"Did you see the telegram he sent me?" I asked.

"Yes, I sent it for him."

"Well, am I on the payroll while I wait or not?"

"Not until Mr. Stone dictates the order to me to be written," Kerby said. "He started to dictate it last week but you stopped him."

Kerby had me there, so I said: "Will you call Mr. Stone and tell him please to dictate the order and what my function is to be?"

That was altogether too much for Kerby. Such a thing had never been done. Mike Moran smiled decorously, and Colonel Durrie stroked his sideburns. The atmosphere of that little room made me more than ever want to hurry—hurry—hurry.

The telephone rang. It was Mr. Stone asking what was in the mail. I stuck in front of Kerby's eyes the telegram Mr. Stone had sent me to make sure he would mention it. Kerby thought the hand that held the telegram was that of Mike Moran and that it was a new message just received, so he read to Mr. Stone the telegram he had sent to me. The telephone service was really good. Anyone in the room could hear Mr.

Stone saying to Kerby: "Oh, yes, take this memorandum to the treasurer: 'I have employed Kent Cooper as traveling inspector. He is to have access to all the records relating to the distribution of news.' "

Kerby hung up the telephone. I listened as he dictated to Moran the note for the treasurer and then I asked him to include mention of the salary. He said Mr. Stone did not dictate it to him so of course he could not write it. I didn't argue with him.

It was then 12:30 P.M. Anxious to get to work, I asked if I could meet the treasurer before he left for lunch. Kerby replied that he had already gone but that he usually got back around two o'clock. I made mental note of the time consumed by such a leisurely lunch, a habit I had not acquired. By 2:30 P.M., however, I had settled down opposite Colonel Durrie with the treasurer's books containing the information on news distribution costs. I was working for The Associated Press that I thought was moribund!

After his return to New York a week later, Mr. Stone did not come to the office for several days. He had not yet put me on the payroll. I asked Kerby to remind him about it the next time he telephoned. He said he could not but that I could write a letter which he would send up with the mail by messenger to Mr. Stone at the Lotos Club; then all Mr. Stone would have to do would be to write approval on it and send it back, and Kerby would turn it over to the treasurer. At the time, I did not express my thoughts about this procedure. I wrote the letter and got my name on the payroll. This was the final step in establishing me in my new work for The Associated Press.

Today I still believe that my experience must have been typical of what was then going on in many old institutions. The new twentieth century wanted to take over and, in trying to do so in a spirit of urgency, it encountered the tenacious hold of the nineteenth century that did not want to give it up. My sense of urgency was that for several years I had been working with the idea that I would retire at forty years of age. To me at thirty, forty was old age!

When I first met the general manager of The AP, he was sixty-two years old—very old, I thought—and he had no idea of quitting though plainly he was a tired man, old beyond his years. The position had lost its glamor for him. As I found out later, some aggressive younger men in The AP membership had formed a special committee to investigate the effectiveness of Mr. Stone's administration. It had completed its report, which contained many recommendations. One of them was that the general manager should appoint traveling inspectors. Thus it eventuated that I was the first traveling inspector The Associated Press ever had up to then or since.

As I look back on it now, I should not have asked for more than $60 weekly. Instead I should have exacted a promise from Mr. Stone that if my work demonstrated my value in the matter of modernizing The AP's transmission of news, I could then, under him, go into news work which I really knew and liked. I shared his high conception of the responsibility resting on those who collect the news.

Even though my news ideas encompassed a wider field than that to which he restricted The Associated Press, I could see that those who did news work under his direction were advantaged and honored. I wanted that advantage and that honor. On occasions I did discuss with him the desirability of looking for some news with more human appeal to brighten up the report. The farthest I got in favorable comment was that if he were young he might try out my ideas. "But," he added with a smile, "I am not young. We will keep the conception of news within the confines to which The Associated Press always has been restricted."

A quick study of the books of The AP revealed that some 75 percent of its total expenses was paid out for telegrams, cables, leased telegraph wires and telegraph operators' salaries—in other words, for news transmission. The treasurer leased the wires. The bureau correspondents hired the operators. I reflected upon the tripod organization then existing in the A.T. & T., comprising three departments under the general manager—commercial, plant and traffic. I thought it should be news, traffic and finance in The Associated Press, but it was two years before I could put the idea over.

The AP was operating at a loss. There were plans for increasing assessments to stop any further deficit which then amounted to some four thousand dollars monthly. It did not take long to see that there was waste in news distribution costs amounting to some one hundred thousand dollars a year. Three months after I had been with the organization, I made a report to Mr. Stone delineating the method by which this economy could be effected. A part of the plan had to be the establishment of competition for the business of The Associated Press between the Western Union, Postal Telegraph and the American Telephone and Telegraph Company, then an entirely new idea to Mr. Stone.

The Associated Press was then, as now, the biggest user of press association leased wires in the country. The Western Union had practically all of that AP business. But as The AP was six months in arrears to the Western Union for payment of wire rentals, Mr. Stone would not consider making any change. Moreover, The Associated Press gave the Western Union its election returns. For them The AP got free telegraph tolls for their collection.

Having the news for sale, the Western Union competed with AP newspapers by selling AP election news directly to the public, even to non-AP members. By obtaining lower wire costs, not only could The Associated Press meet its Western Union bills promptly, but enough could be saved to pay all telegraph tolls for collecting the election news, thereby stopping the Western Union from selling it.

I made a written report to Mr. Stone recommending all of this. Three weeks later it had gotten to the bottom of the pile of letters and memoranda on his desk. He pulled it out and gave it to Kerby for filing. I knew the answer: Mr. Stone was not interested.

At one time I was in Denver negotiating with the Mountain States Telephone and Telegraph Company for a day wire from Denver to El Paso at the rate of $6 per mile per annum for three hours daily. This was one-fourth the standard rate The Associated Press was paying the Western Union. Because of the cost, the evening papers in that section never had been offered a leased wire. There was a Western Union night leased wire. I wrote Mr. Stone by special delivery and telegraphed him that the letter offering a low rate for the day wire and a lower rate than Western Union for the night wire would reach New York Sunday morning. I urgently asked for authority to sign the contract at once; also that the Western Union lease be cancelled.

The letter was not acknowledged. Others were sent pressing for action. I was at the point of being considered an impostor by the Mountain States Company. Finally I wrote a letter to the company accepting the offer, then hurried back to New York to square myself. I had been authorized to arrange for telephone service instead of telegraph service for member papers. I calmed my conscience by telling myself that although this was to be a telegraph service it would be telegraphing over a telephone wire!

I had no idea of what might happen to me for exceeding my authority and I didn't much care. I had waited in Denver for nearly three

weeks and I simply had to know what had delayed Mr. Stone's acceptance of the proposal. Then I returned to New York. I got to the office
early in the morning as some new mail was being stacked on top of
the pile that was always on Mr. Stone's desk. I asked about my Denver
wire recommendation. I was told it was there.

Mr. Stone came in later, and I related to him what I had done. I
expected him to tell me that I had exceeded my authority and that the
contract was invalid. Instead, he merely reached under the pile of correspondence, pulled out my recommendation, checked it for filing, and
said with a pleased smile: "You will have to cancel the Western Union
Denver-El Paso night leased wire when you are ready to switch over."

I wondered whether I could get him to comment on the three weeks'
delay, this being the second one I had experienced. I said: "Mr. Stone,
please tell me why you didn't wire me or write me. I waited for three
weeks for an answer."

"Yes," he said, glancing at the various letters which he was checking
for filing. "Your recommendation came just three weeks ago, didn't it?
I've always said that a lot of things will answer themselves in three
weeks if no attention is paid to them."

That idea of letting communications answer themselves was something to remember. I never forgot it. Thereafter, when action was necessary, I wrote to Mr. Stone and simultaneously took the action I was
recommending. The work was speeded up. Acknowledgments were
unnecessary when, to me, the answers were obvious.

The Denver-El Paso day-and-night leased wire started operation
with the Mountain States Company. I learned later why Mr. Stone,
with nothing more than a smile of satisfaction, permitted me to go
ahead and transfer that lease from the Western Union. It was not that
his smile showed interest in my business ability; rather, he had suddenly developed a dislike for the Western Union on personal grounds.

When I took the Denver-El Paso night wire away from the Western
Union, Mr. Stone welcomed it as an act of reprisal for what he con-
sidered personal discourtesy to him. Theodore N. Vail, of A.T. & T.
fame, and its president at the time, had also become president of the
Western Union that year. He was moving to consolidate the Western
Union with the telephone company and had assumed the presidency
of both. He made Newcomb Carlton executive vice-president of the
Western Union. A minor Western Union official called. I took him to

Mr. Stone. He said Mr. Carlton had sent him to ask why the lease was cancelled. Mr. Stone said:

"You can tell Mr. Carlton that he and Mr. Vail have been in this building as executive heads of the Western Union for more than six months; that the principal customer of the Western Union is and always has been The Associated Press, and that since they have been in this building neither of them has ever darkened my door."

As soon as Carlton was informed of Mr. Stone's resentment, he made a call on the General Manager. While he was in Mr. Stone's office, the cause of it all sat outside, opposite Colonel Durrie, and could not help but hear the apology, its acceptance, and the good-natured banter that passed between them. Before Carlton departed, Mr. Stone called me in to meet him, saying:

"Here's the young man responsible."

It was the start of a close and enduring friendship between Carlton and myself. When the Interstate Commerce Commission turned down the proposed A.T. & T.-Western Union consolidation, Carlton succeeded Vail in the Western Union presidency. He served in that position for over a quarter of a century. But he didn't retain or ever get back the Denver-El Paso lease!

Even with Mr. Stone's explanation that some letters answered themselves, I remained curious about what appeared to me to be lapses in attention to details and correspondence. Finally I concluded they were, in reality, merely evidences of the fact that his early career was contemporaneous with the graceful leisure in business procedures of the previous century. Aspiring youth had to break through the barrier of the customs of yesteryear.

But I knew that Mr. Stone had his business beginnings in the horse and buggy days before the invention of the telephone, the instrument that so quickened American life. Great as was his conception of news —that it be accurate and unbiased and historically important—talking business on the telephone always nettled him.

In his work, however, he also carried over into the new century tactful attributes that made him at once charming and a good companion in elite circles. Business and financial details irked him in a world that had assumed a quickened tempo. Realization of this aroused discouragement in me that brought determination to declare my impatience to someone. To whom? I did not know.

6

IN REMEMBRANCE OF

A TELEGRAPHER

MY FIRST YEAR with The Associated Press ended. I concluded I was miscast in the organization. Nine months after I had given Mr. Stone a full report of how I could save The Associated Press $100,000 a year in its wire rentals, I still could gain no interest in it from him, in spite of the little incident that took one parcel of business away from the Western Union. The fact that I was not on the news side of the press association business completed my dissatisfaction.

In December, 1911, a director of The Associated Press, Valentine S. McClatchy, of the Sacramento *Bee,* who had been active in the Special Committee that two years previously had reported inefficiencies in The Associated Press administration, introduced himself to me as I sat at the desk opposite Colonel Durrie. He said he had seen me there and wondered what my work was. I told him but added that I was not staying with the organization. He asked me why and I replied that the discouragements were too great.

That was on Saturday after the Board meeting had adjourned. McClatchy was leaving the next day for his home in California. He said he would like to have another talk with me and invited me to have breakfast with him at the Belmont Hotel the next morning at nine. The idea of having breakfast as late as nine o'clock and ten

49

miles away from my home in Brooklyn, to say nothing of having it in an expensive New York hotel, intrigued me. So next morning I got up before daylight and showed up promptly at nine o'clock for breakfast.

Director Valentine McClatchy's wide knowledge of the operations of The Associated Press amazed me. In serving on the Special Committee, he had personally visited some of the larger AP offices and had gotten acquainted with the personnel. It was he who insisted upon the appointment of traveling inspectors. I was the first one. I tried to match my knowledge of the organization with his. I told him what I had done in that year as well as the bars to my activity. He seemed particularly interested in the fact that I had been blocked in the matter of effecting the economies on which I had made a full written report to Mr. Stone. He asked me if I had ever told Mr. Ochs about it, and I answered:

"Why, no, of course not. I have never met Mr. Ochs."

He said: "Will you tell Mr. Ochs about it if I take you to him?"

I replied: "Certainly I will, if he asks me."

Mr. McClatchy excused himself. When he returned he said he had telephoned Mr. Ochs at his home and that Mr. Ochs, though awakened from a sound slumber, agreed to see him if he could be there in

Valentine S. McClatchy (1921)—He awakened Adolph S. Ochs at eleven A.M.

an hour. It was then almost eleven o'clock. The publisher of the *New York Times* lived on West Seventy-fifth Street near Riverside Drive. We were at Forty-second Street and Park Avenue. It was a cold but beautiful, sunshiny Sunday morning. We started a brisk walk, timing ourselves to get to Mr. Ochs' house at noon. When we arrived there, we were ushered into the library on the second floor. In a little while Mr. Ochs came in to greet his fellow director. He expressed not a little surprise at my presence when I was identified as an employee of Mr. Stone.

"I cannot conceive what this can all be about, Mr. McClatchy. I apologize for keeping you waiting, but I was out late last night. What in the world is up?"

"If you will ask this young man to tell you what he has told me," said McClatchy, "you will see why I feel it was important to introduce him to you before I leave for California this afternoon."

McClatchy had accelerated matters considerably. I did not relish this dramatic setting to discuss how Mr. Stone operated The AP. Nevertheless, one in my humble position was not going to be the cause of routing the famous publisher of the *New York Times* out of bed on a Sunday morning to no purpose. I also felt I had to make good for McClatchy. Since I had nothing to lose, I repeated the story of the frustration my work had met. Mr. Ochs' astonishment was considerable. He would look at McClatchy and then at me with incredulity. When I had finished and answered all his questions, he said:

"Of course, I have to go to see Mr. Stone about this." Then, with some severity he added: "If what you say turns out to be untrue it will go very hard for you."

I asked him: "What could Mr. Stone do to me other than dismiss me?"

Mr. Ochs replied: "You will lose your position, indeed."

I said: "That's all right. I am resigning, anyhow, although not until I have a chance to talk with Mr. Stone. I intend to resign so that I can spend Christmas in Indianapolis. When will you see him?"

"I will see him," said Mr. Ochs, "as early in this week as I can. But how am I to let Mr. Stone know that I have seen you and heard your story? I should like to give you all the protection I can."

I said: "You mean you wonder how Mr. Stone is going to know I have seen you and Mr. McClatchy today and have told both of you what I have been telling him the last year?"

Mr. Ochs replied: "Yes, that's it."

"Well," I said, "unless you are interested enough to see him earlier tomorrow morning than I do, he will know directly from me that I saw both of you today and told you all."

"I wonder," said Mr. Ochs, "whether that would not be the best way."

"I don't know," I said, "whether it's the best way, but it is what I shall do, anyhow."

The matter having been thus decided, I reported to Mr. Stone the next day. He seemed distressed and said so after a moment, adding: "It is not that I care for myself, but when this gets around among the members it will do the organization no good."

Adolph S. Ochs (1918)—
"I'd be glad to have you
on the New York Times."

I wondered whether I should express regret and apologize for the fact that I was not aware, as indeed I was not, that telling two directors of The Associated Press what they asked me to tell them, and what I had often told Mr. Stone, constituted a wide distribution of my statements. "After all," I thought, "they are directors and a directorship carries responsibility."

The next day, Tuesday, was cold with howling winds and snow. I shall never forget seeing Adolph S. Ochs, wearing galoshes, with snow on his overcoat, enter Mr. Stone's office, having come all the way from uptown. I regretted that he had braved that terrible weather. Mr. Stone closed the door to his office. After a half-hour's talk the door opened, and Mr. Stone asked me to come in. Again the door was closed. Mr. Ochs spoke first:

"Young man, Mr. Stone says he will gladly give you the opportunity to make good on this saving of $100,000 a year, but he wants me to impress upon you that it must be done in strict, confidential relationship with him."

"You see, Cooper," said Mr. Stone, "this organization is a sounding board, and it does not contribute to its well-being to have rumors spread about that there is no watchful economy."

I told him I quite understood all that and gave my word that only the annual reports of The Associated Press would show the net results.

Apparently Mr. Ochs liked my attitude both on Sunday and on that Tuesday, for he said:

"I will say this, young man: If you still feel unhappy here now that Mr. Stone has given you carte blanche, I shall be glad to give you an opportunity at the *New York Times.*"

I thanked Mr. Ochs and told him that press association work appealed to me more than being engaged by an individual newspaper; that I had no doubt Mr. Stone would help me make the saving.

"I will help you, Cooper," said Mr. Stone, "and if you can save $500 or perhaps $5,000 it will be worth while. But $100,000 a year —well, we will see!"

There wasn't much additional work to do other than to carry out the plans I already had recommended. The result was that at a later meeting of the Board of Directors, the following occurred as reported in the stenographic minutes:

MR. OCHS: Has Mr. Cooper made any progress in the matter I discussed with you?

MR. STONE: Yes, we are effecting economies that will approximate the $100,000 he mentioned.

MR. OCHS: Are you going to reward him? I want him rewarded.

MR. MCCLATCHY: Yes, he must be given recognition.

MR. STONE: All right, I shall reward him.

After the meeting adjourned, Mr. Stone told me he was going to appoint me superintendent of traffic at $75 a week, an increase of $10, with jurisdiction over all wires in the service. I was shocked that for a $100,000 annual saving I was not going to get at least $100 weekly and said so. Mr. Stone flushed by way of showing his annoyance but he dictated the notice that my salary was to be $100 weekly. I became the first superintendent of traffic The Associated Press ever had—also the last.

Both Mr. McClatchy and Mr. Ochs were interested in my proposal to Mr. Stone that The Associated Press be departmentalized: news, traffic and finance. McClatchy particularly liked this idea, and at a later meeting of the Board of Directors, he urged its adoption.

As a result, late in the summer of 1912 Mr. Stone announced the tripod organization I had been recommending. He appointed Charles E. Kloeber chief of the News Department, Kent Cooper chief of the Traffic Department, and J. Randall Youatt treasurer. My title of superintendent of traffic was dropped.

Dear old Colonel Durrie had by then gotten too feeble to come to the office. I sat at the double desk alone. Mr. Stone decided I should have a private office—private to the extent that only I and my stenographer occupied it. I had a free hand to improve wire facilities, but I had no control over the personnel that operated them. The telegraphers were employed by the correspondents in the various offices. As traveling inspector, I had discovered that in some offices there were gross inequities affecting them.

At our first departmental conference with Mr. Stone, I recommended that the operators be removed from the jurisdiction of the correspondents and placed under Traffic Department representatives in each office, responsible directly to the chief of traffic.

I said a telegraph operator had a profession of his own and that his immediate superior should be a telegrapher competent to judge his efficiency, not a newsman. I insisted that the system of operations then in vogue was archaic and had brought a lamentable strike against The Associated Press in 1907. The operators lost that strike and sullenly went back to work with no improvement in their working conditions. Five years later, there had been no change in the conditions that caused the strike.

"The operators should be rewarded with better pay and shorter hours," I said. "In their confining work they should have as short hours as the newsmen, and positions should be created to which they can be advanced in recognition of efficiency."

Mr. Stone declared there would be trouble if the correspondents had no control over the operators. He dramatized what would happen if a correspondent ordered an operator to send a news dispatch, and the operator refused and held himself aloof from the correspondent's discipline. There were comments by others which I endeavored to answer. A minute of that first conference in September, 1912, reads:

After Mr. Cooper explained the plans he had for the Traffic Department, Mr. Stone said he felt he saw clearer than before the opportunities and advantages and he accepted fully Mr. Cooper's plan for the Traffic Department.

I had developed a real affection for the first press association telegraph operator I knew, Jack Coleman, who worked in the office of the Indianapolis *Sun*. It was he who sent my first story on the Scripps-McRae Press Association wire after telling me how to schedule it. Jack was fatally ill then with tuberculosis. He never complained in spite of his racking cough.

Worrying about him, I went to the SMPA Chicago office one day and got acquainted with E. F. Wilson, an operator of agreeable personality and a big heart. I told him about Coleman's illness. While I was there, he had the Western Union cut off the Indianapolis *Sun*'s connection with the wire so that Coleman couldn't "hear." Then Wilson "talked" on the wire by telegraph to all SMPA operators throughout that section of the country.

They made up a purse and got a leave of absence for Coleman to go West for a "cure." He went but had to return to his job when the money ran out at the end of his leave. Two months later Coleman "opened" his telegraph key. That "broke" the entire wire circuit, and the operator in the control office at Chicago had to stop sending the news. In the next instant Coleman "closed" his key so his faltering hand could send his farewell message to all the boys on the wire. Slowly he tapped off only two words:

"I'm dying."

We got him home before he passed away. My admiration for Coleman's fortitude for months in the face of death, coupled with later friendships I made with many Associated Press operators, instilled in me an enduring concern for the latter's welfare. When I advocated Traffic Department supervision of the operators, I was thinking of Coleman and of those hundreds I had met in AP offices all over the country. I resolved to get the chance to improve their working conditions as Associated Press employees.

7

HEARTFELT THANKS

FOR PENSIONS

I HAVE OFTEN wondered whether any other executive at thirty-two years of age when first given the responsibility for hundreds of employees had the feeling I did when in a flash of a second, I unexpectedly became the boss of seven hundred Associated Press telegraph operators. Yet I had never been a telegrapher myself and didn't even know a telegraphic dot from a dash.

My first reaction to Mr. Stone's acceptance of my plea for proper recognition of Associated Press telegraphers lifted my spirits to the heights. It was the thrill that comes when opportunity is offered. But my second thought brought me heavily down to earth. I realized that I not only had become responsible for the work of those employees, but also for their happiness and indirectly for the happiness of their families—hundreds of them.

Naturally I wanted all of these telegraphers to like their jobs and to be contented. To find a formula for insuring this was the problem. I knew what I wanted to do but I didn't know how to accomplish it. Up to then I had never been an employer. In several jobs, however, I had envisioned the kind of boss I would have liked—one who would give me the happiness that unrequested reward for merit brings.

In twenty years of working for newspapers and news agencies, I had never gotten an increase in salary voluntarily given. So I planned to do for Associated Press telegraphers that which I had never gotten for myself. If I could do it successfully for them, perhaps I could assure their happiness. With that as my formula, I decided to try.

This conception of my responsibility first for the traffic personnel and later for all Associated Press employees guided my actions for a period of over forty years. I may not have entirely succeeded, but whatever success I did achieve, I owe to this concern for the employees. With The Associated Press telegraph operators placed under supervision of the newly created Traffic Department, steps were taken to make them realize that the change promised their betterment. The first step was to send out requests in October, 1912, asking all telegraphers to write and send to me, as chief of the Traffic Department, brief autobiographies, which would be the bases for personnel files of each individual.

They were asked specifically:

(a) to give their ages and the state of their health

(b) to set down why, when and where they first took up telegraphy

(c) to say if they went out on strike at the call of the Commercial Telegraphers Union of America in 1907, and if they did so, to say frankly why, with assurance there would be no reprisals whatever

(d) to give their ideas on how their work could be made more agreeable

(e) to make suggestions, if they had any, on how operations of Associated Press wires could be improved

(f) to state their ambitions

(g) to ask questions

The replies came. Each letter served as an autobiography to start the employee's personal file. He became definitely, and for the first time, an identifiable individual. And with those hundreds of autobiographies came ideas, a few of them practical. When possible to try one, the man who suggested it was given the opportunity personally to test its worth.

One inquiry was in most of the letters: "Would The Associated Press ever have a pension plan?"

Answering that one required learning what the Western Union was doing. It had thousands of telegraphers. The Associated Press had only 700. I promptly discovered why I had been asked about pensions: a few days before my circular letter was mailed, the telegraph company had notified all of its employees of the adoption of a pension plan.

I immediately recommended to Mr. Stone that The Associated Press take the same action for all of its employees, since it would be unthinkable that only the telegraphers who were in my department should be so recognized. No action was taken. I continued my interest and compiled actuarial tables for a plan to be financed by The Associated Press itself, not by any of the insurance companies which were then experimenting in the pension field at exorbitant rates. I proved to my own satisfaction that if The Associated Press financed the plan, the cost would be less, since there would be no margin of profit involved which the insurance companies included in their figures.

Year after year I continued to plead for action. In four years the only progress I made was approval, in 1916, of sick-benefit allowances for operators!

To make my AP pension plan guarantee half pay at retirement, there had to be a limit upon the annual allowances paid. This limit I fixed at $5,000 per annum because it did not exceed 50 percent of the highest salary paid to any employee, the general manager and assistant general manager excepted.

Not until 1917, after five years of pleading for pensions, was I told in confidence by a member of the Board that a plan which might fix the general manager's pension, if and when he retired, at not more than $5,000 a year would not be approved. I explained that any retirement allowances in excess of the $5,000 yearly maximum could be paid, not out of the pension fund, but out of the general fund, by order of the Board. That seemed to settle the problem satisfactorily to take care of the general manager, assistant general manager, and any other employee who at some time in the future might receive more than $10,000 per year.

Still, adoption of the plan was postponed. There were members of the Board who wanted it adopted but they were in the minority. Adolph S. Ochs and William L. McLean, of the Philadelphia *Bulletin,* were the most outspoken in this group. When I pleaded to be told the basis of further objections, I learned that a majority of the Board felt it would be improper for The Associated Press to venture into the pension field when not a newspaper in the membership had taken a single step in that direction.

To the objectors, voting as AP directors, to adopt an Associated Press pension plan would be laying publishers open to demands from their employees for similar grants. They were sure that if The Associated Press had a pension plan, the newspapers would have to have pension plans. They felt that if a majority of the newspapers ever established such benefits, then would be the time for The Associated Press to follow, and not the other way around.

Yet newspaper publishers were far from heartless. They had been liberal in individual cases with their own employees but without any fixed plan. The practice of some was to take care of valuable superannuated and ill employees but not to establish and announce an obligation to do so, regardless of their feeling for the individual employee or of the degree of merit he had earned.

Another fact on which opposition was based was that newspaper publishers generally had contracted with unions in their mechanical departments. None except the two Associated Press directors named wanted to grant pensions to any of their employees who had memberships in unions. Their white-collar workers, including some newsmen who twenty years later went into the American Newspaper Guild, were not then unionized. They didn't see how they could give pensions and insurance to a nonunion group and not to a union group, which latter they did not want to favor in any way.

I pointed out that there was no such situation in The Associated Press, since the organization had no union contracts. Still, the fear remained that voting pensions for AP employees would lead to imposing upon the newspapers the obligation to do the same thing for all of their own employees, union or nonunion.

In 1918, it was necessity that convinced the doubting directors that The Associated Press must adopt a pension plan. Leaves of absence for war duty were being granted among the youngest, and some of the most competent employees were leaving The AP. It was not easy to fill vacancies. Working for The Associated Press usually meant the transfer of applicants from their home cities to other areas. Some balked at that idea. Also, there was the fact that AP salaries did not compare favorably with those paid by newspapers, nor did advancement in The Associated Press seem promising. And AP telegraph operators eyed the Western Union pension plan.

Given its legal name of "The Associated Press Employees' Benefit Plan," the proposal, just as I had written it six years earlier, finally was adopted in 1918. It provided that The Associated Press would meet the entire expense involved. This meant there would be no contributions from the employees. Not only were pensions authorized, but life insurance of $1,000 (later increased to $5,000) and payment of salaries during illness were granted.

An initial appropriation of $100,000 was made to start the fund. Because of the accrued liability for age and length of service, this $100,000 approximated only 2 percent of what was needed to make operation of the plan actuarily sound. So the Board approved meeting the cost of each year's pension, insurance and sick allowances out of the general fund without expenditure of any part of that $100,000 nest egg. Additionally, in the six years that followed, $226,000 was allotted. This approximated 8 percent of what my actuarial figures called for.

Ultimate stability and permanence of the plan, however, came with the nation-wide economical installation of teletypewriters to take the place of the depleted ranks of telegraphers.

The most generous provision of the plan was full acceptance of the obligation to make grants applicable retroactively for the years of service prior to 1918, a provision which the insurance companies refused to consider. Granting pensions for service before that year meant that an employee who entered in 1900, at forty years of age, for example, would retire in 1925 at half-pay without having contributed a cent toward his pension.

In 1938, the fund had been increased adequately to cover all of these accrued liabilities for service prior to 1918. A new contributory plan was then established, the original fund ultimately being trusteed. For forty years it has been paying pension allowances for the total years of service of all employees on the payroll prior to 1938. At the end of 1957, there was still $4,380,075.22 in the trusteed account.

These generous payments were effective nearly twenty years before there was any United States Social Security legislation. Profound appreciation, therefore, was eloquently expressed in writing by some employees. Only three picked at random will be quoted. One was written March 5, 1940, to Howard Blakeslee, another AP employee, by H. E. Milhollen, an orange-grove owner in Clarcona, Florida. He had been a filing editor in the New York office for twenty-six years when he retired in 1926. An excerpt from his letter follows:

When I went with The AP nearly forty years ago, there was no half holiday, six straight days, a fifty-four-hour week. We had no grievance over that. But the depressing thing was the outlook: no life insurance, no pensions when working days were over, no welfare work for incapacitated or sick employees. Yes, rather a cheerless outlook. But to cut this recital of known facts very short, before the Government in a hit and miss way dabbled with the question of "security," The Associated Press in a purely voluntary way, without Government compulsion, and long, long before there was any Newspaper Guild in existence, inaugurated a welfare plan, insurance, pensions, etc., which for fairness, justice, generosity and absence of red tape, is better than anything the Government or other agency has to offer. And the moving spirit in all this was Kent Cooper. I do not wish to be mawkish, but a thousand times I have felt like rising up and calling him blessed. I have enjoyed these dozen years too greatly not to feel supremely grateful to K.C. and the old AP management.

The second letter was written to me March 12, 1940, by George W. Turner, a New York editor, who entered the service in New Haven in 1915 and retired in 1943. The last paragraph of his letter follows:

Some day, in due course, you will hand over the torch to another. You will be remembered for many brilliant and outstanding accomplishments in our profession; but none will sparkle more than your devotion to the best interests of the men and women who make up The AP. Far ahead of your time, you have had the vision to secure a measure of happiness and security for those in the twilight of life. That monument, in the hearts of AP men, will endure.

The third was the following memorandum from L. F. Curtis, the treasurer of The Associated Press, written August 29, 1944:

In a letter written at Needham, Mass., where he is living in retirement, Harold Martin says:
". . . I do appreciate what The Associated Press has done for me many years in the past. It has added immeasurably to our security, well-being, comfort, and happiness. The later years of the lives of both my wife and myself have been made secure and unworried by the continued and generous attitude of The Associated Press, and I feel convinced that the system under which I have been, and continue to be, rewarded is traceable to the thought and action of Kent Cooper."
I was pleased to have this expression from Harold. From his own ex-

perience he knows—as I know—what you did to create, build up and liberalize the pension plan so that men like Harold might have the security, well-being, comfort and happiness for which he is so grateful.

There have indeed been compensations for my AP work—far, very far beyond any financial recognition given me or that I could have obtained elsewhere: the employees' appreciation for the Employees' Benefit Plan is only one.

Teletypewriters, through which sufficient economies were effected to finance the Employees' Benefit Plan, were first installed on The Associated Press leased wires in 1914. They afforded the first improvement in the transmission of words since Morse demonstrated the telegraph in 1844. In the step then taken, The Associated Press was ahead of all the news agencies in the world.

There were four experiments in teletypewriters being made at the time by Dr. Louis N. Potts, of Baltimore; by Edward E. Kleinschmidt, of Brooklyn; by two Chicagoans, Charles Krum, a mechanical engineer, and his son Howard, an electrical engineer; and by The American Telephone and Telegraph Company.

The two teletypewriters farthest advanced were those of the Krums and The American Telephone and Telegraph Company. To establish commendable rivalry, I simultaneously gave an order to the Krums for installation of their machines in the seven Associated Press evening newspapers in New York, and to the A.T. & T. for the seven New York morning Associated Press newspapers.

I did not tell either of the two companies that I was dealing with the other. The A.T. & T. efforts were still lumbering along when its officials read an illustrated story in New York evening papers about The Associated Press' installation of the Krum teletypewriters in their offices.

Enraged at having been caught lagging, the A.T. & T., more than a year later, delivered to the United Press the equipment which I originally had ordered. Before the telephone company made this delivery, however, I got the Krums to install their machines in the seven Associated Press morning paper offices.

In 1921, Howard Krum told me that the same typed pages could be reproduced on a teletypewriter by radio. The idea was altogether too eerie to contemplate. To convince me, he let me be the first individual outside his organization to send a wireless message by teletypewriter. Thirty years later, The Associated Press was sending and receiving news all over the world by wireless teletypes.

The results of the engineering work begun inconspicuously by the Krums in 1902 had, by mid-century, completely superseded the original Morse method of telegraphy. Our children are taught to remember the names of the inventors of the telegraph, the telephone, the electric light, the cotton gin, the sewing machine. The name of Krum belongs in that galaxy.

8

THE TURNING
POINT

THE WAR PERIOD of 1914 through 1918, with its record of wholesale slaughter of driven youth and wreckless blunders and designs of its "statesmen," stands as the bloody prelude to a half-century murder mood that brought death to the armed and massacre to the unarmed.

Prior to 1914, it was easy to see how the Kaiser's Government, through the Wolff Bureau, its national news agency, was turning news into propaganda to create a jealous rage against anything not German. It was done so effectively that for the first time in history a government incited its people by propaganda to ask for a declaration of war before they were ordered headlong into it.

I never thought the American Government would ever secretly scheme to plant propaganda for war in the news here at home. I was wrong. In 1917, our own Government followed the German lead and became the second in history successfully to use news to incite the people to demand war.

Not wanting to be blamed for instigating this demand, President Wilson and Secretary of State Lansing gave The Associated Press, for its exclusive publication, what turned out to be a propaganda "plant," the government source of which The Associated Press agreed not to disclose. Through this artifice The Associated Press, instead of the

United States Government, stood sponsor for the accuracy of a German Government coded message to Mexico that incited Americans to demand our entry into the war.

The message was intercepted and decoded by the British Intelligence Service, which gave it to President Wilson. It asked Mexico to seek adherence and military support from Japan for a Mexican-Japanese attack on the United States from the Southwest if America went to war against Germany. Lansing, in his memoirs written seven years later, confirmed that he and Wilson secretly schemed to use The Associated Press solely to incite public demand for a declaration of war:

The "cold-blooded proposition" of Germany's secretary of foreign affairs in one day accomplished a change in sentiment and public opinion that would otherwise have required months to accomplish. From the time the telegram was published, or at least from the time its authenticity was admitted by its author, the United States' entry into the war was assured, since it could no longer be doubted that it was desired by the American people from Maine to California and from Michigan to Texas.

Repetition of the word "accomplished," the dictionary definition of which is "to bring to an issue of full success," and the phrase "the war was assured" make Lansing's statement a plain boast of having driven our country to war!

If Wilson and Lansing had not so planned it, they would have exposed the coded message themselves instead of secretly getting The Associated Press to do it. Moreover, they would have coupled the disclosure with their firm assurance that there was nothing to fear from the tottering Caranza Government in Mexico or from Japan, which had already allied itself with Britain and France against Germany.

During World War I, The Associated Press, which had an exclusive contract for use in North America of the news of government-subsidized European agencies, could not always avoid delivering their tainted news to American newspapers. Because of this I took a dislike to the foreign agency relationship. But there was more reason for the dislike than that.

In the general office correspondence in September, 1914, I found an unanswered cablegram from *La Nación,* the great Buenos Aires newspaper. It asked for Associated Press news service. There was a notation on the cablegram that a copy had been given to the New York correspondent of Havas, the French news agency. The original was about to be filed away and forgotten.

I took the unanswered message to Mr. Stone and said I would be glad to arrange the service. He said that I could not because South America was the exclusive territory of the Havas News Agency, and The Associated Press was prohibited by contract from sending news to that continent. I was astonished and said so. He only smiled when he added that the European news agency contracts prevented The Associated Press from sending AP news anywhere in the world outside of North America.

The fact that Havas, a small, government-subsidized French news agency, could prevent the great Associated Press from sending news to South America was bad enough, but that The Associated Press could not present the news of my country to all the rest of the world shocked me. I resented the fact that The Associated Press submitted to such degrading news repression.

The contract had been signed in 1893. Ever since then The Associated Press had been a fettered member of that European cartel. Composed of all twenty-five of the national news agencies of Europe, its leaders were Reuters of England, Havas of France, and Wolff of Germany. These three had allotted among themselves exclusive exploitation of various geographical sections of the world outside of Europe. Reuters had the British Empire and North America, also Japan and China. Havas had the French Empire and South America. Wolff had no territory outside of Europe but it did have control over the Austrian and Russian news agencies. It also shared Scandinavia equally with Reuters. In 1893, Reuters, for a consideration, sublet to The Associated Press its North American rights.

With a feeling that The Associated Press, potentially at least, was the giant of them all, my resentment increased with each succeeding month and year. The giant had been chained!

With a rising tide of war excitement here that ultimately took us in, I may have been moved by a degree of ardor I would not have felt in peacetime. But I believed The Associated Press ought not continue solely as a domestic news service catering only to the provincial tastes of its own country and denying itself the right to portray America to the rest of the world. The more I thought of it, the more I was aroused into a crusading spirit. There had been crusades before —there could be another one.

It seemed essential either to end the exclusive right The Associated Press had granted to the foreign news agencies to send American news abroad, or to terminate the contract altogether. Most important to me was that The Associated Press should have its own world service and aspire to become the world's greatest news distributor.

There was a sound reason why this should be done. American newspapers compose the largest and most prosperous group of journals in the world. I insisted that they could, if they would, make The Associated Press the instrument of world-wide truthful news dissemination. By so doing, all countries would be made aware of the intellectual, ethical and material progress of America. This thought occurred to me constantly during the next twenty years. Nothing, however, could be undertaken then without modifying or annulling The AP's contract with the cartel. To accomplish this was not going to be easy.

In the first place, I knew Mr. Stone would ardently oppose any change. His management had been the beneficiary of the cartel's acceptance of The Associated Press as an ally in 1893 to replace the old UP. He never forgot that The AP had been thus favored, and he firmly believed that otherwise The Associated Press, instead of its adversary of the nineties, would have succumbed. He felt this so keenly that he dramatically told the Board on one occasion, when the foreign agency hold on The Associated Press was being discussed, that he hoped he would not live to see the day when the contract was broken; nor did he.

Three months after I found the *Nación* cablegram, the Board of Directors gave consideration to modernizing the European news agency contract so that The Associated Press would be free to deliver its news to South America. Having succeeded in getting it discussed first at that Board meeting in December, 1914, there rarely was a meeting of the Board in the next twenty years at which I was not in some way able to get the matter on the agenda. I shall never forget that after one of the Board's discussions, Director W. L. McLean, a quiet, unassuming, undemonstrative gentleman, came to me, put his hand on my shoulder and whispered: "Don't lose heart!"

I never did. But after two years no reply had been sent to *La Nación*'s query. By that time *La Nación* had contracted with the United Press, which thereupon took the news agency position in South America that I wanted The Associated Press to have.

In March, 1916, an offer was made to me which, if accepted, might have made it easy for me to try to establish a world news service for an American press association. Roy W. Howard, who then had been the United Press president for four years, asked me to return to that organization. We both had been reporters in Indianapolis when our friendship began. The idea of being associated with him was attractive.

My position with The Associated Press at the time was several degrees below that of Howard with the UP. Apparently it was going to remain so. Discouragement faced me from all directions. At thirty-six years of age, I had been foreclosed against accomplishing many of the things in The Associated Press that called for action. There seemed to be no future for me unless I could be made responsible for the establishment and management of something of transcendent importance. That, I decided, could be an Associated Press world service. I envisioned that longingly with the probability of world-wide traveling.

As Howard and I talked, that idea either for The Associated Press or the United Press was uppermost in my mind. It would have been easy enough to have gone to the UP and applied whatever ability I had to make the United Press services world-wide with no opposition from a chained and bound Associated Press. I would not have been missed at The Associated Press if I had done so.

But what troubled me was that if I made the change, I would have a feeling of not having completed something I had resolved to do, a feeling somewhat akin to being a traitor to myself, though not to The Associated Press, since Mr. Stone was resolved not to permit the establishment of any activity which might be competitive with the world news cartel, to which he and President Noyes were extremely loyal.

A year and a half had passed since I first discovered the fetters that bound The Associated Press to a provincial status, yet I had made no progress toward removing them. Nevertheless, I stayed with The Associated Press and hopefully continued to try.

Forty years later, as I look backward at what has happened in the interim, that decision to try to make The Associated Press the world's greatest news distributor looms as the turning point of my career; for eventually it was accomplished.

When I wrote my declination to Howard I was vague in giving my reason:

New York, March 16, 1916

Dear Roy:

I have thought this thing out very thoroughly and have finally decided to stay where I am. A good many considerations enter into the thing and it is useless to try to twist them around. I believe that financially speaking I am giving up the greatest opportunity that will ever come to me; the loss is to be all mine, however, as I know that your work will go on just as prosperously without me.

Personally I want to thank you for your patience and to wish for you the greatest personal success, just as I know that—having decided—you wish the same for me.

Sincerely as ever,
Kent

His reply follows:

March 18, 1916

Dear Kent:

I have your note of the 16th and I want to thank you for the promptness of your decision.

While I regret, more, possibly, than you can imagine, that you are not going to be associated with us in the bully fight which we have ahead, I want you to know that you have our very best wishes for the big success of which we know you are capable.

You will not misunderstand me when I say that if we can't have you in our organization, nothing would suit us better than to see you at the head of the other one. I don't say this because I think that your big success would make things easier for us. I say it because I believe you are the one man in the other organization who appreciates the uselessness and the waste of energy in much of the so-called competition between the UP and The AP. I believe that you and I realize thoroughly that neither organization can be or should be put out of business, and I believe that when the day comes that you become the head of the other organization, many of the raw deals that are put over on both press associations now, because of the common knowledge that we will not get together even for defensive purposes, can be stopped very quickly.

I thank you for your personal good wishes—expressions which I feel certain are genuine—and I want you to believe me when I tell you that they are reciprocated *in full*.

Now that we have laid for once and for all the ghosts of this possibility of your coming back with us, I hope that I can see you a little oftener and that the distance from Park Row to Chambers Street may be materially reduced.

Faithfully yours,
Roy

I never asked Howard why he thought, in 1916, that I would reach the top at The Associated Press. I certainly did not think so then myself!

On his seventy-fifth birthday, January 1, 1958, I sent him a greeting recalling our friendship of nearly sixty years. In all that time, although in keen business competition, nothing has marred that personally congenial relationship. I reminded him of the exchange of letters in 1916. In response he referred feelingly to the late W. W. Hawkins, his associate and successor as president of the UP. Hawkins was my good friend, too, for nearly forty years. Howard wrote:

I have thought many times how very different things might have been in many ways, had your decision been different. Bill Hawkins was a tried and true friend. Possibly few people will understand what I mean, as well as you will, when I say that a very considerable part of any credit that has come my way for professional success was credit that by rights should have gone to Bill. I've always realized that, by reason of our wide difference in temperament, we supplemented each other, and complimented each other, to a degree that is not always found in partnerships such as ours, not even in those that lasted for forty years, as did ours.

Even so, I am certain that had you elected to go along with us, the results that would have been developed by the three-way team would have been something of which we could have all been proud.

Hawkins, thirty years after I decided to stay with The Associated Press, meant to be equally generous in complimenting me with this:

"The whole history of the press association business would have been radically different if you had never gone with The AP. You lifted a co-operative news service out of a self-satisfied lethargy and made it strong enough to survive a whole half-century, something that never had been done before, and you certainly made it tough for us."

Perhaps things would have been different, as both Howard and Hawkins said, but at any rate, Howard's was the first of three offers, acceptance of any one of which would have led me into new fields and away from The Associated Press, where, for some reason, I felt I must energetically press on.

The only three important things I had authority to do for The Associated Press without first having to appeal for approval from the Board were to improve the wire facilities, the morale of the Traffic Depart-

Roy W. Howard (1958)—
"How different things
might have been."

W. W. Hawkins (1942)—
"Considerable credit
by rights should have
gone to Bill."

ment personnel and to install teletypewriters when good telegraphers were hard to find.

By the fall of 1916, the Traffic Department had gotten far enough in its accomplishments to try a spectacular undertaking. All AP circuits were, at the time, regional in length with many relay points. There was no such thing as a transcontinental wire.

By the time of the baseball World Series of 1916, between the Boston Red Sox and the Brooklyn Dodgers, I put the Western Union to a real test by connecting every AP telegraph circuit in the country to one telegraph sending key in the Boston park; also for the games when they were played in Brooklyn.

There was no relay anywhere. Associated Press operators and Western Union officials were sure such a single circuit of 26,000 miles of wire with connections in 700 newspaper offices all over the country would not work. They remembered the Johnson-Jeffries fight of 1910. For that event, ringside at Reno, Nevada, was directly connected to the Denver-San Francisco wire. Railroad and Western Union operators wanting to listen to the account of the fight "plugged" in at every tank town between the two cities. They did the same on the wire from Denver to Chicago and, in fact, on all wires all over the country, with the result that the circuits were weakened, being heavily overburdened with receiving instruments. Neither The Associated Press nor the hundreds of telegraphic eavesdroppers got much of a story of the fight.

To prevent this from happening in the World Series of 1916, the Western Union, at my request, cut out all such connections in railroad and Western Union offices so that there were no connections to the circuit except to AP offices and newspapers. The company's action made the plan work. AP play-by-play accounts of the Series were carried from the Boston and Brooklyn ball parks directly to newspapers from coast to coast and lakes to gulf. It was all done so well that an old telegrapher by the name of Thomas A. Edison was interested. He sent this message:

KENT COOPER

AP NY

THE ASSOCIATED PRESS MUST BE WONDERFULLY WELL ORGANIZED TO BE ABLE TO ACCOMPLISH WHAT WAS DONE IN THE BALL GAMES. UNCLE SAM HAS NOW A REAL ARTERIAL SYSTEM AND IT IS NEVER GOING TO HARDEN

EDISON

The circuit was the longest in mileage, with more connections than had ever been operated successfully any place in the world. When it was set up and ready, I asked Mr. Stone to make one of his rare visits to the telegraph newsroom in New York. There, in hopeful but fearful anticipation, I listened as he dictated this message to an operator who sent it to every city in the country:

YOU ARE NOW BEING DIRECTLY CONNECTED WITH THE BOSTON BALL PARK.

M.E.S.

When the game was over, he got many telegrams of appreciation. Late that afternoon I was told that Mr. Stone wanted to see me in his office. I went in. He closed the door and we walked over to the large directors' table. There was a tray with a napkin over it. He removed the napkin, exposing two cocktails.

"I deeply appreciate what you did today and ask you to drink with me in commemoration," he said.

Never before had he commended me. And never before had I tasted a drop of alcohol. As I downed my Bronx cocktail, I noticed no difference in its taste from that of a small orangeade. If I went back to my office inspired to accomplish other demonstrations of efficient wire operation to please Mr. Stone, I prefer to assume it was because of the evidence of his satisfaction rather than to any exhilaration I got out of the cocktail—one cocktail!

9

THE YEARS OF
WORLD WAR I

AN OMINOUS SITUATION for The Associated Press developed with the United States' declaration of war in April, 1917, when newspapers that had never before received any press association report demanded service from The Associated Press. If the predicament in which the organization found itself had not been successfully met, the United Press would have gained the lead in the number of papers served.

What faced The Associated Press was that requests for service started to come from scores of newspapers which could not get AP memberships because the so-called territorial franchise rights of the large metropolitan papers prevented their election. Even if the number of papers was considered unimportant, the right to the local news of all of these additional newspapers certainly was important, since papers are obligated to furnish their local news to the press association that serves them.

These "franchise" rights covered circular areas as wide as 300 miles in diameter in which no newspaper could be elected without the consent of the "franchise" holders, who rarely gave it. The map of my home state of Indiana, for example, was covered with circles of "franchise" rights 120 miles in diameter that even overlapped each other. They had been granted to Associated Press members in Cincinnati, Louisville, Evansville, Indianapolis, Terre Haute and Chicago.

Mr. Stone told me nothing could be done to correct the ominous situation. Shortly thereafter I took occasion, while in Washington, to make a courtesy call on Frank B. Noyes, publisher of the Washington *Star,* who served as president of The Associated Press from 1900 to 1938. When he asked me about my work, I told him there were two things about which I was greatly concerned.

One was the need for an equitable assessment plan to replace the one established in 1900. As a result of our talk, the assessment plan I proposed was adopted by the Board in 1918. It is still in use in 1958.

The other matter of concern was the situation in respect to the "franchise" rights. I showed Mr. Noyes how these rights were adding new clients for AP competitors and repressing the growth of The Associated Press. I was able to convince him that it was an alarming situation. With his help, waivers were obtained from "franchise" holders that cut down these areas to a radius of ten miles from the cities of publication. As a result, The Associated Press membership increased in the next ten years by a net of 300, a percentage gain of 33⅓ percent.

If the waivers of the vast exclusive areas had not been secured,

Frank B. Noyes (1930)—
A.P. president (1900-1938).
In Washington, a courtesy call.

The Associated Press membership in 1925 would have been numerically less than it was in 1917 because of losses due to consolidations and suspensions, and The AP's chief competitor would have had a gain of approximately 50 percent. Without question, the UP would have been serving more newspapers by 1925 than The Associated Press, and the vast reservoir of news of all those newspapers would have gone to the United Press.

Some twenty-five years later, in a Board discussion of these exclusive "franchise" rights, President Noyes commended me for having stressed "the necessity of getting the territorial waivers in 1917." He told the Board that "if this had not been done when it was done, I seriously doubt whether The Associated Press would be in existence today."

By the time America entered World War I, the United Press had been established in South America for nearly a year. While The Associated Press was restrained by its cartel contract, the United Press was able to send news to Japan. Later it established the British United Press, which operated in Great Britain and the British Commonwealth. The United Press was also established in several other foreign countries.

By exerting continued pressure, I was given permission to travel throughout all of South America in the summer of 1918. On my arrival in Chile I had an unusual offer. Germanophile South Americans were operating a propaganda news agency which they called Prensa Asociada, the Spanish equivalent for AP. They represented it to be The Associated Press of the United States. The German Government was financing it.

Before I got off the ship at Valparaiso, representatives of Prensa Asociada undertook to negotiate with me for the South American rights to The Associated Press service. Their proposals disclosed the magnitude of the German Government propaganda campaign. As I was interested in knowing the extent of their backing, I asked what amount they would offer. They wanted me to fix the amount. When I declined they named $10,000. I only smiled. Quickly they tripled it. I shook my head. Then they offered $100,000.

"Not if you offered me ten thousand times that amount could you purchase The Associated Press rights in South America," I said.

Proceeding to call upon the larger and more prosperous newspapers,

I found a fertile field for AP development which I reported to the Board upon my return. But the foreign agency contract still barred the way. The next step, therefore, was to get the French Havas Agency to consent to The Associated Press serving newspapers in that continent. To discuss this, Charles Houssaye, managing director of that agency, was invited to New York in the fall of 1918. I was asked to negotiate with Houssaye.

In my talk with him I recounted as dramatically as I could the Prensa Asociada offer and appealed to his French patriotism for co-operation with his American ally to let The Associated Press suppress the German Prensa Asociada by giving the papers the genuine AP service. My disclosure of the German propaganda operations shocked him. We had been conversing in Spanish. Excitedly expressing the outrage of it, he changed volubly from Spanish to his native tongue, so I got a good lesson in French, the second foreign language I had undertaken to learn in anticipation of being allowed to establish The Associated Press world service. The appeal to his patriotism had its effect, for within a half-hour we had concluded matters satisfactorily.

On November 7, 1918, every city in the Western Continent where there was a newspaper that received the United Press service was thrown into a paroxysm of rejoicing by the famous UP false armistice. The Associated Press had no word of any cessation of hostilities. I had a luncheon engagement that day with W. W. Hawkins, vice-president of the UP. He failed to appear. After waiting a half-hour, I went back to The Associated Press office to telephone him.

. The place was wild with excitement. A newsroom drama was being enacted. Painfully I witnessed the intense emotion that can be worked up in a newsman who is devoted to the idea of never being beaten on a hot news story. Jackson S. Elliott, the news editor, was shouting into the telephone to someone that The Associated Press bureau in Paris had been badly "scooped" by the UP, which had announced the end of the war. After he hung up the telephone and turned to me, Elliott's face was red with disappointment and anger at The Associated Press Paris bureau.

I tried to calm him. "Four years ago," I said, "a member telephoned Mr. Stone and loudly protested that his opposition United Press paper was on the streets with the death of Pope Pius X. The member excitedly asked at the top of his voice what was the matter; why didn't

The Associated Press have it? I heard Mr. Stone reply that since The Associated Press didn't have news of the death, the United Press must have anticipated it. 'Well, then,' said the member hotly, 'for God's sake, Mel, why in hell don't you hire their anticipator?' You remember, Jack, that it was not until the next day that the Pope died, according to the official announcement then carried by The Associated Press."

Carl Brandebury, Harold Martin and Fisher Curtis were in the room. They started to smile, looked at Elliott and decided not to, for my little anecdote didn't calm his rage. Still angry, and even pre-

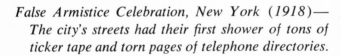

False Armistice Celebration, New York (1918)— The city's streets had their first shower of tons of ticker tape and torn pages of telephone directories.

tending not to have heard what I said, he again tried to get someone, anyone, in authority in the government at Washington to make the announcement of the armistice so that The Associated Press could carry it from Washington and take the edge off the United Press scoop. Messages were coming from everywhere by telegraph and telephone demanding that The Associated Press send the news that the war was over.

Meanwhile, New York streets were jammed with people celebrating the end of the war. Adding to the excitement in the streets, New York had its first great shower of tons of ticker tape and torn pages of tele-

phone directories. With some difficulty, Mr. Stone returned from lunch to The Associated Press. Excitement was at a high pitch in the big newsroom. Mr. Stone asked: "What is it all about?"

"We are utterly beaten, Mr. Stone," Elliott began, almost shouting.

"Is the war over?" Mr. Stone quietly asked.

"Yes, our Paris bureau has failed us completely, Mr. Stone," Elliott replied.

I never saw a more touching exhibition of personal distress over a story than Elliott's. Nor do I recall ever having seen such a striking example of poise in an emergency as Mr. Stone showed. He referred to the excitement in the streets:

"Well," he said, "since we haven't any news of the end of the war, let me see what we have sent out about this wild excitement in the streets."

"You don't think we would be sending out anything about that, do you?" asked Elliott. "We already have sent out an informative note that we are not reporting these demonstrations because we have no news that would justify them."

"Elliott, what is going on in the streets is news. I never saw such a demonstration."

"But, Mr. Stone, the story is the end of the war, not what is going on in New York streets," exclaimed Elliott.

"I want the story of this demonstration written at once," said Mr. Stone. He turned to Brandebury, city editor, and said: "Brandebury, I'd like to have a running story sent out about this wild street demonstration and I want you to say that they are celebrating a report of the signing of an armistice, of which The Associated Press has no news."

Mr. Stone's remarkable judgment never could have been demonstrated better than it was then. He sat down, lit a cigar, and waited for copies of the running story of the celebration, which Brandebury hammered out with a speed he had not shown since he wrote the coverage of the Harry K. Thaw murder trial several years before when he was an employee of the UP.

When he saw the first part of the story, Mr. Stone said: "Elliott, now send a message to other cities to put on stories of what is happening there."

Elliott silently complied, though still suffering with rage.

Thus The Associated Press had good stories on the riotous celebrations of an armistice, the signing of which it had not reported. That was the story of the day. There was no other news of consequence, for a few hours later the Government in Washington announced there had been no armistice.

Four days later, on November 11, 1918, the Eiffel Tower radio station in Paris cryptically and dramatically flashed: "Fermez les portes, fermez les portes." Twice in each sixty seconds the flash was repeated: "Fermez les portes, fermez les portes." All of Europe was waiting as radio-receiving operators, professionals and amateurs, listened to hear the news that the war was over. John L. Hart, an American boy who was in Holland with his parents, heard the words: "Fermez les portes, fermez les portes." He thought at first it must be a code message. All of Europe's listeners, including the American boy in Holland with a simple little radio-receiving set, had to guess the meaning of "close the doors."

Was it code? No, but it might as well have been except to those who remembered Janus, the ancient Roman god of gates and doors. Suddenly its meaning clicked in the American boy's brain; that in ancient times the doors of the Temple of Janus in Rome were thrown open when the warriors went to battle and were closed when they returned victorious. With "close the doors" the Eiffel Tower station kept on signaling victory.

A few minutes later, at 2:46 A.M., Associated Press wires all over America were singing the news: "Flash—armistice signed." But the French had not put it into plain words like that until some time afterward. Then the message was: "The war is over."

The French had gone to war dramatically, they had fought dramatically, and they had announced the end of the war dramatically, just as they celebrated Bastille Day dramatically on the following July 14.

The war ended November 11. I sailed from New York to South America three days later with high hopes of a new conquest on behalf of The AP. I succeeded. Seven weeks later, The Associated Press had received into membership many of the important newspapers in South America, and delivery of its service began.

Before I returned to New York, the AP annual meeting of April 22nd had been held. The proceedings had been turned into a celebration of my success. One of the most eloquent of The AP's new South American members, Señor Augustin Edwards, owner of the Mercurio newspapers of Santiago, Valparaiso and Antofogasta, paid as beautiful an oratorical tribute to The Associated Press as exists in its archives:

"We are, gentlemen, living in wonderful times. The people at large have taken into their own hands the broad lines of the policies they consider best suited to their national purposes. And the press today constitutes really and truly the channel of communication which conveys to governments the impressions and thoughts of the people, and to the people the difficulties encountered by those in power. As long as that channel of communication is kept clear and clean, the press is nobly using the power that destiny has thrown into its hands.

"The Associated Press has done perhaps more than any other human agency to keep that channel clean and clear. The news it spreads throughout the world is unbiased. Its news flows as crystalline water springing from the purest fountain. This institution, The Associated Press, has to my mind raised the profession of journalism to a high moral level, in which it begins to lose the appearance of a trade and to shine with the glory of the priesthood.

"The Associated Press has just come through a test, perhaps the most severe that it is ever to undergo, in these four and a half years, in which the quality of every institution—and perhaps the quality of every single individual—has been tested.

"Ancient empires have fallen; crowns and thrones have crumbled; systems of government have disappeared, showing their dangers and immoralities, and even the machinery of international intercourse has had to undergo repair.

"Yet The Associated Press stood the test and stood it well. It has today, as it had before the war, the respect of the whole world."

When I returned to New York and read the stenographic report of all the speeches at the luncheon, I felt that I had been a crusading knight in foreign lands. What was said was an immediate reward given during my lifetime for the beginning of The Associated Press world service which I had advocated for four years. The press of South America had come to know that although the United States was a foreign country, The Associated Press principle of true and unbiased news without a tinge of propaganda could be accepted with confidence in its integrity. "The highest original American moral concept ever developed in America" had been welcomed in its sister continent.

10

MUSIC HERALDS

A SUNRISE

IMMEDIATELY AFTER REACHING New York in the spring of 1919, I went to Paris, where the peace treaty was being negotiated. I was very much impressed by what I was able to observe of the methods by which the treaty was being put together. I wondered if anyone had thought about the matter of the inclusion of an article declaring for a free press and freedom of international news exchange.

I had heard about the utopian approach on every other subject affecting the welfare of the peoples of the world: there were considerations of how to protect their health, their right to live; also about the suppression of their right to wage war. But I could not find that anyone had projected for consideration the welfare of the people as to guaranteeing that they could have true, unbiased news to read in their newspapers about either world or domestic affairs.

Believing in truthful, unbiased news and a free press, I felt that a world peace treaty, in the writing of which America had a part, should do no less than extend that idealistic concept throughout the world. This thought—that good will among men depends upon truthful news exchange—seized me with such force as to become the dominating idea of my stay in Paris.

I had become acquainted with Colonel Edward M. House, President Wilson's advisor, before I went to South America the first time, and had told him the whole story of how The Associated Press contract with the great European news agencies, headed principally by Reuters of London, had confined Associated Press activities to the United States. He had listened attentively. Learning that he was at the Hotel Crillon in Paris, I called on him and told him what I had done in South America.

I asked him if he knew whether anything respecting freedom of the press and freedom of international news exchange was being incorporated in the treaty. He asked me to explain exactly what I thought ought to be done, and I told him. He said he would make inquiries, and with high hopes I left him. A week later I called on him again. He had raised the question but was told somewhat cryptically that "the matter had been taken care of privately." I gathered the impression that the European agencies themselves were going to handle the affair.

Naturally I assumed this meant that Reuters of England and Havas of France would impose their will on the German news agency and those of all the new countries that were being created by the peace treaty. My guess proved a good one. That is exactly what happened. Not only that, but the subject of freedom of the press was not dealt with in the peace treaty.

I was disappointed and wondered then whether in my lifetime The Associated Press would gain freedom of action abroad. I wondered whether in an expanding world The Associated Press could always remain domestic with only a restrained expansion of its activities in the Western Hemisphere.

Confronted with this disappointment, I decided to try to get inspiration from the idea that freedom of news exchange between peoples would foster peace. Since England had suffered its most devastating war and surely didn't want another one, I hoped that Reuters would be interested in my conception of a transcendent opportunity to advance a great cause in a world recovering from its greatest catastrophe.

After the signing of the peace treaty at Versailles in June, 1919, I went to London, where, for the first time, I met Sir Roderick Jones, managing director of Reuters. He was wholly unresponsive even to a discussion of the principle of a world free press and freedom of news exchange. I had no idea what my next step should be.

And then something happened that renewed in me a resolve to rededicate myself unfalteringly to freeing The Associated Press so it could make its own international exchange of news the medium of acquaintance and friendship among all peoples. That resolve was due to what I observed in Paris a few days after returning from London. They told me that the Allied troops were going to parade through the streets of Paris on Bastille Day, but I had no idea that merely watching men march would affect me as it did.

I had an excellent vantage point from which to view it all, from a window overlooking the Arch of Triumph, built by Napoleon, who issued a decree that none but conquerors were to pass under it. Constructed over a hundred years before, no French troops until that day, July 14, 1919, had earned the right to march under it. Into the celebration went all the enthusiasm pent up in them since their last Bastille Day five years earlier.

The French are nothing if not dramatic. Perhaps the spectacle of that day may never again be equaled. First through the Arch were the French wounded. Carried on cots, rolled in wheel chairs, those pitiful fragments of bodies were borne through, many of them clasping hands in prayer as they passed. Others tried to shout or sing as they heroically attempted to lift their pain-racked bodies.

Heroes indeed, for I was told that several had died during and immediately after the parade. All had pleaded to be allowed to lead that procession; they would willingly die if given that one chance for glory in life. So from the hospitals they were brought, even as life ebbed out of them.

They were followed by the commander-in-chief of the Allied forces, Marshal Foch. Then came the marching hosts: First there were the Americans, headed by the color bearers, for the detachments representing each country proceeded in alphabetical order. Pershing led this picked body of men, all of whom seemed to be exactly the same height and weight, wearing shining helmets and new uniforms, marching briskly to the music of the band. Next came the Belgians, their uniforms and equipment quite drab in comparison with the Americans. Then the British, Italians, and so on through the list of Allies until, as a courtesy to all the rest, the French came last.

The procession already had taken hours to pass and yet the packed mass of spectators waited expectantly. The day had been cloudy, but as the French officers rode through the Arch, the sun came out to shine upon their sabers as they whipped them toward the heavens in dramatic salute. The people who had waited became hysterical with their cheers when the French infantry followed, not in new uniforms and shining helmets, but in bluish gray, bespeckled with mud, just as one might expect to see them emerge from trench warfare.

When the day was done, I had witnessed an aggregation representative of the greatest war strength ever gathered to meet a common enemy. And as I watched, I thought that the soldiers of any one of the nations might have fitted into the ranks of any other nation by the mere change of uniform.

The same thought struck me later when I went to Germany and

saw discharged German soldiers still wearing their trench clothing. But language, environment, and something else had driven them to war. The type of civilization that each had known was the same in its broad aspects; yet there was something that compelled them to occupy from one to four years of their lives in trying to kill each other.

The only time that millions of them had ever been near to the other millions was when they were at death grips. They had come from all corners of the world for one purpose, and that was to kill! And yet these men as children had played much the same the world over. They had grown into manhood under the care of mothers who

Bastille Day Parade, Paris (1919)—
First the Americans, picturesquely
headed by the flag bearers.

were all of the same instinct. And those who had survived would take up a workaday life much the same regardless of nationality.

They had come to fight and they fought like demons because the propaganda their governments fed them back home made them believe they had reason to hate. The propaganda, masquerading as truthful news, reached them from the news agencies, many of which were owned outright or were subsidized by governments which intentionally tried to create war fever. These governments were well aware that the decision as a result of their propaganda ultimately would rest on the number of dead on the field of battle.

The parade of the Allied powers on Bastille Day, 1919, formed in me the resolve to disregard discouragements and to do what I could to rid international news exchange of controls that intentionally feed men's prejudices, and to see that all men everywhere could read truthful news. I vowed to myself again that there eventually would be an Associated Press world service to make that possible. That was the only effort I personally could make to erase one of the causes of war.

That night the city of Paris was *en fête*. The boulevards were filled with merrymakers. Not for five years had Parisians been allowed to celebrate their "Fourth of July." There was no organized effort to promote the jollity the thousands upon thousands engaged in. No police control was imposed. It was all good-natured fun.

I watched it until midnight from a vantage point near the opera house, then turned down a side street to go to my hotel. Suddenly I was encircled by a half-dozen teen-aged girls singing and asking me in French for "one kiss" for each. Without hesitation I complied. I was about to kiss number one the second time when they all cried in French: "No, sir, that's all!" They broke their circle and I was left free to go my way.

That was one Parisian story I thought I could repeat to my wife and daughter when I got home. I told about kissing the first teen-ager, then the second, without noticing how shocked my little daughter was. As I said I kissed the third, fourth, fifth and sixth, she was about to break into tears of rage as she cried:

"Papa, why didn't they pick a young man!"

In 1920, I was named assistant general manager. Again that year and the next I spent several months in South America and Europe.

From 1922 to 1925 I made several prolonged trips in the United States visiting AP members in connection with radio broadcasting, a novelty that had ominously injected itself into the business of news dissemination. Some newspaper publishers feared that oral broadcasts of news into the home would diminish newspaper circulations. Others thought such broadcasts might ultimately supplant newspapers entirely.

Both fears proved groundless. But moves toward meeting the novel, competitive method of news and advertising publication did create a division of views among The Associated Press membership. Some members thought the menace could be fought and overcome if the news agencies refused to furnish news for broadcasting. Others installed their own radio stations and insisted they be permitted to broadcast the news the press associations were serving to their newspapers. It took The Associated Press membership more than twenty years to harmonize its attitude toward radio. Its first concession was to make its news available for broadcasting through contracts with the stations. Then it amended its by-laws and admitted the stations to membership. Acceptance of this solution by the stations was effected through the admirable ability and tact of Assistant General Manager Oliver S. Gramling.

When the Atlanta *Journal* had installed its radio station, my visit there in February, 1925, to discuss radio news broadcasting had a surprising result for me personally. For it was then I realized once more that my longing to compose music could not be permanently suppressed, although more than twenty years had passed since I completed the waltz the first four bars of which Victor Herbert had written on his cuff in my presence.

John S. Cohen, president and editor of the *Journal,* and I were discussing the popularity of musical broadcasts. He deplored the fact that not since Stephen Foster had anybody written such beautiful southern music. I said probably no one ever would. As we talked, I related the Victor Herbert incident. Then I happened to think of his newspaper's slogan: "The *Journal* covers Dixie like the dew!" I asked him how he would like to broadcast something with a title like "Dixie Girl," the words and music of which I would write. "Great!" he exclaimed; "provided, of course, you can write it!"

"Dixie Girl" had its first rendition on the Atlanta Journal radio station four weeks later. Sixteen years after that, I happened to play it for Niles Trammell, president of the National Broadcasting Company and a Georgian himself, being a native of Marietta in that state. He liked it and had it put on the air on one of the Cities Service programs.

"Dixie Girl" really went to town. Lanny Ross and Dinah Shore

K.C. in Illustrious Company—An Edwin Cox panel drawn by Bliss, Washington Post *(1941).*

premiered it on the Columbia Broadcasting System May 7, 1941. It was then recorded by Sammy Kaye for Victor and by Rogers for Columbia. It was played and sung on the "Hit Parade" and by orchestras across the country. It was also sung for three weeks at New York's Radio City Music Hall by Earl Wrightson. Royalties were donated to the Girl Scouts of America.

My musical urge was aroused anew. I then wrote several other numbers, all of which were broadcast many times. They included ballads like "Sunset," "America Needs You" (a patriotic song dedicated to the Girl Scouts), orchestral pieces like "El Olano," marches for bands like "The Spirit of Freedom" and "Mardi Gras Parade," beautifully premiered by Paul Lavalle's Band of America. Also, there was an operetta, for which I wrote the book, lyrics and music. It was broadcast over the entire Mutual Broadcasting System from Station WGN in Chicago. Membership in the American Society of Composers, Authors and Publishers was conferred upon me.

The original broadcast of "Dixie Girl" on the Atlanta *Journal* radio station in March, 1925, proved to be an omen of good fortune for me. It heralded the sunrise of a golden opportunity in The Associated Press just one month later.

11

INTO THE HIGHEST POSITION

When Frank B. Noyes, Adolph S. Ochs and Victor F. Lawson, serving as a committee of The Associated Press Board in April, 1925, asked me if I would assume the general managership, my answer must have been Yes. At least Mr. Noyes told me afterward that I did express what he defined as a gracious and appreciative affirmative, but that my thoughts appeared to be far away.

They were indeed. They shot back instantly to the day I gave up news work, then they leaped forward through the years into thankful realization that at last I was returning to it with the further opportunity of increasing membership loyalty that would aid in advancing The Associated Press into new fields of achievement while holding its highest executive position.

For the best twenty years of my life I had been absorbed in expediting delivery of news but not writing it, nor even having authority to say what kind of news should be sought or how it should be written. And for fifteen of those years I had been trying to develop loyal interest in the welfare of The Associated Press on the part of its members. I was pleasantly associated with newsmen everywhere—in The Associated Press and on newspapers. I also continued sincerely cordial relations with my old friends who were conducting the United

*Kent Cooper—Appointed general manager of
The Associated Press (1925).*

Press services—Roy W. Howard, W. W. Hawkins and Karl Bickel.

I gave ideas to others in The Associated Press, which they put into effect in their own way if the rigid rules of AP news treatment permitted. I hoped I was sowing the seed for the news report of tomorrow, wondering if for me tomorrow in news work would ever come —a tomorrow that would give me authority to enlarge the news picture of human activity with the color such an important product so richly deserves.

Even before Messrs. Noyes, Ochs and Lawson had left the room, my thoughts were restlessly anticipating changes. Within a week I had written an outline of what The Associated Press report would have to be. Before the year 1925 ended, what I then wrote was expanded into an address which I personally repeated to all state and regional membership meetings throughout the country. These gatherings were attended by representatives of more than half of The Associated Press membership. Excerpts of what I said follow:

The high principles upon which this news service is conducted were conceived long ago. Briefly, these principles have required that the news to be reported must be important, written with dignity befitting its importance without reportorial bias, and that it be an honestly compiled day-by-day history of the world. Respect for and loyalty to those principles shall guide us. But there also will be a fervent determination to expand what the word "important" means in news coverage.

That calls for a new policy that will embrace as important such news as interests all the people. With this new definition of what news is important, I know of nothing which has interest that need be banned. This leaves a tremendously large field. Never forgetting to continue the sound treatment we always have given the basic news of affairs of state, commerce and politics, we shall venture further into this tremendously large, heretofore untouched mine of information.

We shall develop special writers to induce men of science and inventive genius to tell us on what they are working to give us better opportunity to enjoy better living; how men of medicine and chemistry are developing new protections against disease and methods of prolonging life. There shall be writers regularly assigned to report news of the stage, screen, radio, the arts, labor and industry, as well as the people's religious devotions and religious movements.

Perhaps another way to say what I have in mind is that hereafter man—

in high or low position—what he feels, what he does at work or play, what he says that interests others, his fears, his hopes, his aspirations, his prayers, how he is facing and meeting his destiny also take positions of importance in the news. In other words, we must prove there is nothing so important, nothing so fascinating as the true day-by-day story of humanity. We shall tell this whole story insofar as we have the ability, so that the news report shall become a stronger, more practical force that will strengthen, invigorate and sustain this venture in journalism which we call The Associated Press.

To acquaint American newspaper readers with life as it is lived by the hundreds of millions on the other continents, the foreign staffs shall aid in bringing about this change. They shall tell what is happening in and what interests the people of the countries to which they are assigned. They shall continue to report the news of governments, of course, but they also shall present fully for American readers a picture of the lives of the people, their varied activities and interests, their joys and their sorrows, their amusements and their devotions, their work and their play. In other words, the members of the foreign staff are to give us news concerning the people of low as well as high estate. To do this they must go out of the beaten paths of travel to observe and write of life in the towns and villages of which readers in this country may never have heard. We are to have date lines from wherever spot news or features can be found, not just from the capitals of a few countries.

In short, the emphasis is that the news must be about people—all the people, both at home and abroad, but never forgetting continuance of the same sound treatment of the only kind of news heretofore designated as important.

I could give many reasons why I struck out so definitely, if not defiantly, on these changes. First of all, I wanted members to take more pride in their Associated Press service so that they willingly would pay for the striking improvements I had planned. With more money, I could make The Associated Press a more attractive place for competent men to work. A well-rewarded staff would produce a better news service, which in turn would increase membership loyalty —indeed, such a firm loyalty that when the members lost their so-called exclusive "franchise" rights, as I then feared one day they surely would, not one of them would resign his membership because of that loss, since by that time the service might be so valuable as to be indispensable to them.

In the one matter of "humanizing" the news, The Associated Press was not the sole pioneer. Individual newspapers here and there were doing it with their local news in the century's first two decades. Under the presidency of Roy W. Howard, the youthful UP, held down by no retarding restrictions as was The Associated Press, also was doing some trail blazing of its own with the news it delivered to its clientele, smaller numerically compared to The Associated Press membership. I had the good fortune to have been one of the first of the group of United Press pioneers who started out on these new trails as early as 1903.

But it was the broadening of Associated Press news policy that galvanized interest in a new national standard which was promptly embraced by AP newspapers, which synchronized its publication throughout the country. How quickly they embraced it was marked by the prompt co-operation of Associated Press newspapers which began contributing human interest stories of their own localities, which harmonized with the news The Associated Press staff was writing.

Less than eight months after I started this modernization of the service, the Kansas City *Star* of December 14, 1925, declared editorially:

Until recently The Associated Press has conceived its field to be restricted to the chronicling of serious and important news. From its standpoint, a catastrophe, an election, a congressional debate, the death of a distinguished man, an important trial, pretty much exhausted the topics of human interest.

Until recently. An attentive reader of the *Star* must have noticed a change in the last few months. The Associated Press by-line now is appearing over dispatches that are gay as well as grave. The whole range of human activities has been covered. From remote quarters of the earth have been flowing dispatches revealing quaint and interesting phases of foreign life. The correspondent with the Amundsen relief expedition has told the story of his adventures in trying to get elusive news. From Commander Rodgers has come the story of his thrilling hop to Hawaii. A woman correspondent has written her impressions of Mrs. Coolidge at Chicago.

The Associated Press has begun to live up to the Greek philosopher's saying that nothing human was alien to him. It has not lowered its standards. It has simply enlarged the field of its interests. It is striving to report every phase of the human spectacle.

The transformation has been due to the vision and imagination of the new general manager, Mr. Kent Cooper. Mr. Cooper is impressing his fresh conception of the functions of a world-wide news gathering association on his far-flung reporting staff. The resulting changes should bring to the reading public a new and vivid conception of this strangely interesting world they live in.

Best of all in support of maintaining the new policy against its critics was the response of readers in the attainment of the greater newspaper prosperity which resulted in part from these changes. The role was a striking one. The readers really took their newspapers unto themselves with a friendly, familiar feeling because the newspapers contained what interested them told in the way they talked to each other. They appreciated having sports news written in the vernacular even though it meant the inclusion of slang.

They liked Anson referred to as "Cap," not "Adrian C." They liked Cobb referred to as "Ty," not "Tyrus"; Bender as "Chief," not "Charles"; Evers as "Johnny," not "John J."; Simmons as "Al," not "Aloysius"; Speaker as "Tris," not "Tristram E."; Waddell as "Rube," not "George Edward"; Wagner as "Honus," not "John Peter"; Young as "Cy," not "Denton T." They also wanted batters reported as having hit "two-baggers," "grass-cutters," "Texas Leaguers," "homers," etc.

In the mid-century years, it was difficult to believe that news of the tremendously broadened human field was ever banned from The Associated Press report or that the vernacular was taboo in reports of sports events. It was difficult to believe that it had ever been necessary to countermand orders that the nicknames of the National and American League baseball clubs were not to be used.

In The Associated Press code, nicknames were considered to be slang. So the terms "Cubs" and "Yankees," for instance, were not supposed to appear in news reports on baseball. The first was supposed to be called the "Chicago National League Baseball Club"; the second, the "New York American League Baseball Club."

The use of nicknames, a critic once declared, constitutes a practice of catering to lower intelligence. If that is so, the riposte may well be that the well-educated family that lives next door, the nice fellow one meets on the street, the lawyer, the merchant and the school teacher, are all of lower intelligence for they use such terms and they are good Americans, too. God bless them every one!

The first AP general order on the use of slang in 1905 was:

Correspondents will be careful to avoid the use of slang phrases in the service, particularly in connection with sporting and markets.

After five years of infractions of this order, a further warning went out as follows:

The use of slang in the report should be avoided. If not carefully controlled it is apt to degenerate into the coarse and vulgar and it is very seldom indeed that any adequate end is served by slang expressions. Vigorous and incisive construction is desirable, but the line should be drawn against slang terms and phraseology.

In spite of such repeated orders and the sending of numerous corrections by wire, batters occasionally were still "whiffing" out, "popping" flies, "beating it" safely to the first "sack" and "purloining" second. Also, there were "grass-cutters," "Texas Leaguers," "homers," etc. There was also this order of 1910:

Basketball being merely a form of exercise and, therefore, not news, the scores of the various teams should not be included in the news report.

When this injunction was issued, basketball was neither a professional game nor was it played in many universities. After five years the increase of public interest in it, however, brought a slight modification in the order:

The reporting of basketball events should be limited to contests between universities and colleges.

The clamor of members for sports news resulted in a trial of a special baseball wire as early as 1910. That, it was hoped, would keep sports stories off the regular wires. But even on the special wire, slang and nicknames were not supposed to be used. So patronage of it dropped until 1913, at which time a special sports editor was employed to try to enliven it.

But with the start of the war in 1914, the special wire disappeared and sports news was carried on the regular wires in conventional form thereafter until the 1920's. By then the order not to use nicknames and slang terms in sports news just died from total lack of observance.

The work of alert, critical AP news supervisors brought compliance with the requirement that other than sports news be told in the conventional form, as a promising young journalist learned soon after he entered The Associated Press service in 1910. Being a Princeton man and well acquainted with' Woodrow Wilson, then governor of New Jersey, he was assigned in 1912 to report the news of Wilson's candidacy on the Democratic presidential ticket. Wilson, a liberal, had an eye on the vote in New York State. Word came that Judge Alton B. Parker, a conservative and the Democratic nominee of 1904, had been selected as temporary chairman of the New York State Democratic Convention.

With the other correspondents, the AP man asked Governor Wilson if he had any comment. The Governor didn't want to say anything about it, but he told the reporters that they could say he "frowned." The "lead" to the AP man's dispatch reported that Governor Wilson "frowned" when he learned of Parker's selection. When it reached The Associated Press in New York, the "lead" was promptly killed on the ground that unless Governor Wilson was ready publicly to say he was displeased and to be so quoted, The Associated Press would carry nothing at all on the matter.

For reporting what the Governor said he could report, the young AP man got a lecture on how important it was "not to read other people's minds." In his six years with The Associated Press this reporter never had a by-line. Since then he has had many of them—elsewhere. A nationally known columnist, his by-line is "By David Lawrence."

Having launched human interest stories, another change that was enthusiastically received after 1925 by AP members was the reporting of motion picture news. That industry's development had reached the point of popular interest and patronage at the beginning of the First World War. Readers were interested in news of the war but they were interested, too, in motion picture news, which at that time was not being printed by newspapers on the ground that it was "free advertising." By demand of its member newspapers, The Associated Press promptly adopted the policy of excluding motion picture news and rigidly adhered to it. Indeed, it continued to adhere to it long after the newspapers, having gotten motion picture advertising, unanimously changed their attitude.

The film industry itself did no advertising before the First World War, and local exhibitors, many of them showing movies in converted storerooms, never had patronized the newspapers. They merely announced their attractions with display cards in "downtown" store windows. In return, the storekeepers got passes to the movies. But inability to get motion picture advertising was not all that confronted the newspapers. Their readers began to demand movie news.

With the newspapers and their AP remaining obdurate, came the nuisance of a trickster type of press agent. His news stories exploited the names of movie stars both in newspapers and The Associated Press. Motion pictures in which they were starred, however, were never mentioned. Yet the stars as individuals were reported as actually having suffered occurrences in love affairs or peril which their screen vehicles later depicted. No expense was involved in getting movie stars mentioned in this way except for the salaries of the press agents and the cost of their typewriters.

The newspapers and The Associated Press were taken in. This was long before the day of the public relations experts. The news profession then knew, and once a year welcomed, the open and aboveboard circus press agents who, with an ample supply of passes for the show, dealt in superlative adjectives. They also knew the more restrained type of advance theatrical representatives. But until the motion picture trickster came along, neither The Associated Press nor the newspapers had ever encountered the type that would concoct an untrue story solely to get his employer's name mentioned in the news reports.

Entirely responsive to its newspaper masters in their efforts to avoid free advertising, The Associated Press, leaning over backward to avoid it, was nevertheless taken in on the "news" of these press agents, not once but often. Finding that it could not always detect whether this news was true or not, The Associated Press solution was the establishment of a rule that the name of no screen actor or actress be allowed to appear in the news report. The exception was that if one were arrested, seriously injured or murdered, the police record, briefly recited, was admissible. Even an obit at death was not!

Yet before and after this policy was adopted in 1914, there certainly were practices inexplicably at variance with it. Except for the screen, there was ballyhoo in the news that was admissible and brought fame to many. With or without publicity conceived and stimulated by press agents, heroes of romantic ventures and daring achievements came to be nationally known, their deeds being related in the AP news reports. There was no embargo against using their names or telling what they did. With their fame thus made secure, they prospered later by stage appearances or books of autobiography that might never have held any interest whatever if The Associated Press news reports had not made their names household words.

Then, too, year after year, prize fighting and horse racing were projects that could have been labeled entertainment for which, like the movies, admission was charged; yet even though outlawed in some states, such events were publicized in The Associated Press report and printed in the newspapers.

An instance of this in the fight game was that the first million-dollar gate for a pugilistic contest, the Dempsey-Carpentier fight in 1921, resulted from news build-ups and ballyhoo, not from paid advertising in newspapers. Of race-track events, mention need only be made of the amount of free news space that was devoted each year to the Kentucky Derby. AP news stories, not paid advertising, annually attracted thousands to Louisville from all over the country.

News of criminals, due to reader interest, often produced surprising results, too. Jesse James' name in the news made him famous, but not until after his death were his widely reported exploits capitalized by the simple means of "dime" novels and admission fees to exhibitions of wax figures representing him.

In 1922, in a statement I read to the Board of Directors, I told how The Associated Press fully reported the activities of another desperado, the notorious Pacific Coast bandit Roy Gardner, while it still refused to carry a word about motion picture stars. Having escaped from prison, Gardner did not commit a desperate deed every day, but until he was caught, The Associated Press was reporting enough diversified criminal activities, of which he was suspected, to make his name known far and wide.

On the other hand, while Gardner's name was appearing in large block-letter headlines over AP stories in this country, a screen star of that day, who had not then lost his popularity here at home, was getting big headlines in England over stories of his welcome to that, his native land; but not in the United States.

Thirty years before Charles Chaplin turned against the America that had made his fortune for him in motion picture pantomime, the screen comedian arrived in London. The year was 1921. Thousands hailed him at Paddington Railway Station. More people surrounded him begging for autographs, the London papers reported by way of comparison, than greeted President Wilson on his London visit in 1919. There had been published here much cabled news from London on the Wilson visit.

Not one word on Chaplin's rousing reception or on his being entertained by royalty, as was Wilson, went over The Associated Press wires, which were then carrying detailed stories about Roy Gardner throughout the country. When Gardner finally was seized and returned to prison, there were AP stories printed up and down the Pacific Coast announcing that "Mrs. Roy Gardner, wife of the most famous bandit of modern times, had decided to make a vaudeville tour to tell about her daring husband!"

Why did The Associated Press carry dispatches on Roy Gardner and not on Charlie Chaplin? The answer: The latter would have been country-wide free advertising for a Hollywood actor.

There were other instances in The Associated Press news that presented some novel comparisons with this omission of famous names of the screen; for instance, the treatment of operatic and stage stars. Mary Garden, operatic soprano, arrived almost yearly in the century's first three decades and, gifted with tart phrasemaking, recited what was good enough to be a memorized script about the operas in which she would sing "this trip." It was publicity and free advertising for Mary Garden but it winged its way to all newspapers on The AP wires and was printed in news columns all over the country, including cities where Miss Garden had never sung and never expected to sing.

A while earlier, the arrival of Sarah Bernhardt, French tragedienne, was treated the same way. Then Mary Pickford and her husband, Douglas Fairbanks, came to New York from Hollywood. They posed for pictures and commented on the films in which each would next be seen. Not one word went out on The Associated Press wires. Yet for every person who had then heard of Mary Garden, there were hundreds who were devoted Pickford-Fairbanks fans.

Cancellation in 1925 of the order which had precluded AP use of motion picture news corrected the inconsistency of making famous the names of prize fighters, race horses, opera singers and criminals, while news of motion picture stars was excluded. Not a single AP member complained of the inclusion of motion picture news, which all of them by that time were printing from wherever they could get it. Yet even then the order of suppression might not have been withdrawn as early as it was had it not been for the late Will Hays, president of the Motion Picture Producers Association. Hays earned public credit for making the movies respectable and keeping them so.

But the accomplishment for which I respect his memory is that at my request he promptly killed the "faking" of news stories by motion picture press agents. I had written him that unless he did so, I was fearful of an adverse reaction from newspapers when I removed the ban as I proposed to do. Hays gave his personal assurance to me in writing that motion picture news would be truthful. Having confidence in him, The AP began to use it. Publication of it caused reader interest in motion pictures to sweep the country at the same time the "faking" press agents were swept into oblivion.

The industry was well on the way toward becoming one of the country's largest. There was news about it as a great commercial development. It went in for newspaper advertising in a big way. With this pleasant but unexpected windfall for the newspapers, more and more news of the screen and its stars went into the AP report. In 1926, two AP reporters were assigned by me to live in Hollywood and write as motion picture columnists. At first their contributions were sent by mail to newspapers all over the country. Later, by demand, they went by telegraph. The readers not only were getting the news they wanted of the stars they worshiped, but they were getting it hot off the wires.

Giving the names of those who write the news—"by-line" is the word used—always had been prohibited in The Associated Press.

There had been one instance showing that a few newspapers wanted by-lines over AP dispatches. When Kirke Simpson's stories of the burial of the Unknown Soldier were sent from Washington in 1921, three requests for the name of the author were answered by a leased wire message to all points. The message did not authorize the use of Simpson's name as a by-line, but he won the first Pulitzer prize awarded to an AP man.

His record of the three-day event was truly a masterpiece of news writing. To meet numerous requests, The Associated Press published a booklet containing the seven Unknown Soldier stories. Permission was granted for republication of the series in school readers. From pulpits ministers extolled the simple beauty of the work, and students in public speaking learned the sentences by heart. The requests for copies continued for the next eighteen years.

The stories certainly deserved a by-line. They didn't get it! Not until September, 1925, did the name of a writer appear over an AP news story. Even then I gave the by-line to a story by a writer who was not an Associated Press employee. He was John Rodgers, a Navy aviation commander. Rodgers and his crew had made the first attempt to fly from California to Honolulu. Their craft fell in the sea short of their goal.

The "item" in the Navy Bureau of Aeronautics Official Calendar of naval aviation records the then unprecedented flight as follows:

Commander John Rodgers in a PN-9 attempting a flight San Francisco-Honolulu, was forced down by lack of fuel shortly after 4:00 in the afternoon. Lost at sea for 10 days in spite of extensive air and sea search, Commander Rodgers and his crew of 4 rigged sail from the wing fabric and set course for Kauai. After covering about 450 miles, they were sighted on 10 September by the Submarine R-4, 10 miles from their goal. The 1,841 statute miles flown before the forced landing was an official world's record distance for seaplanes.

When they reached shore, their story could have been pumped out of them by questions from AP reporters and written either as a news story or in the form of an interview. The former was permitted under the old rules; the latter, as will be referred to later, was not.

The order countermanding this rule had not been issued when the Rodgers flight was made. I could have ordered an interview to prove the change in policy. Instead, I went beyond that and personally cabled Rodgers asking him to write his own story for The Associated Press.

I did this because when a man of the sea, or the air, or the mountains, or the plains, sits down to write a story of a perilous adventure that was his very own, in his own words, the reader gets something more than just what happened. He learns what manner of man met peril and how he faced it. He gets the clear ring of a personality, modest and humble, braggart or ostentatious. What the reporter writes tells much; what he leaves unsaid tells something, too. There is even interest in how he tells it. This was the message sent to Commander Rodgers:

Commander John Rodgers (center) *and his crew* (*1925*)— *The whole country welcomed his story.*

The whole country would welcome your own story, told in your own way, and published under your name, as the author. Therefore, please write it and send it to The AP, New York, cable tolls collect. Thanks.

An excellent story came and was printed throughout the land and abroad under the name of Commander John Rodgers. I presented him with a gold watch and made him an honorary member of The AP staff. He was the first individual to be so recognized and so rewarded by the organization. At the next annual luncheon of The Associated Press in the old Waldorf-Astoria, Rodgers was a guest of honor. Both my introduction of him and his response, as reported stenographically, follow:

MR. COOPER: The members of The Associated Press will recall one day last September when there was great suspense as to the fate of some flyers who were making a flight to Hawaii. At that time we were trying hard indeed to locate them—both The Associated Press and the Navy Department. When they were found, I requested Commander John Rodgers to tell the public of the flight. In a style worthy of any newspaperman, he sat down and wrote. The story appeared in all Associated Press papers—the first Associated Press story ever to have over it the name of the writer. For this excellent work, I had the honor of appointing Commander John Rodgers an honorary member of the staff, and on behalf of The Associated Press I presented him last year with a gold watch in appreciation of what he did. I asked him to come here today so that you might see this new employee. I introduce Commander John Rodgers! (Great applause and all arose)

COMMANDER RODGERS: I did not think I would be expected to speak but I am going to say a few words in appreciation of what The Associated Press has done for me.

I think it is a well-known weakness of mankind that man takes a greater pleasure in his amateur successes than he does in those that are strictly professional, and so you can see that my great pleasure at knowing that as an aviator I am a good reporter is quite natural. (Laughter) Especially when the news comes from no less authority than the general manager of the greatest news-gathering and disseminating organization in the world.

Also, I would like to show you my watch, which I take great pleasure in carrying on occasions. (Laughter) I got it out of the safe deposit last night to wear here and attached it with a heavy chain around my neck. (Laughter) The chain is a present from my mother, so you can see that not only I, but my mother and my family appreciate the gift. (Great applause and laughter)

Rodgers was a magnificent type. Four months later he met death tragically in an airplane crash near Philadelphia, the cause of which has never been explained.

12

THE AP'S FIRST

INTERVIEW

IT WAS ONLY two months before the Rodgers by-line story appeared
that I had wanted to give a by-line to a story by an Associated Press
veteran, John Bouman, of the London office, and thus make him the
first Associated Press staff writer to have his name appear above his
own story. I had keenly regretted the refusal of my predecessor to give
Kirke Simpson a by-line for his masterpiece. The Board did not cen-
sure him for refusing.

But with the Bouman story before me, recollection of my ardent
feeling that Simpson should have been so recognized made me pause
because Simpson, not Bouman, should have been the first in The Associated Press with a by-line. But Bouman, too, could well have been
credited for his story even though it was just a letter to me and not
written for publication.

In May, 1925, Amundsen and Ellsworth failed in their effort to fly
over the North Pole. The Norwegian Government sent a ship to rescue
them. Since Amundsen had sold the newspaper publication rights to
his story, I knew The Associated Press could not get him to talk, but
I sent Bouman out to sea to get the story of the rescue, which could
not have been any part of Amundsen's salable story.

Bouman went out and stayed out several days far at sea beyond

Spitzbergen, part of the time in small boats making their way through icy waters. Bent upon protecting Amundsen from an inquiring reporter, not even the commanders of the Norwegian Government vessels would tell Bouman about the rescue.

On his return to London, he wrote me a letter telling fully what happened to him. The letter was not filed away and forgotten. It was promptly sent on Associated Press wires for publication in full .and was widely printed as an Arctic adventure story. I did not give him a by-line but I personally wrote a note to precede his letter for transmission on the wires. In it I mentioned his name as follows:

Editor's note:

How a staff correspondent of The Associated Press, who was sent to the Arctic regions to learn the fate of the Amundsen-Ellsworth North Pole expedition, unflinchingly braved the perils of the icy seas can now be told.

Less than a month ago, when the world was praying for the safe return of the Norwegian explorer's party—believed by many a forlorn hope— J. A. Bouman, of the London Bureau of The Associated Press, was encountering hazards as great as those of the explorers. His risks were in the line of duty. He had no thought of fame. His work, like that of all employees of his organization, was to be anonymous. His reward was to be only the knowledge that he had done his best. He met courageously the hazards that beset his journey. The public is entitled to his story.

When the Amundsen party hopped off from Spitzbergen on May 21 in two airplanes in an effort to fly to the North Pole, their aim was to be back within two or three days at the most. When days and weeks passed without any word from the adventurers, there was insistent demand that a relief expedition be sent to Spitzbergen and as much nearer the Pole as ships and airplanes could reconnoiter. The Norwegian Government finally responded, and it was arranged to send airplanes and fliers to Spitzbergen on the coal carrier *Ingertre*.

Meanwhile, Mr. Bouman had been sent from London to Oslo, the capital of Norway, where the Norwegian Aero Club had bought the exclusive rights to the personal narratives of Amundsen and members of his party. Bouman, a man of fifty-two years and not particularly robust, cheerfully accepted the assignment to proceed with the relief ship, notwithstanding that he suffered severely from a cold caught on the fifty-hour journey from London.

The Associated Press had applied to the Norwegian Government for permission to have its representative go on the rescue ship. Finally, the permission, including the promise of the ship's wireless, was obtained. Later, the rescuers left the ship, eventually transferring to another Government ship, the *Heimdal,* and Bouman was not permitted to board it. He was left stranded at Advent Bay, where ships rarely touch.

This constituted the only instance in the history of The Associated Press where any government has not willingly accorded facilities for obtaining the story of an effort to save human life.

What struck me about both the Rodgers and the Bouman stories was that they were written as each man might have talked. By comparison, AP men were not writing their stories as they would have related them in conversation; they were following a stylized AP code that barred individuality. To change this, attention was first given to sports writing. All the restraining orders, rules and warnings in the first quarter of the century about how to write AP dispatches on sports were wiped out. AP sports writers joined their associates of newspaper sports pages in original and novel expressions.

It was this pioneering that led the way to the change in writing many classes of news. Far from being raspingly discordant each with the other by breaking away from the restrained method previously in effect, individual styles personal to the writers began to shine with occasional brilliance. By thus distinguishing themselves, AP reporters, as the years rolled on, were accorded by-lines. At first the names were sent on the wires "for optional use if desired." Soon it was obvious that they were desired and the "optional use" phrase was dropped. Though by-lines were then a novelty in The Associated Press news report, some newspapers had been using them for a long time, particularly for sports reporting.

In recognizing by-line merit, memories of my own experience as a reporter in Indianapolis early in the century often recurred. As a result, by-lines were never given to AP writers as a reward instead of an increase in salary! I never forgot what my editor told me when I got my first reportorial by-line in 1902. He said that I "needn't get puffed up with reportorial egotism and expect a raise." Then he added, with the trace of a smile: "Your name was printed over that story solely because it recounted something unusual, so unusual that it probably isn't true. If proved untrue, everybody'll know you're the liar, not the paper." By-lines or not, a salary raise for me never came.

No wonder I remembered this when the opportunity arose to reward Associated Press men financially.

Of all the special reportorial assignments created in conformity with my announcement to the staff and membership in 1925, the two that were hailed most enthusiastically were science and medicine. Of these two, AP science reporting evoked the most interest. It was entirely without precedent in the press association field.

But getting scientists and physicians to talk for publication or to disclose on what they were working proved very difficult. Men in those two professions had always been taciturn. They insisted that it was unethical for their work as individuals to be paraded before the public. Physicians had known of doctors who had advertised for patients. The great body of medical men recoiled from this method of self-exploitation. To them it was objectionable notoriety. They even resented the columns on health written by members of their profession which some papers in the country were publishing prior to 1925. To get scientists to disclose any news at all was even more difficult.

In the effort to launch these two departments, I assigned a man who was not afraid of discouragements. He was Howard W. Blakeslee. Besides being a good reporter, he was friendly and diplomatic with the scientific and medical men upon whom he knew he had to rely. He got acquainted with them first as friends, and on the basis of friendship he got them to talk. In helping him on his way in the science field, I personally appealed to Alexander C. Humphreys, then president of Stevens Institute of Technology. He promised to help in his own wide circle of acquaintance among scientists.

In the medical field, I dealt with physicians of great accomplishment who unselfishly had imparted to their fellows in lectures, but not for public consumption, what their experiences had taught them. I asked for their co-operation on the grounds that what they did would be for the public welfare. I promised that what we published would be told with dignity and even with anonymity if they insisted. At first they were quoted anonymously. From then on, however, Blakeslee took over. When they all found that his efforts proved to be constructive, they permitted him to quote them by name. It came to be that Blakeslee's by-line attracted readers as much as did the newspaper headlines over his stories.

In an address on "Science and the Press" at the dedication of the

William J. Murphy Hall at the University of Minnesota in 1940, Blakeslee said:

Some twenty years ago Kent Cooper, then head of the Traffic Department of The Associated Press, was looking at a typewriter standing on a table. There was nothing else on the table, no wires attached to the machine and no human being close to it. But the keys were typing a news message. Wireless directed those keys.

Mr. Cooper thought then, and at many other times as he looked at other industrial results of scientific discoveries, that science itself would be a great news source. Afterward, when he became general manager, one of his first innovations was to appoint science editors.

Within two years science became front-page news in Associated Press member newspapers throughout the nation. The volume has grown steadily. Many men have begun to write of science pioneering, the same as other news.

Last week, on a day when war news was big, I noticed five science

Kirke L. Simpson

John Bouman

stories in one New York afternoon newspaper. Scientists have told me
that in no other country is science covered as in the United States. In
the great European nations, where science was mainly centered until the
last two decades, there is by comparison almost no science news in the
daily press.

Until his death in 1952, Blakeslee's career as a medical-science
reporter was studded with generous compliments from those professions and acclaimed by AP members. Awards were given him by scientific and medical societies. As a result of this plan, executed almost
wholly by Blakeslee, news of science and medicine took, and still
takes, a high place in general reader interest, far above special news
of commerce, finance, sports and the amusement field.

For while a large group of newspaper readers is interested in commerce, each individual in it is also interested in medical progress toward maintenance of health, and in scientific success in providing con-
sumer comforts. The same can be said of groups of financiers, athletes,

Howard W. Blakeslee   *O. B. Keeler*

entertainers and all others. Their interest, next to their immediate professions, is found first in news of medical and scientific achievement.

Of these two the first is concerned with human health; the other with human contentment. As Dr. Humphreys said to me: "Science has given us bed-spring mattresses, for example, instead of corn husks and straw." Yes, and it has given us every convenient gadget there is—a truly endless list.

Damascus, a place of antiquity, flashed into the news in 1925 when France used heavily armed forces to carry out its mandate to control Syria. From my Sunday-school days, I had remembered the Biblical account of Paul's flight from this oldest inhabited city in the world. To escape persecution as a Christian convert, he was let down from the city's walls in a basket to go forth and extend the religion of Jesus Christ. The importance to posterity of Paul's escape with his life has been emphasized by H. G. Wells and other historians who have claimed that while Christ was the seed of Christianity, Paul was its founder.

Those ancient historic walls! That oldest of cities! Belatedly the French disclosed that for two days in October, 1925, they dropped shells inside the city's walls. Then, for some reason, they desisted without having won control of the city. In May of 1926, when the attack flared again, I sent Thomas Topping of The Associated Press Paris staff to Syria with a contingent of French reinforcements. I told Topping to let me know of any move to renew bombardment of the city. His first dispatch said the shelling had started and was probably doing enormous damage.

Up to then the world had paid little heed to the Syrian situation. There was no concern about the ancient city. The French declared they were merely enforcing their mandate. But there was no news from the forces of the besieged Nationalists and Druses. Wanting Topping to contact them, I asked him to request of the French commander the right to go to the city's walls under a flag of truce to talk to the Druses and Nationalists and get their story. To back up this request, I cabled Aristide Briand, then foreign minister of France:

Excellency: I have asked Thomas Topping, The Associated Press correspondent with the French troops in Syria, to request a white-flag escort to the gates of Damascus to get a statement from the Druse leaders on the reason for their resistance. I hope you will feel that the peoples of the world, especially the friends of France, have the right to know the Druse side of this story before the French Army destroys them and the oldest inhabited city in the world from the walls of which Paul, the great evangelist, was let down in a basket to escape persecution. It well could be that what Topping learns could lead to an avoidance of the city's destruction for which, if it occurs, history will place the blame upon the Republic of France. Your co-operation in our effort to reach the Druses is asked.

The French Government thus became the first of several foreign governments to which, in the ensuing years, I appealed for availability of news on the theory that the public had "the right to know," a phrase which became the title of a book I wrote in 1956. Those words, in communicating with officials of foreign governments, seemed easier for them to comprehend as a basis for demands for information than were other terms of American origin like "the rights of the press," "freedom of the press," or "freedom of information."

No reply came to me from Briand, but a representative of the French foreign office promptly called upon Elmer Roberts, chief of The Associated Press Paris Bureau, and gave assurances that before the city was destroyed, if, indeed, it had to be, Topping could make the visit under a white flag as a symbol of world interest in the fate of the city, if the "enemy" would so allow. My message to Briand may have had nothing to do with the fact that after that day the shelling ceased. The French then made contact with the rebels and not long afterward the resistance was nearing its end. While the city had been heavily damaged, its ancient walls remained intact.

It was also in 1926 that I reviewed the rule which precluded The Associated Press from carrying interviews in its news report. No one seemed to know definitely the origin of the ban. One AP veteran made a guess. He assumed that it was because if anyone has anything important to say he should say it without waiting to be asked! When I inquired of Mr. Stone, he answered that it was a policy which existed when he became general manager in 1893 and he never saw any reason to change it.

Before removing the ban, I gave consideration to all the objections for not doing so that I could think of. One was that the function of The Associated Press is to report the news, not to manufacture it; for an interview could be conceived to be the manufacture of news. To extract comment from prominent figures in the interview form could mean probing their minds about something upon which they may have expressed no opinion.

Besides, a news-conscious reporter would always ask interesting questions and thus evoke newsworthy answers, which, by being published, would enhance the individual's reputation—a form of personal advertising. But regardless of what I could conjure up to justify the exclusion of interviews, they never had appeared in The Associated Press news report—and that was that!

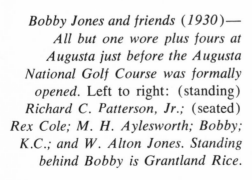

Bobby Jones and friends (1930)— All but one wore plus fours at Augusta just before the Augusta National Golf Course was formally opened. Left to right: (standing) *Richard C. Patterson, Jr.;* (seated) *Rex Cole; M. H. Aylesworth; Bobby; K.C.; and W. Alton Jones. Standing behind Bobby is Grantland Rice.*

Having weighed all the objections that I could think of, I decided there would be interviews. That form of news presentation seemed to me to make interesting reading. In my youth, being the son of a lawyer, I enjoyed listening to interrogations of witnesses in controversial court trials, especially when questions were adroitly worded, as I thought they always were when my father asked them.

Perhaps that was what prompted me in my reportorial days frequently to use questions and answers in my reports of police court trials. They seemed to make my stories read well. So I not only removed The Associated Press ban on interviews with interesting public

figures in all walks of life, but I personally planned all nine of the outstanding ones obtained by The Associated Press that year. Each may have been a case of an interview "making news." If so, I saw no objection since each turned out to be newsworthy.

The first interview carried in The Associated Press news report was the one with Bobby Jones. In 1926, Jones had won both the British and American open golf championships. That achievement was said never before to have been accomplished by the same player in the same year. No one previously had asked Jones for publication how he had learned to play good enough golf to accomplish that feat. Being a golfer of sorts myself, one of millions, I wanted Bobby asked *how* he did it. I thought there would be more permanent interest among the millions like myself in how he did it than in the fact that he did it. Moreover, anything the champion said about golf would make good reading.

The interview which I wanted was obtained and written July 14, 1926, by O. B. Keeler, Jones' "Boswell," who excelled in sports writing as Jones did at golf. With the Jones interview having shown the way, interviews were then obtained by or under the direction of Sports Editor Alan J. Gould with tennis champions Bill Tilden and Helen Wills. Add to these the two remarkable interviews with Mussolini by Robert H. Davis and Percy Winner, and an interview with George Bernard Shaw by James P. Howe.

Finally, James A. Mills had interviews that totalled a good poker hand—three kings and two queens. The interviews were with Queen Marie and King Ferdinand of Rumania, King Alexander and Queen Marie of Yugoslavia, and King Boris III of Bulgaria. All were later dethroned and are now dead. As Mills discovered, they were living in fear of their lives when he talked to them.

"Each of them," Mills wrote me, "had a peculiar tendency of watching the movements of my hands. Constant dread of assassination obviously ruled their subconscious minds, even in the presence of a friendly visitor. I noticed that merely reaching into a pocket for my handkerchief completely disconcerted Boris of Bulgaria by exciting his suspicions. So I finished that interview with my hands in my lap. Then I purposely experimented with the same motion while Alexander of Yugoslavia, who later was assassinated, was talking with me. He stopped abruptly but resumed a few seconds later and kept on talking after I put my hands in my lap and kept them there. With the others I did not experiment."

With this array of interviews, the rule that they were permitted surely was well established.

Then there was an event arranged to produce news. It was in the form of a golf tournament of a kind never before and never since undertaken. I planned it to be an exclusive for The Associated Press and it was. On September 20, 1926, at my request, champion Bobby Jones played an eighteen-hole contest against the "best ball" of woman national champion Glenna Collett, and Maureen Orcutt, New York Metropolitan woman's golf champion. The three teed off at the Oakland Golf Course near Bayside, Long Island.

No previous mention of the contest had been made in any quarter. The first the opposition press services or Associated Press members knew of it was when the story was ticked off on The Associated Press leased wires all over the country.

Playing the "best ball" of these two women experts was not an easy assignment, even for Jones. The three of them played from the tees located back of the women's tees. The match reached the eighteenth tee with Jones one up, as it had been from the fourteenth.

Jones really wanted to win. It was a 485 yard par five hole. Assuming a chivalrous role not out of character for him, surely with no thought that what he said would adversely affect his opponents' games, he suggested to Glenna and Maureen that to give them a better chance to even the match he would concede them the right to drive from the women's tee on that last hole some sixty yards forward. Their resentment to the suggestion was voiced long and loudly. They would show Mr. Jones! After Bobby's drive landed in the rough, they said they were going to try for a birdie four. They would show Mr. Jones, indeed!

Maureen almost did. All, however, were on in three and down in five, Maureen barely missing a thirty-foot putt, making Bobby the winner. Perhaps his chivalrous suggestion did cause them to press and thus played a part in the result! Anyway, The Associated Press had its exclusive story.

13

AMUSING A
PRESIDENT

IN THAT MEMORABLE EFFORT to blaze new trails in 1926, there was another instance of "making news" when I assigned myself to arrange for an unprecedented type of news story—an interview with the President of the United States.

Henry Van Dyke, in his *The Ruling Passion,* said that Raoul Vaillantcoeur, in order to show his strength, "would start to chop a log just at the spot where there was a big knot." Remembering Van Dyke's dictum, I was not thinking of myself as being a "brave-heart" when I moved to set a presidential precedent. Nevertheless, there was no one in public life at the time from whom it would be harder to extract an interview than Calvin Coolidge.

The President was not known to be talkative. I recalled that in a message to the Congress, he had given his view of the proposed Veteran's Bonus in six words: "I do not favor a bonus." On a visit to the White House earlier that year, I asked him if he had changed his mind on that matter. Before he answered, and remembering that he had disposed of it in six words, I added: "I think you were somewhat garrulous in the way you referred to it in your message to Congress!"

My remark brought a smile from one I had never before seen smile. I felt there was something hidden in the character of this silent, un-

120

communicative man that should be explored. That was why I wanted a personal interview consisting of questions and answers on anything except domestic or international policies or politics. The President had gone to White Pine Camp near Paul Smith's in New York for the hay fever season. That camp, from my point of view, presented a more pleasing scene for a human type of interview than the cold formality of the White House in Washington.

The President's close friend was Frank W. Stearns, of Boston. I made an appointment to discuss my idea of the interview with Mr. Stearns. He became ardently enthusiastic. The President's secretary made an appointment for me. Generously the President and Mrs. Coolidge asked me to bring my daughter Jane with me to the camp for lunch. It was late in July when we motored over to White Pine Camp from Lake Placid.

By pre-arrangement Mr. Stearns was there. After lunch, also by pre-arrangement, Mrs. Coolidge took charge of my daughter. Mr. Stearns disappeared. The President and I were left alone in the large sitting room. He sat on a comfortable two-seated swing hung from the ceiling. I sat about ten feet in front of him in a comfortable chair. We both were enjoying our cigars. I said:

"Mr. President, does anyone ever report to you the amusing stories that are told about you?"

"No," he replied.

"That's too bad," I said, smiling reflectively as I continued smoking. In a moment he said: "What kind of stories?"

"Just funny stories, Mr. President," I said, still smiling.

There was a long pause, and then he said: "Tell me one."

"Oh, no, Mr. President," I protested with feigned presentiment. "At least not unless I have the presidential pardon in advance, and, being a newsman, I want to quote them if you will tell me they are true."

"You can have my pardon, all right, but you cannot print them. Tell me one!"

This time he spoke imperiously. I began with the mild little anecdote about his trip to Chicago in the drawing room of an ordinary sleeper and when he ate in the public dining car "just like other folks." I did not remind him of how his little plan to gain acclaim by this evidence of his democratic ways brought only a laugh from the newsmen who accompanied him in the next car. For, although the President was not traveling in the presidential private railroad car, he might as well have been since all of the pullman accommodations in his car,

Jane Cooper—Mrs. Coolidge
was a gracious hostess to her.

Bruce Barton (1926)—Made an
honorary member of The AP staff.

except his drawing room, were occupied by secret service men and
White House personnel. It was the same when he went to the "public"
dining car. Secret service men and White House personnel had taken
all the seats but two, which were kept unoccupied until the President
and Mrs. Coolidge came in for dinner.

All I did tell him was: "After you had been served, the dining car
steward solicitously asked: 'Is the steak all right, Mr. President?' and
in turn you asked: 'What do you think's the matter with it?' Did that
happen, Mr. President?"

Coolidge neither smiled nor answered my question but kept on
smoking. After a while he asked: "Is that all?"

A little discouraged I said: "Well, Mr. President, I understand that
a congressman brought one of his constituents to your office. On being
introduced, the constituent said: 'Mr. President, this is the first time I
ever have been in the White House; the first time I ever have met
a President of my country, and I would like to have some little me-

mento of the occasion—for instance, one of the bands off of your favorite brand of cigars.'

" 'Why certainly,' you replied. Reaching into a drawer of your desk, you got out a large box of cigars, took out a cigar, took off the band, handed him the band, and returned the cigar to the box, the box to the drawer, and closed the drawer."

I laughed. The President did not. He just said: "That's what he asked for, wasn't it?"

Hoping for a smile on the next one, I told him about the time when he had been nominated as vice-presidential candidate at Chicago in 1920. "I understand," I began, "that you and Mrs. Coolidge were in your room at the Adams House in Boston when one of your friends knocked at the door, was told to enter, and upon entering, exclaimed with his right hand in the air: 'Hail to the next Vice-President of the United States!' and that you said: 'Thank you very much.' Then Mrs. Coolidge nudged you and said: 'Calvin,' and nodded toward the trunk in the corner of the room, and you said: 'Oh, yes.'

President Coolidge (1928)   *President Harrison (1899)*

One President was interviewed; one refused to be.

"So you went to the trunk, unstrapped it, unlocked it, opened the lid, took out the top tray, the second tray, the third tray, and from the bottom of the trunk extracted a small bottle of brandy; that you got a brandy glass and poured out one drink, which you gave to your friend; that he drank it down with gusto as you went back to the trunk, replaced the bottle, the third tray, the second tray, the first tray, closed the lid, locked the trunk and strapped it.

"As you turned, there was another knock on the door and another friend came in and exclaimed: 'Hail to the next Vice-President of the United States.' You thanked him. Mrs. Coolidge nudged you again, and you went to the trunk and repeated the process of getting out the little bottle. You poured a drink for your second friend, and as he drank it, you started back to the trunk, whereupon Mrs. Coolidge said: 'Calvin' and pointed to the first visitor, whereupon you protested: 'Oh, he had his!' Is that what happened, Mr. President?"

His smile broke into a quiet laugh, as he guiltily remarked: "I want to forget that one. Prohibition was then the law of the land."

I went on with one or two other anecdotes, intermittently switching some questions to a character that would evoke answers on the more personal things that concerned any man. We were having a good time. He told me that well-known little anecdote about the time he went to church alone. Upon his return home, Mrs. Coolidge asked what the preacher's sermon was about. The President answered, "Sin." Mrs. Coolidge asked what the preacher had said about sin. The President answered: "He's 'agin' it."

As the pleasant hour came to an end, I had in mind the interview that I wanted with questions and answers and the right to publish the interview exclusively. I said:

"Mr. President, this has been a wonderful visit with you. I have just been thinking how satisfying it would be to you if every citizen in the United States could get to know you as I have come to know you this afternoon."

His comment was just what I had hoped for when he said: "What can I do about it? I can't have them all up here for lunch like I've had you."

"No, Mr. President," I said with eagerness, "but I can take you to them if you will submit to an interview about the things we have discussed today."

"Would you write and publish what I've said today?" he asked.

"No, Mr. President, and for three reasons: First, I haven't your consent; second, you are in public life. You have been a candidate for President once, and you are eligible to be re-elected two years hence. Candidly, I believe that the kind of interview I want would not increase your fame as a statesman, but it could portray to your fellow citizens what the President of their country thinks on simple things of life that concern and affect us all, and they would love you for telling them. Third, it may surprise you to know that I have never written an Associated Press story.

"If I would write the interview and if it were published under my name, some Democrat promptly might say that the executive head of The Associated Press is out to sponsor your re-election. On the other hand, The Associated Press man regularly assigned to you here and at the White House, or the chief of our Washington Bureau could do it, as they both are writing the news." I stopped. He made no comment. I added:

"Another name I would like to suggest is one of my dearest friends, a good friend of yours, a graduate of Amherst like yourself, a writer of distinction—"

The President interrupted with: "You must mean Bruce Barton."

I did indeed. The President said he would give the matter consideration and let me know. I bade him good-bye.

The next thing was to sell the idea to Bruce Barton. Bruce said that he would be keenly interested in doing the interview provided that I would help by supplying some of the questions and get a definite understanding with the President that it would be a real interview in which he would be quoted.

I wrote to the President and got his assurances that it would be what Bruce and I wanted.

In my lifetime no president of the United States during his incumbency has sold for publication his views on public affairs or revealed public documents for a price. But several did both or were willing to do both after their terms expired. I got my first evidence of this in carrying out a self-assignment as a reporter on the Indianapolis *Press* in 1899.

Ex-President Harrison's home was in Indianapolis. The Venezuela-British Guiana boundary dispute had just been settled after five years of effort at arbitration. Threats of war between the two nations had been made as early as Harrison's term as President from 1889 to 1893.

It seemed to me, therefore, that his views on the settlement that was reached would be newsworthy.

I went to see him and told him what I wanted. A little imperiously the short, squat, gray-bearded, sixty-six-year-old father of a baby girl, which his young bride had just presented him, said nothing for a full moment as he looked at me. Then:

"Young man, do you realize that what I would say in comment on this matter would be worth money—a considerable amount of money? Any reputable magazine in the country would gladly pay me at least one thousand dollars for it. Yet you expect me to give you my comment gratis. Good day! "

He turned and left the room. I wrote a little story and quoted what he said. My city editor liked it but he said it would be an indignity to the Ex-President to print it.

The interview with Coolidge, which Bruce Barton obtained, was published on September 22, 1926. It was an all-time presidential first and was acclaimed by Associated Press members.

The President's great and good friend wrote the following letter:

Boston, Sept. 23, 1926

My dear Mr. Cooper:

Your idea was a stroke of genius and the way it has been carried out is another stroke of genius. Please present my compliments to Bruce Barton when you see him.

Sincerely,
F. W. Stearns

I made Barton an honorary member of The Associated Press staff. "I would rather have that recognition than anything," he said.

The late Ray Long, then editor of *Cosmopolitan* magazine, went to see President Coolidge shortly after publication of the interview. Long offered to pay the President an amount that he described to me as being fabulous, if the President would write a human interest story for the *Cosmopolitan*. The President accepted the offer. His story included comment along the line of the Barton interview. Long was elated. He was so much elated that he decided not to write to inform W. R.

Hearst, owner of the *Cosmopolitan,* who was then in California, of the magazine's good fortune. Instead, he prepared to take the long trip out there to tell Mr. Hearst personally of his success.

On the day Long was to take the train for California, the President's secretary telephoned to tell him that the President wanted to see him. Long said he would be in Washington the next morning. The appointment was made for twelve o'clock. Convinced that the President had changed his mind about permitting the story to be printed in the *Cosmopolitan* magazine and intended to ask for the return of the manuscript, Long arrived in Washington after a sleepless night, went to the Mayflower Hotel, walked its corridors and around the block until exhausted, waiting for twelve o'clock to arrive.

Each hour had added to his fears that the President had decided to cancel the agreement. So sure was he that this was the reason he had been asked to come to Washington that Long worked. himself into extreme nervous tension, which he later said must have been visible when he was finally ushered into the President's office. The President looked up and, in his clipped way of talking, said:

"Oh, yes, Mr. Long. Here's another article for you. I assume you will pay the same price for it as the other one."

Stunned that the visit turned out as it did, Long afterward said that he gulped, "Yes, Mr. President," took the manuscript, sat at one side of the President's desk, wrote an order on White House stationery asking the *Cosmopolitan* magazine treasurer to send another check to the President for the same amount, and asked the President's secretary to mail the letter himself.

Leaving the President immediately, Long took the train from Washington direct to California to see Hearst. Long told me afterward the results of his enterprise:

"When I told W. R. what I had gotten from Coolidge, he upped my salary to thrice that of the President of the United States. So thanks for getting Calvin started talking with The Associated Press interview!"

14

NEWS FEATURES AND
NEWS PHOTOS

AN EXPERIENCE in my reportorial days just after the turn of the century led The Associated Press in 1927 to be, not only the first press association in the world to collect and distribute news photos, but to become by far the greatest distributor of them in both hemispheres.

There were in that year several large news photo services for newspapers and magazines, but none of them was connected with or operated as a part of any telegraph news agency. Yet with The Associated Press having blazed the trail, this idea of one single agency delivering news both in words and pictures, which was then without precedent, had by mid-century become standard practice here and abroad—even with Reuters in England, and with Tass in Russia.

Proving that imitation is the sincerest form of praise, the United Press finally, after delaying for twenty-five years, copied The Associated Press by absorbing Scripps' Acme picture service and sending out pictures for publication over the name of the United Press.

I originally got my idea of illustrating news stories when Kin Hubbard, the artist, and I were contemporaries on Indianapolis newspapers. While working for the Indianapolis *News,* he originated the drawing of a Brown County, Indiana, philosopher whom he named Abe Martin. Kin would make an Abe Martin sketch in varying poses

128

each day to be printed with two unrelated sentences contrived by him containing humorous observations on the ever changing times.

Earlier, Kin had started as a cartoonist. He was as good as anyone I have known who could connect a cartoon and caption with telling effect. Later, with his Abe Martin sketches, he would test each of his one-sentence observations by quoting it to one or more of his friends. He tried out many on me. I recall one of these at the time when the motorcar industry had passed the experimental "gas buggy" stage and had gone into production of highly priced four-cylinder motors, like the Winton, Peerless, Premier, etc. This particular whimsy I have never seen printed since then:

"How's this one?" Kin asked: "Tel Binkley cranked up his four-thousand-dollar motorcar yesterday and drove over to the poorhouse to see his mother."

Now with me it was only a step from Kin's drawings to a yearning to get my own news stories illustrated in some novel way. But our paper, the Indianapolis *Sun,* had no photographer, no artist and no equipment for making half-tone engravings, a process then comparatively new. Not being an artist myself, I dreamed up and put into exe-

BROWN COUNTY FOLKS

Ther haint nothin' as hard as a easy payment.

Abe Martin—One of Kin Hubbard's thousands of sketches of the Brown County, Indiana, philosopher.

*K.C.—Drawing by
Louis Richards (1899).*

cution a plan to induce some well-known individuals to do some rough
line drawings to run with my news stories, giving them credit in the
newspaper for their "art."

If I did not have a story to be illustrated, it was not difficult to create one by asking anyone in public life to make a line drawing of what
he thought a horse or some other animal looked like. I once asked
Police Chief Hyland to draw a sketch of the fiercest-looking criminal
he could recall having been taken in by the Police Department. There
never was a horse that looked like any of the sketches I got. Likewise,
no thug ever appeared as horrid as Chief Hyland's drawing. But they
were talked about. They made people pay one cent for a copy of the
Sun to get a laugh.

The line drawings were reproduced through the use of the long-
since-discarded but inexpensive "chalk plate," by which a simple
sketch could be turned into a lead casting that could be locked up in
newspaper page forms, to be matted for the high-speed cylinder
method of newspaper printing.

Anyone could reproduce a line drawing with "chalk plates" by the
use of a tracing inscriber. I had known about the process because it
was used for cartoons by the *Republican,* a newspaper back home in

Columbus, Indiana. When I went to Indianapolis as a reporter, I was worth a "chalk plate" cartoon in the *Republican*. Louis Richards was the *Republican*'s cartoonist. He depicted me in high-water pants and derby hat, asking of the mayor of Indianapolis: "Anything for publication today, Mr. Taggart?" Richards was a talented boy who drew pictures for the fun of it. He was a bellhop in the St. Denis Hotel, which was across the street from the newspaper office.

Kin Hubbard's art, my own experience in getting my news stories amusingly illustrated, and what a young hotel employee could do with a "chalk plate" made an impression that I carried with me until I went with The Associated Press in New York. There the newspapers, like the big metropolitan press elsewhere, were printing really good pictures on local news stories in "half-tone" engravings.

The telegraph news was not illustrated by pictures sent by wire. Such pictures from afar as were printed came by mail from one to several days after the printing of the story. They were serviced through the mails by one of the news photo agencies, none of which, as previously mentioned, was operated by a press association. Pictures were just not considered as being any part of a press association's work.

Thinking about this situation, I convinced myself that it was as much the obligation of The Associated Press to deliver the news in picture form as to deliver the news by telegraphing words, since pictures often had proved to be the best way of telling the news.

Obviously this meant that sooner or later The Associated Press, if it was to thrive, ought not only operate its own news photo service for its newspapers, but also arrange instantaneous country-wide distribution of the pictures by wire.

I hesitated, however, to give future sending of pictures by wire as the real reason for wanting to establish a news photo service. I did not in my first year as general manager want to arouse fears in the Board that the establishment of a picture service was merely the inexpensive first step toward the second and more costly one of sending pictures by wire.

I knew there would be members of the Board who would object to an Associated Press picture service on the ground that the organization had built its substantial, eminently dignified reputation as the reliable transmitter of news by words alone. I had heard some of them express horror at the appearance in some newspapers of the pictures of Miami Beach bathing beauties in abbreviated swim suits. Steve Hanagan, an energetic promoter hired by that resort city's authorities for the purpose, was flooding newspaper offices in the North with bathing-beauty "art" for publication, while the icy winds and snow were blowing outside.

Some readers complained about newspapers printing pictures of "nude women." With this going on, surely any recommendation seriously made for The Associated Press to have a picture service would bring bathing beauties to the minds of some members of the Board as probable objectionable subjects for future AP photos.

Realizing that this was bound to happen, I decided to prepare the way for the definite proposal I would submit later. In 1925, I said I wanted to establish a picture service and informally, even humorously, recited how I had conceived the picture idea long ago when I had been a reporter in Indianapolis.

I got some laughter, as I had hoped. But I also got the unfavorable comment about the Miami Beach bathing beauties. Even pictures of the *Police Gazette* type were brought into the informal discussion. So I dropped the idea temporarily and went on with presenting and gaining approval for the less revolutionary plan of establishing The Associated Press illustrated feature service. I confessed both regret and concern that we would have to go to other news photo services to buy old pictures to illustrate Associated Press features. No one expressed himself as sharing my regret or concern.

When The Associated Press feature service was started, over 1,000 of the 1,200 members subscribed to it and paid additional assessments therefor. It replaced a "mail" service which was not illustrated and was generally dull. For it no charge was made.

When reporting to the Board, in 1927, the enthusiastic use of the new feature service by the membership, Mr. Ochs said that The Associated Press name on the material gave the impression that it was sent by wire although it was sent by mail. Moreover, he said that identifying it in any way with The Associated Press reflected on the dignity of the organization's serious function of rushing important news to the membership by wire. I said that even though the Board might be ashamed of the feature service, I was not, and that obviously neither were the members who paid for and used it.

I quote the stenographic record:

DIRECTOR OCHS: I want to say that I have no desire to reflect on Mr. Cooper in this at all. We simply differ as to how it should be done, that is all.

MR. COOPER: There are no ideals higher than mine on what The Associated Press ought to be, and I repeat I am not ashamed of the feature service. That is the first thing. The second is that we be concerned as to how far in a practical world The Associated Press can continue to exist and hold itself aloof and unresponsive to modern ethical newspaper standards. Take one paper like the *Times,* that has standards. We cannot possibly meet the standards of the *Times* in all respects in a general news service. Take any other paper, and we cannot meet its standards with a general news service. In the broad concept that I have of this work for 1,200 newspapers, I have tried to keep a median line which is still a respectable line and still an honest line, in order to give publishers what they need for their newspapers and thus gain their loyalty so that The Associated Press can endure. I go on the theory that you want The Associated Press to endure, but it cannot endure if it does not have members. And it cannot have members if it does not give them the service they feel they need. The general comment, as you have seen from what I have read to you, is that the way we have fulfilled our task is generally commended.

DIRECTOR OCHS: I am not speaking of any special item of news; we are just discussing the principle of it.

MR. COOPER: I am discussing the principle of it. I do not believe The Associated Press can be utterly oblivious to the trends that are making newspapers more appreciated by more people than ever before. Yet The Associated Press still will not do a great many things that some newspapers do and that many newspapers want it to do. It has kept to the standards, as I have outlined them to this Board, to the staff and to the membership. I think frankly these standards are higher than the general standards of newspapers in this country. I am not ashamed of what The Associated Press is doing, either in its news report or in its feature department. I do regret the human errors that it makes. But what actually has happened? I have to put modesty aside, but I will state a fact to you: Five years ago The Associated Press was rapidly disappearing out of the columns of many of its own member newspapers. They were taking other news services to get what they wanted. Today The Associated Press is displacing the dispatches of other services. The

New York Times itself, for example, is printing more AP news today than it has for twenty-five years.

DIRECTOR W. H. COWLES: The fact is, Mr. Ochs, lots of these newspaper fellows like these human interest stories.

MR. COOPER: The *New York Times* likes them. It is one of the best users we have of them. But what you say is very, very important to me because I have a commission here, and with the ability I have I am trying to fulfill it, but if I am out of harmony with the Board . . .

DIRECTOR OCHS: I think you are perfectly right in asking an expression of the Board with respect to these matters.

MR. COOPER: I do so because if I am in error I can resign or I can change—one or the other.

DIRECTOR OCHS: I think there is another obligation upon you. I think you should go a step further and persuade the Board that what you do is the right thing to do. The Board has ordered that The Associated Press credit line must appear over all Associated Press news. How important do you think it is to have this credit on the feature service? Can't we omit that credit?

DIRECTOR MCLEAN: Absolutely.

DIRECTOR OCHS: Why should not "AP" be understood to be a news service and not used for the purpose of features? It is of no advantage to The Associated Press.

MR. COOPER: The Board will have to answer that because we have been conducting all the services in accordance with the Board's approval of my recommendations.

PRESIDENT NOYES: The feature matter is not anything we want to protect and not anything that particularly would inure to the prestige of The Associated Press.

DIRECTOR OCHS: I would like to suggest that in the feature service The Associated Press credit line be omitted.

MR. COOPER: Will you just give me a reason? Is it because you think it is derogatory matter?

DIRECTOR OCHS: You are taking unnecessary risks in crediting it. You can omit the date line.

MR. COOPER: If we omit the date line it will not be practical to put The Associated Press credit on it.

PRESIDENT NOYES: The motion is that the date be omitted in the feature service. Director Howell so moves.

DIRECTOR RAY: I second it.

The motion prevailed.

MR. COOPER: That means there will be no credit line whatsoever in any feature service matter of The Associated Press!

Thereupon, even though it had a larger list of patrons than any other, The Associated Press feature service became the only one in existence without a name!

But in spite of the omission of The Associated Press credit line, the members inserted it when printing the features. The Board decided not to discipline them for so doing. Many years later, authorization was given to restore use of the credit.

At the time the credit was removed, however, I got comfort from editorial expressions that were being printed by many members in approbation of the various departures into new fields which I had already developed, the feature service among them. They were encouraging, of course, though I never knew whether the members of the Board ever saw them. A sentence in a long editorial of approval in the Boston *Herald,* for example, on May 7, 1928, read:

The Associated Press news service today, under the energetic management of Kent Cooper, excels anything that has ever been known before by American or any other newspapers.

And this excerpt from an editorial on December 26, 1927, from the Bristol (Virginia) *Herald Courier* read:

Under the leadership of Kent Cooper, The Associated Press has grown and developed more in the last two years than in the past two decades.

Finally, as to the treatment of features which the Board did not want credited to The Associated Press, the Indianapolis *News* on November 10, 1927, declared:

Facts, to The Associated Press under the management of Kent Cooper, are as staple as potatoes, but they do not always have to be served raw. The Associated Press now presents its news so that it will be interesting as well as true.

After making the feature service a success, I again brought before the Board the idea of an Associated Press news photo service. This time I spoke seriously about it. I warned of what could happen to The Associated Press if competitive press associations were first to take the step of co-ordinating delivery of news in pictures with delivery of news in words. I purposely avoided mentioning wire delivery of the photos at that Board meeting.

Seriously presenting this revolutionary idea to the Board had to be done diplomatically. Mr. Ochs, of the *New York Times*, long before had established Wide World Photos and sold news pictures to a large clientele among The Associated Press membership.

I knew that an AP photo service would result in orders to cancel Wide World. Mr. Ochs was not only a director of the organization but also one of my staunchest friends and supporters, who, as I have related, was responsible for my remaining with The Associated Press fifteen years earlier. I didn't anticipate it then but I had presented a plan that ultimately was to cause The Associated Press to take ownership of Mr. Ochs' Wide World picture service.

Moreover, two other large AP newspapers—Colonel McCormick's Chicago *Tribune,* and Captain Patterson's New York *Daily News*—owned and operated a news photo service which they called Pacific and Atlantic Photos. Colonel McCormick was a member of the Board. Like the *New York Times'* Wide World, Pacific and Atlantic sold its pictures everywhere. Nevertheless, I was proposing that The Associated Press compete with a second picture service owned by two other loyal friends, who later, because The Associated Press did go into news pictures, had to wind up the affairs of their Pacific and Atlantic Photos.

There was, however, still another AP member who operated a news photo service. It then was the biggest of all. Even prior to the creation of either Wide World or Pacific and Atlantic, William Randolph Hearst had owned and operated the Hearst Photo Service, which later took the name of International News Photos.

It was not strange that word of what I was urging privately within the Board reached the managements of all the competing services. As an AP director, Mr. Ochs knew about it of course. At first, he doubted the wisdom of The Associated Press' embarking on such a venture. But he said that although the *New York Times* owned Wide World, he would not let that fact influence him against whatever action his fellow directors wished to take.

Captain Patterson learned of it from Colonel McCormick and came to see me. Avoiding my troubled gaze as he looked out of my office window, he said: "I understand you want to start an AP news photo service."

In an effort to avoid what I expected to be a competitor's declaration of war, and to be truthful at the same time, I said: "Yes, Captain Patterson, and I'm so glad you came to see me, because with your vast experience with pictures, which your amazing success with a picture newspaper in New York so brilliantly evidences, I am sure you can advise me as to how to make The Associated Press photo service the biggest and best in the world."

If Patterson really came to me to declare that war, I hoped my generous compliment would give him pause. For several anxious moments he said nothing, as he still avoided my gaze. Then:

"Do you have any idea that you can make it the biggest and best news photo service in the world like you say, and will you give me that assurance?"

"Certainly," I said. "Why should I want to undertake it if the effort is to result in leaving The AP product no better or even not as good as that of its news photo competitors?"

Another long silence followed, with Patterson still looking out of the window. Finally he said: "With that ambition on your part,

Joseph M. Patterson (1939)—
He said: "Good day."

I guess it will be worth The Associated Press trying it. I wish you success."

He turned, looked at me smilingly, reached out to shake my hand, and said: "Good day."

That was all. But I was encouraged enough by Patterson to go directly to William Randolph Hearst, the biggest financial underwriter The Associated Press has ever had, and one of its charter members in the reorganization of 1900. Since he owned International News Photos, I wanted his blessing, too.

"You are embarking upon an adventure that will lose The Associated Press a lot of money," he said. "I have always lost money with my photo service, so have all my competitors—Wide World, Scripps' Acme, and Pacific and Atlantic. However, my papers, all being large ones, can meet the loss. The many small papers in The Associated Press whose money you will be squandering cannot."

"But," I protested, "the small papers will be benefited equally through my plan. They are equitably meeting their share of the organization's expense for the news in words. No one ever before has offered them an equitable plan for obtaining news in picture form and I propose to do just that."

"You are too optimistic," Mr. Hearst said, "but who am I to object? With a score of newspapers, all of them interested in news pictures, there cannot be too many sources of picture news in existence if they are available to me. I want pictures. Nearly all of my papers are in The Associated Press, so I will have AP pictures if I want them. Good luck!"

"You shall have them," I exclaimed in final realization that not one of The Associated Press members who owned picture services was going to try to stop The AP development.

I believed that with my report on these visits, surely the Board would approve, and that one day The Associated Press would indeed have the biggest and the best news picture service in existence. Yet still there was indecision.

I finally gained the Board's approval for the news photo service in spite of my disclosure, reluctantly made, that I expected to deliver the pictures to all member newspapers on wires running parallel with the wires that carried the news in words. That meant simultaneous transmission of pictures and news into the offices of Associated Press newspapers from coast to coast. Since in reality I wanted no news photo service at all unless I could send the pictures by wire, I finally concluded I might as well risk everything and disclose my plan for this seeming impossibility.

The declaration that this was to be the ultimate development obviously stunned the Board. I was accused by Director Frank MacLennan, of the Topeka *State Journal,* of fantastically involving The Associated Press in an expense that would result in its disintegration and bankruptcy. After considerable talk, some in whispers one to another, Director W. H. Cowles, of the Spokane *Spokesman-Review,* came over to me and in a whisper asked how soon I could begin sending pictures by wire directly into newspaper offices. I answered aloud:

"I have just been asked how soon I could begin sending pictures by wire directly into newspaper offices. My answer is I cannot do it until the Board first approves my recommendation that a news photo service be established, since no pictures can be sent by wire if we have no pictures."

There were many more hours of discussion at that time and at succeeding meetings. Then, in 1927, the Board approved starting AP news photos. Satisfied that my ultimate goal was the sending of pictures by wire, Mr. Ochs voted for it with some enthusiasm. The Associated Press promptly entered the field by mailing pictures, by tipping pullman porters to carry them, and by motorcycle deliveries to airplanes, just as its news photo competitors did in trying to be first into each newspaper office.

When Pacific and Atlantic News Photos dropped out of the field in 1930, it sold its European operations to the rapidly growing AP foreign photo service, and its domestic news photo service to Scripps' Acme, together with the registered word "Telephoto." Some ten years later, the *New York Times* sold to The Associated Press its long established Wide World Photos, which still is operated by The Associated Press as a photo feature service. Long before these transactions, however, the output and patronage of The Associated Press photo service had surpassed all others.

As a member of the Pulitzer prize board, I convinced my fellow members in 1941 that news photography had risen to the point of distinction for which an annual Pulitzer award should be given. In the next twelve years, eleven first prizes were given to photographers whose pictures were included in The AP news photo service. Some of the pictures were contributed by Associated Press members. Associated Press photographers who received awards were Frank Noel (1943); Frank Filan (1944); Joe Rosenthal (1945); and Max Desfor (1951).

In 1931, when The Associated Press had not yet gotten the consent of its European allied news agencies to serve its news abroad, I gained approval from the Board to incorporate The Associated Press in Great Britain and in Germany, as wholly owned subsidiaries to originate and service AP news photos throughout the world. The allied news agency contracts still restrained The Associated Press from serving news abroad in words, but the contract itself, made before newspapers used news photos, was so antiquated that it never included reference to news in picture form.

The Associated Press world picture service was so successful by 1938 that its excess of receipts over expenses helped finance The Associated Press entry into world dissemination of news in words.

15

MY ONLY AP

DISPATCH

CHARLES LINDBERGH and Gene Tunney were very much in the news in 1927 when Lindbergh became the first to fly nonstop from New York to Paris, and Tunney repeated his 1926 victory by defeating Jack Dempsey in a second world heavy-weight title match. Had it not been for that flight and that fight, the plans they each had for matrimonial bliss would not have brought them to me at different times during 1928 with the same request, an unusual one. What they wanted was quite a large order to fill for two national heroes of the day!

Of the two, Tunney came to me first, accompanied by Bernard Gimbel, a mutual friend, who started the conversation:

"Gene," said Gimbel, "has had his last fight. Confidentially, he is retiring from the ring and wants to retire from public notice at the same time. He has a reason which he also will tell you in confidence."

"He can retire from the ring," I said. "That he can do. But if he wants to retire from public notice he has not had his last fight. To do that would be harder than fighting again with one arm tied behind him. But I'll keep the confidence. What's the reason for trying the impossible?"

"My future life," said Tunney, "will have no connection whatever with the fight game. I have made great and good friends in that career.

Gene Tunney (1927)—
"My future life . . ."

and I hope they always will be my friends. But I am entering on a new life that has no relation whatever with my ring career."

Having found that strong, daring and successful men are the most reticent and embarrassed when victims of Cupid's darts, I took a good look at the strong, daring, successful Tunney and ventured to ask:

"Some other kind of a ring?"

"You guessed it," said Gimbel. "You see, she never fell in love with Gene because of his ring prowess. Instead, she admired him for deciding to give it up. It would not be fair to the girl and would be altogether wrong if the impression gets out that she fell in love with him for being a great prize fighter. Actually she fell in love with him in spite of that fact. It is not that she feels he has been engaged in a degrading occupation. She has not asked him to retire from the ring— that is his idea, just as it is his idea to drop out of public notice before the engagement is announced."

"And the girl is—?" I asked.

"Polly Lauder," said Gimbel. "You met her at our home in Greenwich."

Since it was time for lunch, I asked them to join me at the St. Regis Roof, where I thought the clientele would not be rushing Gene for autographs. I realized that he must have been observed entering The AP building, so I suggested that we use the freight elevator in order to avoid being encountered on our way out.

We did, only to be delayed by an aggressive but pretty young lady on the watch at that exit. She was from Bruce Barton's advertising agency on the floor above, and wanted Gene to sign an endorsement for a food product which Commander Byrd was to test in his forthcoming Antarctic explorations. We dodged that by not letting the lady ride down in the elevator with us.

Tunney was easily recognized on the street, and his handsome, manly figure caused people to turn and stare. He seemed oblivious to it, but I was not. At the St. Regis Roof, we had no more than been seated when waiters began bringing menus from women admirers asking Tunney to autograph them. He was gracious and signed them. I watched it all.

"Don't you see, Gene, what all of this means?" I asked. "Your engagement is going to increase public interest in you because all the world loves a lover. Despite anything you can do you are going to be romantically in the newspapers, and the more you try to prevent it, the more you are going to be talked about. I am sorry, but you are going to have to meet it head on. It is a first-page news story which also will get attention on the sports pages. I admire your modesty, but if you are married secretly it will be an even bigger story. Therefore, I suggest you get me a picture of the bride-elect for The Associated Press to use with an announcement of the engagement by Miss Lauder's mother."

By the time the lunch was over, my suggestion was accepted. He sent me the picture. That was late in July, 1928. On August 1, Tunney announced his retirement from the ring, and on August 8, from Bristol, Maine, The Associated Press received the following telegram from Polly Lauder's mother:

Mrs. George Lauder, Jr., of Greenwich and New York, wishes to announce the engagement of her daughter, Mary Josephine Lauder, to Mr. Gene Tunney of New York. No date has been set for the wedding, which will likely take place in New York in the late autumn or winter.

When it developed that the marriage would take place in Italy, I gave Gene a letter of introduction to The Associated Press correspondent in Rome.

Some twenty-five years later, I sent Gene a Christmas card on which I reminded him of our talk that day. He replied:

"My, but you have an excellent memory! I remember the things you outlined. You very graciously gave us a letter to Mr. Cortesi, The AP man in Rome, and we were accordingly entertained by him at a lovely dinner. His son, incidentally, witnessed our wedding party dressed as a waiter; of course, The AP coverage was the most accurate and complete."

I had met Lindbergh in the fall of 1927. He had just finished a unique flying tour of the United States under the auspices of the Daniel Guggenheim Fund for the Promotion of Aeronautics. I requested, and he gave me on November 11, a statement for The Associated Press of how best to promote aviation in America, the first on the subject he had written for publication.

One month after writing this for me, he made the nonstop flight from Bolling Field, Washington, to Mexico City. More than a year later he came to my office to ask a favor. He wanted me to tell him how he could drop out of the newspapers completely. Having remembered that his mother visited the Morrows shortly after he flew to Mexico City, and having been asked the same thing by Tunney, I thought of orange blossoms.

"Is it Miss Morrow?" I asked. He was astonished. My question almost brought him to his feet.

"How did you get that word!" he exclaimed.

Since I did not want blame to fall upon the bride-to-be for having disclosed the news, I told him about the similar experience with Tunney, and I connected Miss Morrow's name with Lindbergh's request because Ivy Lee, a mutual friend, had told me that Ambassador Morrow's daughter was the one who first suggested to her father that it would be a compliment to the Mexican people if the transatlantic hero would make a flight to Mexico City.

We had a long talk. To prevent a repetition of what occurred when I took Tunney and Gimbel to a public restaurant, I offered to have lunch brought to us while we continued our conversation. He asked for a sandwich and a glass of milk, which is probably why his nick-

Charles A. Lindbergh (1927)—A sandwich and a glass of milk.

name was "Slim." I never earned that nickname myself, which was probably why I remained hungry after also confining myself to a sandwich and a glass of milk.

Finally I told Lindbergh that what he wanted just could not be done. "As a matter of fact," I said, "you will be more in the news than ever." He seemed distressed that there was nothing I could do.

I recall that Lindbergh had asked me, when we first met, to make a flight with him. I declined, giving fear as my reason. He said that no one had given him that excuse before. Because he seemed disappointed, I promised him that if I changed my mind he would be the first to take me up. I never changed my mind and so, more than thirty years later, perhaps I might claim to be the only person always too frightened to go up with Lindbergh.

In 1948, I similarly declined to fly from Frankfurt, Germany, to Berlin with General Lucius Clay, then commander-in-chief of the

United States forces in Europe and military governor of the United States zone in Germany. It was at the time of the famous airlift to Berlin. There was then no way to get to Berlin except to fly, and since Mrs. Cooper and I didn't want to fly, General and Mrs. Clay and Ambassador Murphy paid us the compliment of flying from Berlin to Frankfurt to see us. At dinner, General Clay got Mrs. Cooper's consent to fly back to Berlin the next morning if I would fly with them. Having in mind the controversy with Russia which was currently a world news story because of the successful airlift, I declined, saying:

"General, you would be the last man with whom I would fly to Berlin." He appeared perplexed, perhaps affronted until, citing the angry Russian attitude toward the airlift, I said:

"If I flew with you over Soviet-occupied Germany, and the plane were shot down, Mrs. Cooper and I would not even be mentioned in the news story! It would be all about you, Mrs. Clay and Mr. Murphy. If I ever break my resolve against flying and I am killed in a crash, I want my name in the story even if it is not in the head- lines."

While abroad in the summer of 1927, I met and talked with the chiefs of state of nearly all the European governments. There were three that year that were ruled by dictatorships—Spain, Italy and Russia. I talked with Dictators Primo de Rivera of Spain and Benito Mussolini of Italy. I also observed the Soviet dictatorship of the pro- letariat at close range; there, personal discussion was not practical!

Primo de Rivera, a handsome man of military mien, had been do- ing what he could to bring order out of the economic and political chaos his lovely Spain was suffering. When he took over as dictator, the people had no work. Idleness was breeding revolution. Primo de Rivera planned to connect all the cities of Spain with fine highways, of which the country had none except for the few the Romans built two thousand years before. He was pleased with the progress being made. We conversed in Spanish.

"The Romans," he said, "knew that there could be no commerce and, therefore, no prosperity and contentment without good roads." For the same reason, the dictator ballasted with stone the roadbeds of the Spanish railways and electrified many miles of them. "When we complete this road building we can next start the wheels of in- dustry, and ours will be a happy country," he said.

He tried. But the best he could do was to postpone the inevitable revolution. He died in exile three years after my visit.

Mussolini was inquisitive. He was learning English and asked me to use my language. We got on very well.

"Were you in Italy before our fascist years?" he asked.

"Yes," I replied.

"Do you notice any difference?"

"Yes," I answered.

"What difference?"

"Well, for one, the streets of Rome are smoothly paved and clean."

"And what else?" he continued.

"It seems to me," I said, "that an Italian, instead of idling down the street, has his head up walking briskly like he is going someplace, and I guess he is. Don't you think so?"

"Good. Indeed he is. What else?" he asked.

"Well," I said, "I do not seem to be afraid to walk the streets of Italian cities at night."

"Ah, the bad men—the Mafia," he said. "All of them we have sent over to your country. You are not as safe at home as you are here!"

I asked him what his ambition for his country was. Tersely and proudly he told me: "Italy shall have its place in the sun. That is our destiny."

I have wondered ever since that talk with him what would have happened in Italy if in 1919 America and Britain, to please France, had not imposed upon the German Republic the onerous Versailles peace terms. For it was German hatred of those terms which was responsible for the rise of Hitler, who, having adopted Italian fascism and distorted it into German nazism, destroyed the German Republic, made Mussolini his servitor and elevated communist Russia to its position of eastern world dominance shortly after mid-century.

Aboard the *Leviathan* homeward bound from France that year, I met Richard E. Byrd and drew from him a story of the devotion he felt for his mother and for his wife, Marie, who lovingly gave their benedictions to his plans for all his dangerous adventures. With their blessing, he and Floyd Bennett made the first successful flight over the North Pole in 1925. Just before I met him, he had been the first with a crew under his command to make a flight from New York to the shores of France.

The story I wirelessed from the *Leviathan* about this venturesome explorer was the only one I ever wrote for The Associated Press. On countless occasions I, as general manager, could have put the spotlight on myself by taking, with my own by-line, the most outstanding news story opportunities away from other AP men. Out of loyal con-

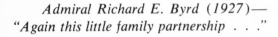

Admiral Richard E. Byrd (1927)—
"Again this little family partnership . . ."

sideration to them I never did so. The Byrd story was different. I was the only reporter on the ship and I gave myself no by-line.

My acquaintance with Byrd ripened into an intimate friendship that lasted until his death thirty years later. Before he embarked upon his first Antarctic expedition, I counseled with him about how to get the best results in arousing public interest in the value of his exploration. Before his second expedition to Antarctica, he confided in me that he was going to spend the long Antarctic winter alone in a well-provisioned hut far in advance of his base but in communication with it. I told him this might well cost him his life. He said that he hoped the observations he could make at a point nearer the South Pole during the long night would be worth the danger involved.

He, of course, survived. On his return, he autographed and sent me a tear sheet from the *National Geographic Magazine* containing an elaborate map of the South Polar Plateau which showed the location of the "Kent Cooper Glacier," which he had named in my honor. "It is a very beautiful glacier," he wrote. "Mount Don Pedro to the westward, and Mount Ruth Gade to the eastward, are marvelously beautiful mountains thirteen or fourteen thousand feet in altitude. The glacier is next to one of the most historical in the world—the Axel Heiberg—and it is far better-looking than its neighbor."

My only Associated Press story, wirelessed from the *Leviathan,* follows:

On board the steamship *Leviathan,* July 17 (AP)—America's mightiest ship, the proud bearer homeward of five transatlantic aviators today took its first marine salute of the voyage on behalf of the fliers. Fittingly enough, the salute came from the *Paris,* a French liner eastward bound from New York.

To the aviators the deep-throated whistle of the great French liner seemed once again to throb with the cordial spirit with which they were welcomed in France, while to the passengers better evidence of the fraternity of these titans of the sea could not have been offered.

The *Paris* hove to a little closer for the brief ceremony, and when she came abeam, her double sirens roared their acclaim. It was as if the power of her great steam signals cried out the enthusiastic cheers of her passengers for the aviators, while the long answering blasts of the *Leviathan* not only acknowledged the salute, but also seemed to send back the spirit of pride and enthusiasm of the aviators' fellow passengers.

The infectious spirit of camaraderie of Commander Richard E. Byrd, which enthralled the passengers, has been everywhere aboard ship, from stem to stern, from bridge to engine room. A talk with him soon develops hopes and aspirations already projected far beyond what can be done in one man's lifetime.

As he says himself, the urge to hazard his life in worthwhile undertakings "has got" him. The urge which sent Byrd the man successfully upon transatlantic and North Pole flights, and which grows stronger as the South Pole exploration looms, was not denied Byrd the boy at twelve years of age when, in spite of his mother's misgivings, he completed a trip around the world. And if it were not for both his wife and mother fully sharing that urge of his today, there would be no homecoming for Commander Byrd tomorrow after his successful transatlantic flight.

Indeed, there would have been no transatlantic flight for him; nor would the North Pole flight have been accomplished and the South Pole plans made, except for the fact that his inspiration in these efforts has been and is in full partnership with his wife and mother.

No interview was sought to gain this information; it came merely from random conversations during the week aboard the *Leviathan,* without any thought at the time of setting down what he said.

The aid the two nearest and dearest to him have given exists as part of the success of each effort he has made, and will continue to play a big part in the future.

Random quotations from these various conversations would read:

"This urge to hazard my life in worthwhile adventures has got me. I suppose I was born with it, for before I was twelve years old I burned with the desire to travel around the world. I may have delayed for a time on account of my solicitous and adorable mother, but with resignation and misgivings she finally consented, and the twelve-year-old boy went around the world alone.

"With manhood, marriage and children, new responsibilities of husband and father, added to those of son, crowded upon me. But, far from the urge lessening, it grew. I could not suppress it, as well-meaning friends told me I should for the sake of my family, which they said needed me. How could I throw my mind wholeheartedly into something else when the appeal of hazardous and scientific adventure consumed me?

"Indeed, I should have gone mad, but for two things: First, my mother's sharing in my fondest hopes, and second, my wife's adroit discovery of the compelling urge within me, which I thought I was concealing. Promptly thereupon she acquiesced in my taking up these hazardous efforts in deadly earnest.

"Convinced that she meant what she said, convinced that even if I lost my life, both they and my children and my children's children would have a heritage that would make them better off without me than with me in my mental turbulence, I have been as free from care upon their account as if they were not here.

"That may sound inhuman to one who does not understand.

"This by way of explaining what, in answer to your question, I thought most of when I returned safely from the Pole and landed safely in France.

I thought, well, again this little family partnership has been successful, leaving body and mind able to try some other worthwhile thing.

"I do hold them as full partners, even as senior partners. They not only wanted me to try, but their confidence carried me through

"As for compensation to our children for the risk there may have been of losing a father—well, some men amass great wealth and generously leave it to their loved ones. I cannot amass wealth. It would be as hard for me to amass wealth as it might be for them to fly to the North Pole.

"Each father must decide what heritage he leaves his children. But, after all, he can leave them only what he can leave, and Fate seems to be so working it out that it will be for my children to judge at their maturity whether their father did well by them by following the urge for hazardous scientific adventure that now impels him."

One thing more of the many things Commander Byrd said should be recorded in order fully to prove the sense of obligation he feels toward others who have helped him, second only to his appreciation of his wife and mother. He stressed the comradeship of the men who have accompanied him upon each endeavor:

"They could not have been greater in the spirit with which they accomplished their tasks," said Commander Byrd. "Three of them are aboard with me now—Noville, Acosta and Balchen. One other ought to be, and that is Floyd Bennett, who was injured worse than I was in our spill last spring and had not recovered in time to make this flight. Bennett is a wonderful fellow."

16

A MARTYR TO
A HOPE

I PREVIOUSLY have expressed my keen regret that I was unable, during Mr. Stone's active years, to gain his favorable consideration of my conception of human interest news: that it consists of accounts of people's joys and sorrows that bring heart interest to the reader who enjoys mentally living the experiences about which he reads.

In 1914, in an address to the Columbia University School of Journalism, Mr. Stone gave his definition of human interest news. Mine, as I have outlined it, differed from his as then given:

I know many news editors who calmly catalogue events saying this is news and that is not, and having done this, they go their way assuming that they are master workmen in the craft. They will say, for instance, that a hanging is always news, a prize fight is always news, a divorce case is always news, a railway accident is always news; in short, that any disaster by flood, or field, or in the domestic circle, is always news.

Now, as a matter of fact, these things are episodes; they are the May flies in the world of news—those short-lived insects which swarm like driving snowflakes in the evening, and, having deposited their eggs, leave their bodies piled in heaps on the banks of their native stream on the morning of the very next day. They are in no sense contributions to the real history of the world. To use another simile, they are like dishes of what the cookbooks call 'floating island,' tickling the palate for the moment, but having no substantial merit. Of such a character are nine-tenths of those news dispatches which, for want of a better name, are called human interest stories.

The highest and best form of news is informative in its character. We should be writing the real history of the world and, so far as may be, we should dismiss the episode and the tittle tattle.

No one would question that news should be informative, that it should be a history of the world. But my belief is that human interest news, not only is informative and important, but is the color in the picture of events that brings a lasting impression on the memory. Besides, if peoples are to know each other intimately, the news ought to record what touches them in the ordinary course, not alone the unaccountable things that happen out of it. I have no apology for making certain that those things were recorded. As I have said, without them the news picture is woefully incomplete.

From the moment of my appointment, Mr. Stone had been watching how I was changing his policies. I always felt that The Associated Press news service was Melville Stone's news service. Its rules were his rules.

Because of this I had a twinge at my heart strings every time I made a radical change, which was often. I would wonder if I were doing something that might distress him. It was that feeling for him that retarded my pressure for change more than the expressed concern of the Board. For The Associated Press was everything in his wakeful life, just as it had become in mine, and as I knew it would be as long as I lived.

In October, 1926, five months after my first year as general manager ended, I got from Mr. Stone a benediction for which I devoutly wished. He then told me, with the affection of a father speaking to his son, that he understood and wholeheartedly approved of my course. The Coolidge interview and the story Commander Rodgers wrote particularly impressed him.

During the years of Mr. Stone's general managership as well as mine, The Associated Press news report was accused of being partisan. For instance, a reader of an AP newspaper said to be owned, not by one, but by three railroads charged that the railroad owners had an insidious control over The Associated Press, which, of course, they never had and could not possibly have attained. At another time, Senator Foraker of Ohio, an attorney for the Standard Oil Company, wrote a letter to the company that it should acquire "a healthy control of The Associated Press."

The senator didn't specify how it could be done. But in some quarters there was still a feeling that those who had other interests besides owning newspapers required their newspapers to be conducted in harmony with those other interests, and that indirectly The Associated Press was involved. I received comment based on that contention quite as often as did Mr. Stone in his day. But neither Mr. Stone nor I could ever get a bill of particulars. All we got were statements of suspicion couched in general terms.

The Associated Press membership always has consisted of large and small newspapers with varying editorial policies. That has been one of its points of strength. The ability of newspaper owners has ranged from incapacity to genius. Some of them inherited their properties and led them either to greater prosperity or to oblivion. Others, by sheer dint of genius and without capital to purchase any newspaper properties, nevertheless ultimately did so. Still others tried and tragically failed. Some individuals published newspapers because newspapering was their natural bent. Fortunately they are in the majority in The Associated Press membership.

Some newspapers are indeed owned by copper mining companies, by railroad companies, news print and a wide variety of other manufacturers, by bankers, politicians, oil companies, church organizations and men of great wealth who have wanted to own newspapers to satisfy their ego or just for the fun of it. When charged with having used their newspapers to control public thought and action to protect and advance the welfare of their other investments in the areas where the newspapers were published, the history of the newspapers involved furnished the answer. For the solution in all such cases rested upon a discerning public. If such newspapers did these things, they were eventually shunned and driven into oblivion for lack of patronage.

I do not, however, refer to this diversified character of newspaper ownerships to point either to the morality or immorality involved. I do it to emphasize the fact that such diversified interests are joined into one group under the name of The Associated Press. With an investment of billions in newspapers, their private interests and their personal convictions run the gamut of human activity and human thought. What I mean to point out is that it could be assumed that all of them would seek favorite treatment from the news service that they own and that furnishes the principal informative element of their newspapers.

Did any one of them request it? Did any one of them demand that The Associated Press publish or suppress news that affected their major corporate interests adversely or favorably? Did any one of them get favorite treatment on news of their major investments?

The answer to the three questions is a positive No. This is so because The Associated Press general manager alone could not pervert the news without instructions to the employees who write and edit it. To effect perversion, he would have to conspire with them. Even then the conspiracy could not succeed, because the entire news product is subjected to the critical eyes of all its newspaper members as well as the intelligent reading public. A better way to maintain the integrity of the news has not yet been discovered. If ever it is I imagine The Associated Press will promptly adopt it.

Getting their names favorably or romantically into the news is a usual avocation of Americans. Wanting to keep their names out of it, as did Tunney and Lindbergh, is unusual. Having said that, there are two main reactions of a layman toward news with which news executives must contend:

First, the demand for suppression before publication of any unfavorable allusion to some individual, some corporation or government official, local, state or national; second, the favorite American pastime known to newsmen as the practice of damning news items after publication for what they have disclosed in their truthful, unbiased presentation.

In respect of both of these reactions, the press association is in a different relation with the public from that of the newspaper or radio station. These two news publication media exist on the patronage of their advertisers. Because of this there is the frequent charge that some of them cater to their advertising patrons even to the point of suppressing news. Each individual newspaper or radio station is quite capable of furnishing its own answer to such accusations. The AP's revenue comes from the newspapers and radio stations, not from advertisers. It is thus not subject to any such demands.

In the matter of news suppression, I did, however, receive requests affecting momentous matters. One was made by President Hoover in January, 1933. He was the ninth of the twelve presidents I have known, but not until Harding and Coolidge, his immediate predecessors, had I been upon fairly intimate terms with any of them.

Hoover's love for Leland Stanford, Jr. University, his alma mater, is well known. One morning at breakfast in the White House, where I had been an overnight guest, I told him how Leland Stanford got its first president—David Starr Jordan. Though he knew Jordan intimately he had never heard the story which my father got from the Reverend Dr. Atwater, who had officiated at my parents' wedding in 1872 in Bloomington, Indiana.

Mr. and Mrs. Stanford came East in their private railroad car seeking a president for the university they were founding in honor of their late son. They wanted the best president regardless of cost. Their first choice was Dr. Eliot of Harvard. Dr. Eliot declined but told them the most competent man he knew was Dr. Jordan, then president of the alma mater of my father and mother—Indiana University.

Mr. and Mrs. Stanford went to the university town to see Dr.

President Hoover (1930)—He was trying to keep open 4,000 banks.

Jordan. They arrived there early one Sunday morning unknown to anyone, even Dr. Jordan, who did not know they were coming. Their private car was shifted to a siding near the Monon railroad depot. They strolled up Kirkwood Avenue to attend service at the first church they saw, which happened to be the Christian Church.

Stanford was the innocent cause of considerable consternation in the church when its treasurer asked the pastor, Dr. Atwater, to announce that one of the brethren had by mistake dropped a twenty-dollar gold piece in the collection plate but could have it back upon application to the treasurer.

That afternoon recital of this little anecdote by Stanford to Dr. Jordan pleasantly opened the negotiations that ended with Dr. Jordan's resigning from the presidency of Indiana University and becoming the first president of Leland Stanford, Jr.

In making a request for suppression of news, President Hoover disclosed to me in strict confidence that he was trying "to keep open four thousand banks that tragically are faced with closing at any hour—even today." He then asked me not to permit AP men to report speeches of alarmist congressmen who, even though Roosevelt had been elected two months earlier, were still "carrying on their political attacks in the halls of Congress on my administration while the country's economic fate hangs in the balance."

Needless to say, not one word went from me to The Associated Press Washington staff to suppress anything in compliance with the President's request, made, as it was, with the high purpose of the country's welfare in mind. Fortunately, however, all worked out to the President's satisfaction, since it eventuated that most of the congressional speeches the President felt were injuring the economy were repetitious, therefore not newsworthy and not reported.

In the matter of damning news items for what they disclosed or the way they were worded, criticisms of The AP took the form of letters, denunciations in public addresses or demands for corrections accompanied by threats of libel suits. Over a period of twenty-five years I am sure I heard from representatives of every form of public activity. Before the Volstead Act was repealed, the anti-Saloon League was a constant critic on one side, with representatives of the brewers on the other.

I once heard from an officer of the American Bar Association. The reason was that I had done the simple little thing of changing the news form for reporting the pleas of individuals charged with crimes.

When at the bar, the judge always asks the accused: "How do you plead—guilty or not guilty?" There was one unsuccessful libel suit against The AP for having said a man pleaded "guilty" when his plea was "not guilty." In transmission the word "not" was inadvertently dropped from the news story. The defendant was thus reported as having pled "guilty." That once was enough. To forestall a recurrence, an order was issued that pleas were always to be reported as "guilty" or "innocent" in The AP news report. A few weeks after this order was given, the protest arrived:

"For a thousand years or more in English and then in American courts the pleas have been 'guilty' or 'not guilty.' Therefore, your reports are inaccurate since no one ever has been heard to plead himself 'innocent' or ever will. The term is 'not guilty.' "

Nevertheless, the term "innocent" instead of "not guilty" has become universal in news reports. In court rooms, however, the plea of innocence remains "not guilty."

It was in the eventful year of 1927 that I had an unexpected opportunity to even a score with Dr. Martin W. Sampson, who was professor of English at Indiana University, where I matriculated in 1898. I had been writing news stories for my home-town newspaper and I went to the University solely to learn to be a better writer of news.

There was no journalism course at Indiana University, nor anywhere else in those days, so I enrolled in Dr. Sampson's English class. Our first study was Longfellow's "Hiawatha." We had to write a thesis defining the poet's "purpose." With printer's ink in my blood, I wrote an imaginary interview with Longfellow in which I asked him what his purpose was in writing the poem. In my thesis I quoted this answer:

"I had two good reasons," the poet said. "First, the idea of depicting mutual love between two individuals of a savage Indian tribe intrigued me; and second, I frankly hoped it would sell."

There were other questions and answers in my reportorial thesis. My paper came back from Dr. Sampson with a zero on it. The class next took up Matthew Arnold. I wrote an imaginary news story about Arnold. Sampson sent for me and said he didn't know whether I was dumb or trying to be smart but that I had no place in his English

class. So I became an English student casualty because I yearned
for my university to teach me how to write for newspapers, something
in which it and many other great universities specialized in a grand
way a few years later.

At that time, however, I was just a martyr to a hope and could do
nothing about it but transfer to a German class. Shortly afterward
my father died, and I had to leave the University and go to work.
Twenty-nine years later I was invited by Frank Gannett, then president of the New York State Publishers' Association, to be the speaker
at a dinner of the association in Willard Hall on the Cornell campus
at Ithaca.

Wanting to honor me, Gannett invited the entire Cornell faculty
to be present when I spoke to the publishers. Now I think I can talk
shop to newspapermen when I've got them alone and I think I can
talk to the public when it wants to be imposed upon by a speech
from me. But I was in a quandary as to how to interest a mixed audience of newspapermen and college professors. Without the least idea,
therefore, of how I was going to start, I arose to Frank's generous
introduction. Since I was seated in back of a bank of flowers, most
of the audience was hidden from me until I stood up.

Then, at the table in front of the dais, I saw a face I had not seen
during all those twenty-nine years. I stared at that face for a full
minute without saying a word, to the obvious embarrassment of its
owner. I then told the audience of my desire to get an education in
news writing at Indiana University and quoted the words my English
professor had spoken to me in derision of my reportorial efforts.

"But," I said, still staring at that face, "as I was determined to be
a newsman, I decided there was nothing for me to do but to leave
the University and go out and become the chief executive of The Associated Press with its long list of brilliant writers."

Gesturing, I pointed my finger at the owner of that familiar face,
saying: "And I did just that, Dr. Martin W. Sampson!"

Dr. Sampson didn't remember me. He had long before left Indiana
University to go to Cornell as professor of English. Nevertheless, when
I finished speaking, he came up on the dais and embraced me:

"I am proud of you," he exclaimed. "You are one of my boys!"

The year 1929 is memorable for the Wall Street crash. To me it
also is memorable because in February of that year Melville E. Stone,

my illustrious predecessor, died. Since I was away from New York on business at the time, I sent the following statement on The Associated Press wires for publication throughout the country:

It would be superfluous for anyone on The Associated Press staff who has worked with Melville E. Stone to allude to his genius or his greatness as a journalist. All that is well known. The members of The Associated Press staff today are thinking most of the affection in which they held him and in which we all know he held us. Our loss is irreparable.

17

AN ASTONISHING
SUGGESTION

In march, 1930, I stopped to think of the past and the unpredictable future. Fifty years of age could be a good time for taking stock of one's self. I tried to do so.

The first thing that came to mind was that I had not started in an authoritative position in The Associated Press young enough in life; that I had been retarded in what I wanted to do by the practices and prejudices of the previous century, more so, I thought, than I would have experienced in any other organization. Nevertheless, in spite of being retarded, every recommendation I had made except two ultimately had been approved.

One exception was that after sixteen years I still had not been allowed to develop The Associated Press as a world service. It was hope for this which had encouraged me to remain with The Associated Press. Fulfillment would be the most important contribution I could make to the welfare of the organization, to my country and to the maintenance of peace in the world.

The other one was refusal to approve my recommendation to build up a large reserve fund as insurance against any adversity that could strike at the co-operative. I hope the day never will come when there will be regret that this was not done.

On the credit side, but not in the order of their importance, I had:

Reduced the cost of and improved The Associated Press wire service.

Organized the Traffic Department.

Established Associated Press delivery of complete full-page tabulations of Wall Street prices, saving members large sums of money thereby. These tabulations have since appeared in hundreds of newspapers throughout the country.

Created a new method of proportioning assessments more equitably among the members.

Stimulated the extension of state and regional meetings of members for discussion to improve the news service.

Visited the offices of almost every member of The Associated Press to discuss how the service could be improved.

Greatly increased the membership numerically by successfully pressing for the constriction of protest rights, thus opening up vast new territories for membership development.

Obtained the consent of the Havas News Agency of France for the entrance of The Associated Press into South America.

Made three trips to South America establishing Associated Press memberships there.

Developed teletype operation of Associated Press wires throughout the service.

Prepared the actuarial tables for and written the entire Associated Press pension plan, establishment of which the Board approved in 1918 and made that plan actuarily sound by paving the way to allot some $4,300,000 to it, which I made available through economies in wire contracts and their operations.

Tried to get included in the Versailles peace treaty when I was in Paris in 1919 a clause guaranteeing freedom of international news exchange and a free press in the conquered countries, hoping to get acceptance of the principle by all of the signatories.

Visited all European countries in 1927 investigating news administrative practices in all of them.

Attended a meeting in 1927 with the managing directors of the Reuter, Havas and Wolff agencies looking toward the modernization of a contract that had been in existence with practically no change for thirty-four years.

Greatly changed the nature of The Associated Press news report into an all-inclusive form of whatever had interest to mankind.

Assigned reporters to specialize in news of science, religion, medicine, literature, the theatre and art.

Established The Associated Press Feature Service, the Washington Regional Service with individual attention to Washington news that concerned each state.

Increased the news staff in Washington to 100 because Washington instead of London had been made the political center of world news for American newspaper readers.

Assigned seventy-five staff writers and photographers from all over the country to the national conventions of 1928 in Kansas City and Houston for the detailed reporting of actions of all state delegations. Formerly only eight or ten men had been assigned to write the story solely on a national basis.

Completely revised the administrative functions by abolishing the four geographical divisions which were then satrapies, each of them presided over by a superintendent.

Appointed forty chiefs of domestic bureaus, all of them responsible directly to the general manager for the news of their respective regions and the personnel in their jurisdictions.

Required all newsmen to send to me confidentially brief autobiographies, which became the bases for the personal file of each individual, as had been done when the Traffic Department was organized thirteen years previously. Up to then, little of the information thus sought had been compiled. With each newsman's autobiography starting his personal file, he became definitely and for the first time an identifiable individual to be encouraged and rewarded.

Secretly launched the American Telephone and Telegraph Company engineers on a project that, when the equipment was perfected, would make possible the later launching of Associated Press Wirephoto.

Laid plans for the incorporation of news distribution by subsidiaries of The Associated Press in foreign countries, hopeful some day to gain approval actually to enlarge that development into an Associated Press world service.

Conceived the idea of an association of managing editors of Associated Press newspapers to constructively aid in improving the news report, with the hope that through mutual fellowship between themselves and The Associated Press staff, a new era of loyalty to The Associated Press would come into being.

Established the news photo service, making The Associated Press the first press association in the world that served news photos.

What I had done evidently had earned the approval of the membership and the respect of the Board, which, deeply concerned with its responsibility, had imposed delays which I could not understand. I had submitted to the inevitability of that concern, which, naturally enough, had been aroused by the scores of changes, big and little, which already had been put into effect.

In spite of the progress made, conditions in 1930 appeared ominous for newspapers. Radio was delivering news directly into the home long before newspapers could be printed and delivered.

David Sarnoff, then president of the Radio Corporation of America, has been a friend of mine for nearly fifty years. He began as a wireless operator in a shed at Seagate near Coney Island, New York, from which place he sent and received messages from nearby ships for the Marconi Company, predecessor of the Radio Corporation of America.

Sarnoff once told me that his first experience with the staid practices of New York journalism was through an arrangement he contrived by which a wireless operator on a tug at the finish line of the Lipton yacht races at Sandy Hook flashed the winner to him at Seagate. Sarnoff said by pre-arrangement he telephoned it to The Associated Press in New York, which sent it out for publication but without any explanation that it had been sent by wireless.

The plan worked beautifully except that the New York newspapers, not having heard from their own reporters at the scene, thought the message was a hoax. Not one used the wireless flash. Their men were aboard boats at the finish line, none of which had wireless equipment.

When the race ended, the newspapers' "dispatch" boats sped as fast as they could to the nearest landing place. Not until their reporters telephoned confirmation of the Sarnoff message, more than a half-hour later, did the newspapers awaken to the speed and efficiency—indeed, to the eerie reality of radio news transmission.

Through my friendship with Sarnoff I kept close to amazing developments in all forms of communication by wireless, a twentieth-century novelty. He suggested in September, 1930, that I join his organization. In telling me of his vision of the future for a more effective publication of news orally by radio, as well as through inexpensive facsimile receivers of typed pages of news directly in the home, he included a vague mention of pictures of events on a "live" screen.

This did not astound me so much as it could have at the time had I not previously witnessed demonstration of a device by which, through the use of several wire circuits, each of two persons conversing by long-distance telephone could plainly see the face of the other on a small screen in front of him. Altogether too expensive, it never was adapted to general telephone usage.

Faced with such certain ultimate presentation of news in words and pictures broadcast directly into the home, I shuddered to think

David Sarnoff (1950)—"I shall for the moment content myself . . ."

where the newspapers would be if they continued belatedly to illustrate the printed words with news pictures sent to them by mail. Radio news broadcasts already had killed editions of newspapers which formerly published word accounts of baseball games, prize fights, and elections in "extras."

However, I declined Sarnoff's offer. My interest continued to be the news. It was then and remained an ardent interest. I wrote:

October 7, 1930

Dear David:

After having considered the matter from every angle, and especially because of my sense of duty to this work, I have decided to continue to carry on here.

In doing this, I recognize I am denying myself unusually remunerative and congenial work which has a great future and am also denying myself what is far more important, namely, the opportunity to work with you. Also I realize that there is no further financial recognition that The Associated Press will give me.

But I began something here that is not finished. A lot of young men who are devoting the best years of their lives are counting on me to continue. Having gotten up a blind alley financially myself, I at least want to see the undertaking here succeed.

Please forgive this long statement. The confidence in me that you have shown deserves an even longer explanation.

With deep appreciation and happy in the continuance of our friendship, I am

Sincerely yours,
Kent Cooper

Sarnoff replied:

October 8, 1930

Dear Kent:

I thank you for your letter of October 7th. While I am naturally disappointed that you could not see your way clear to accept the offer made you, I cannot do otherwise than respect your decision and honor you all the more for the unselfish motive which led you to make that decision.

I shall for the moment content myself with the knowledge that I at least know a good man when I see him, even if I cannot hook him.

Wishing you continued success and happiness in your present position, believe me

Always your friend,
David Sarnoff

As Mr. Ochs of the *New York Times* had induced me to stay with The Associated Press many years before, I sent him a copy of my letter to Sarnoff and his reply. Mr. Ochs wrote:

October 31, 1930

My dear Mr. Cooper:

I have your letter of the 24th with enclosures which I herewith return; except the letter you wrote to Mr. Sarnoff, which I am retaining for my files. (I assume you have a copy in your file.) It's a fine letter and very characteristic of you and I would like to keep it if you have no objections.

It's needless for me to tell you how pleased I am with your decision. I realize you are making a great personal sacrifice. I fully appreciate what it means. You are ably and admirably occupying one of the most important and useful positions in America. The preservation of the ideals of The Associated Press and their practical and efficient application is a job worthy of the greatest talent, and there is no greater opportunity for public service. I congratulate you that you can disregard the "flesh pots" and dedicate your life to a noble enterprise which is deeply impressed with a public interest.

You well deserve the fine letter which I am herewith returning to you.

Yours faithfully,
Adolph S. Ochs

For the second time in fourteen years I had declined an opportunity that exceeded anything in the way of financial reward The Associated Press ever would or could do for me, and I knew it. Then came a third offer—an astonishing one to a newsman without capital.

The late Robert Paine Scripps was heir of the founder of the United Press and namesake of the man who first inducted me into press association work. He was at the time the controlling owner of the Scripps empire of newspapers as well as the United Press, the Newspaper Enterprise Association, a feature service, and Acme Newsphotos.

Scripps, W. W. Hawkins and I were having dinner one evening

at the Lotos Club in New York. Hawkins for twenty-five years had been associated in high positions with the Scripps enterprises.

America was then in the depth of the depression years. Scripps said that in the interest of efficiency and economy the newspapers of the entire country would be benefitted if The Associated Press would agree to confine itself to covering all of the domestic news of the United States for all of the newspapers in the country, and withdraw from reporting news from the rest of the world. If The Associated Press would do that, he said that the United Press would agree

Robert Paine Scripps (1935)—
He was earnest and hopeful.

to withdraw entirely from reporting domestic news and confine itself solely to reporting foreign news for the same newspapers.

Naturally I had to say what he knew, namely, that I could not speak with authority equal to his on a matter of such grave importance, but that I believed the members of The Associated Press, some 80 percent of whom did not then take the UP news service, would never consent to such a plan, as the 80 percent would have to do what the other 20 percent were doing, namely, take two press association news reports; that if any economy resulted by thus dividing the domestic and foreign fields, the beneficiaries, so far as The Associated Press membership was concerned, would be those constituting the 20 percent.

I added that I had been struggling, as he knew, for years within

The Associated Press to obtain its release from the shackles that bound it to the international news cartel headed by Reuters. I said that in anticipation of success, I was impatiently waiting for the chance to embark The Associated Press into world distribution itself, in competition with the United Press. Scripps then said:

"Your first love was newspapering, not the press association business. You can select and I will buy for you any metropolitan newspaper in the United States that can be bought, if it is not published in a city where there is already a Scripps-Howard newspaper. You would be the ostensible purchaser and the real publisher, with no strings attached to your editorial, news or business policies. You would be entirely free from any alliance with the Scripps-Howard newspapers, even to the point of not having to take the United Press news report if you would not want to. Your financial reward would be all of the profits, if any, during the first five years after the purchase, with the agreement that I would each year meet the losses, if any. Thus it would be to your interest not to buy a newspaper that is operating at a loss or is even likely to do so within the time it is solely in your control."

Hawkins, having listened to the entire conversation, expressed amazement, adding that he had never heard of such a proposal made by anyone anywhere. "That," he said, "is better than anything Scripps has offered either Howard or myself," and went on to say that as a friend of mine for a quarter of a century he did not see how I possibly could decline it. I replied that I could not answer at least until we left the club to go home that evening.

Some two hours later my answer was given. I said that with me it was not only loyalty to what I had undertaken in rebuilding The Associated Press so that it could have a successful and prosperous future, but that I had inspired several men much younger than myself to remain with The Associated Press in spite of tempting offers to them from others; that they wanted to play a part with me in the development of The Associated Press of the future; that not one that I needed was deserting, therefore I could not.

"You're a strange one," said Scripps. "You have loyalty to a non-profit organization that never can issue you a share of stock nor pay you a cent in dividends. Not only that, but to maintain your personal position of responsibility for unbiased news in that organization, you get no outside income through investing your savings in any profitable corporate enterprise because you fear it might one day ask a favor of

The Associated Press. Compared to that, Scripps employees can invest directly or indirectly in part ownership in the Scripps-Howard newspapers."

A few weeks later, when I saw Hawkins alone, he referred to the offer Scripps had made me:

"I want to tell you why Bob was so earnest and hopeful in making that offer to you. You see, Roy has been the dynamic go-getter of Scripps-Howard. As such, he has held the center of the stage. He had not, however, been able to get you to join us. Bob thought he could do it and put one over on Roy by doing something that Roy had not been able to do. Moreover, I want you to know that on our way home that night I told Bob you may have believed that the reason he made the offer was to get you out of The Associated Press management with the thought that your departure would reduce the strain of competition on the United Press. Bob said that if that was in your mind, it never had been in his and that he wanted me to tell you so."

I said no such thought had occurred to me. It could not have since certainly no one in The Associated Press had assessed my value to the organization so highly that my departure would benefit the United Press!

While talking with Scripps I kept thinking of those two very important things I had not accomplished; also a certain sentiment that I had begun to feel deeply within me.

First, I hoped I was on the eve of getting the Board to let me start The Associated Press on a great career as a world service; and second, the impending establishment of Wirephoto.

The sentiment was the indefinable attraction of an atmosphere created by the interest and concern for The Associated Press on the part of some of America's greatest newspaper publishers. They were guardians of the organization's welfare and not promoters of change, the latter of which I, to them, was a radical example. They had, however, become my personal friends in spite of the fact that most of them felt I was making too many changes in The Associated Press too rapidly. Yet, though some Board members wanted me to slow down, not one of them ever told me he wanted me to give up trying to convince him.

And then one month after my birthday of that year, I was honored to be the speaker at the annual luncheon of Associated Press members, and I was touched by what President Noyes said in introducing me. Excerpts of the stenographic report of his introduction follow:

MR. NOYES: It is my purpose to introduce to you a gentleman much better equipped than am I to speak of the great burden we lay upon the shoulders of the general manager of The Associated Press.

It has been noted—with satisfaction by our members generally—that in recent years the news reports of the organization have been what I might describe as "humanized" to a greater degree. There has been, also, a great broadening of the scope of our reports, which have covered a much wider field of interesting matter, ranging from greatly enlarged market, business and foreign reports to the lighter human interest stories. Some twenty years ago a new man appeared in the service of The Associated Press in the person of Kent Cooper, who had been appointed traveling inspector and a couple of years later became chief of the Traffic Department. His dynamic activity, his great enthusiasm, his detailed knowledge of the organization and his keen intelligence brought him almost immediately to the personal attention of those of us who were charged with the responsibility of conducting the affairs of The Associated Press, and he rose step by step until in 1925 he became general manager of the organization.

It is a pleasure to me to be able to say to you that Melville E. Stone, my dear friend for nearly forty years up to the time of his death last year, rejoiced in the success of his protégé and gloried in the development of the service under Cooper's leadership. Having in mind my own responsibility in selecting him for the post he occupies, it is with pride and satisfaction that I introduce to you the general manager of The Associated Press, Kent Cooper. (Great applause and all arose)

What Mr. Noyes said was a benediction for what I had done. But more important to me was that it encouraged me to continue to press forward.

18

WHEN AP LOYALTY BEGAN

THE ASSOCIATED PRESS, being a non-profit co-operative and therefore unlike a stock company operated for profit, as is the United Press International, cannot be successful unless its members have a lively, loyal interest in it.

By loyalty I mean a sincere concern on the part of its members that The Associated Press services shall be operated more efficiently than those of its competition, and a determination to contribute all that is necessary to maintain that predominance.

Loyalty was demonstrated in the nineties by the way the co-operative AP membership was aroused to hostilities against the old United Press, which was not a co-operative. The affray that followed took AP member loyalty to heights it never since has attained. Its headquarters were then in Chicago, where the members met. A decline of membership interest in it began after the United Press went out of existence and The Associated Press became a New York corporation in 1900. Its general offices then were moved to New York City and its annual meetings were held there.

In 1910, I often heard veteran AP members of those late nineties talk of the defeat of the UP of that day and refer wistfully to The Associated Press gatherings which were held in Chicago. They never referred to the meetings, but they did refer to the dinners which were held on the evening of the day of the annual meeting.

Victor F. Lawson, the reserved and dignified owner of the Chicago *Daily News* and the president of The Associated Press from 1893 to 1900, said that perhaps those dinners aroused more genuine enthusiasm for The Associated Press through cementing friendships than did the fight against the United Press itself.

Convivial dinners do make for good fellowship provided the company attending them is democratic and not too large in number, and the speeches are not too formal. And if those who attend are brought together in a practical common cause, it follows that increased loyalty to the cause ensues. Friendships that began between the members and the management at the dinners in Chicago undoubtedly contributed to creating a spirit that aroused pride in being a member of a group of successful men in the same profession.

It is worth while first to look in upon them as they dined, and second, to cite a later effort to assure the continuance of loyal ownership interest ten years after the general offices were moved to New York in 1900—a loyal interest which, I repeat, is essential if a non-profit co-operative is to endure.

The first Chicago dinner was held in 1893; the last one in May, 1900. There were three attractive elements that made them a success. First, they started out with less than seventy-five in attendance. Thereafter, there never were many more than 100. Second, practically all of those who attended the dinners got well enough acquainted to address each other by their first names. Third, all of the speakers were members of The Associated Press. If an outsider was present as a guest, he was allowed to tell an anecdote if he first apologized for his presence in such a select group of newspapermen.

Naturally the speeches were more joyous in each succeeding year as it became clear that the fight against the United Press was being won. At the banquet of 1895, Charles Emory Smith, of the Philadelphia *Press,* referred to the fact that the United Press had carried various rumors about the probable demise of The Associated Press:

I want to say that my heart is bubbling over with joy tonight, with earnest congratulations upon the great success which you have had today. Charles Lamb had a friend whose story comes into my mind at this moment. This friend of Lamb was accustomed, as the poet said, to take down gin and water goblet on goblet, sending the first on a tour of observation, sending the second to keep company with the first [laughter], sending the third to find out where the second had gone [laughter], sending the fourth to follow the third, and sending the fifth to announce that it was not the last [laughter and applause].

Mr. Chairman, during the last two months I have heard a great many rumors and reports about this Associated Press. I have heard one story sent out, apparently on a tour of observation [laughter]. I have heard another sent out to keep company with the first [laughter]. I have heard a third sent out to follow the second, and I have heard a fourth sent out to announce that it was not, by any means, the last [laughter and applause].

At the banquet on May 19, 1897, the collapse of the United Press the previous month was suitably celebrated. A loving cup was borrowed for the occasion. St. Clair McKelway, of the Brooklyn *Eagle,* opened his remarks as follows:

My friends, the name of the association from which this [indicating the loving cup] was borrowed tonight, under written pledge of return, which two policemen stand at the door to see is carried out by Major Handy— the name of that organization from which this loving cup is borrowed is the Fellowship Club. It seems to me that is not a bad name for us newspapermen here to appropriate temporarily tonight between those quotation marks, which too few of you use when you take my paragraphs [laughter].

Eloquent clergymen write or speak about the recognition of friends in heaven. I earnestly hope that all my friends will go to heaven, and that if any of my enemies go there they will behave in such a way that I shall be able to recognize them. I could not for the life of me believe that there is anyone here who does not intentionally resolve to go to that place. We would all become reporters and take an assignment to that spot, but our chances are in time, I hope, too remote, and in moral probability, I fear, in the case of some of us, too ambiguous to make that a safe or other than a speculative subject of temporary news gathering. Instead of recognizing our friends in heaven, we propose to recognize our friends on earth, and we are familiar with that environment. It belongs to us; it belongs to us because we are meek, and the meek shall inherit the earth; they ask no more [laughter].

At the banquet in 1898, the major speech of the evening was by Colonel Watterson, of the Louisville *Courier-Journal.* He referred touchingly to the union of the entire press of the country under one banner which "for thirty years has been the dearest aspiration of my heart."

Newspapermen had found that they could have a better time picking speakers from among their own number than by bringing in outsiders to lecture them. General Taylor, of the Boston *Globe,* was selected to make the address at the final banquet in Chicago in 1900. He related forgotten facts about the trail blazing in journalism done by Bennett of the New York *Herald:*

Mr. James Gordon Bennett, the first and greatest of modern journalists, began to report religious meetings in 1839. In 1840, sixty years ago, he began to publish reports of notable sermons on Monday mornings. Strange to say, while in his early days he was denounced by some of his competitors in stronger terms than have ever been applied to any journalist in our time, he was the first man in this country to recognize that religious conventions and meetings and sermons had a news value. Stranger still, some of the ministers of that day resented having their sermons reported, and one went so far as to state to his congregation that he would not begin his sermon until the reporter of the New York *Herald* had left the church [laughter].

May I, in passing, tell you younger men briefly why I think James Gor-

Henry Watterson (1908)—"For thirty years the dearest aspiration of my heart . . ."

don Bennett, Sr., was the first and greatest of modern journalists? You ought to know it as a part of the unwritten history of your profession. He was great because he blazed out the new paths of modern journalism. There has not been a popular paper established in this country in the last forty years that has not followed the lines laid down by the elder Bennett fifty years ago. He was the first man to originate the financial or money article, which is now a feature of every daily in the land. When the telegraph was first introduced between New York and Washington, it was the custom for a banker to hire it for twenty minutes, then a newspaper would hire it for twenty minutes, and then another banker, and so on. The newspaperman always noticed at the end of his twenty minutes that his story left off at the most interesting point. Mr. Bennett called the other newspaper proprietors together and proposed that they take a report of two hours and divide the expense. That was the origin of The Associated Press [applause].

When the first steamer came from the other side to New York, Mr. Bennett was the first passenger booked to go back, and made arrangements for news from the great foreign capitals. He published the first war map in this country in 1838. He illustrated more than sixty years ago, and was really the first man to illustrate a newspaper in the United States. In 1838, an English criminal landed in New York. The authorities could not arrest him or hold him. Mr. Bennett suggested an extradition treaty, and one was arranged later by Mr. Webster and Lord Ashburnham [applause].

The important point in his career for the purposes of this evening is that he was the first man to give religious gatherings and sermons in a daily newspaper. In 1860, a New York daily issued a prospectus, which said: "Not assuming or seeking to be a preacher of religious doctrine, but recognizing in all its judgments on the practical affairs of life the authority and efficacy of Christian principles and Christian truths, all the news will be found in its columns. In all that concerns mental and moral progress and culture this paper will be first and foremost."

That was the prospectus of the New York *World*. And I presume this announcement will astonish no one in the country more profoundly than it will the present staff of that newspaper [laughter and applause].

Of course, as a religious daily it did not pay. More than twenty-five years ago an attempt was made by a very sincere, earnest, and honest preacher to establish a religious daily in Boston. It is needless to say it was a failure. The minister devoted five years of his life to the worries and troubles of an unsuccessful paper, and it ruined his health and caused his death. In the whole five years, he had just one chance to smile. He always owed his help six or eight months. When it came Saturday he would give a man three dollars if he was single, four dollars if he was married, and five dollars if he had children [laughter].

One day it was rumored through the establishment that he proposed to raise salaries. The men got together and signed a round robin to him begging him not to raise their salaries, because it was such hard work to get what he had already promised. They did not want the additional labor of struggling for the increase [great laughter].

Four months after this banquet, The Associated Press was re-incorporated in New York and its headquarters were transferred to New York City. No effort was made to have a dinner until the annual meeting in September three years later; even then it was not a success. After another three years it was tried again, with General Horace Porter, U. S. Ambassador to France, and Mark Twain as speakers.

That affair, though larger than the one three years before, instilled no spirit of camaraderie. It went into history as the last Associated Press banquet ever held. Two years later, in 1908, The Associated Press had changed the date of its meetings in New York from September to April so that they could be held in the same week with those of the American Newspaper Publishers Association, which conducts important services for newspaper publications.

To give themselves a good time with an evening of relief from their "arduous" week of Associated Press and American Newspaper Publishers Association meetings, the two associations held their first joint banquet that year. It got off to a good start as excerpts from the speeches of Rabbi Wise and William Jennings Bryan indicate.

Said Rabbi Wise:

Mr. Toastmaster and Fellow Muckrakers—or, I might say, Fellow Ruckmakers: Like you, I am very happy in looking forward to the opportunity of hearing a noteworthy address by him who, because best, is logically and prudently saved for the last. I rejoice especially, because I expect Mr. Bryan [applause] to disprove something which I lately heard—namely, that while Mr. Bryan was an orator of wonderful power, a public speaker of extraordinary gifts, his speeches had ceased to match his addresses of 1896, for in 1896 he always spoke on his mettle [laughter]. Not very long ago I heard two men engaged in discussion in the street, one of them asking the other: "What is today's celebration, anyway?" "Don't you know," answered the man addressed, "that the 12th of February is Lincoln's birthday?" "Well, but why do we celebrate Lincoln's birthday?" "Because," was the answer, "that's the place William Jennings Bryan comes from." [Laughter and applause]

Perhaps I am tempted to be unkind for a moment, because a good woman in the synagogue came to me not long ago and said: "Rabbi Wise, I have a very great compliment for you." I was delighted. "What is it? Tell me quickly," I said. "Well, I heard someone say that if only you were the least bit good-looking you would very slightly resemble Mr. Bryan." [Laughter]

I am to speak to you tonight on the power of the Press. I remember some years ago I was crossing the ocean, and a friend, who is a distinguished journalist—all journalists are distinguished—and I happened to notice that a general of the Civil War was pacing the deck with one of the millionaire pork packers of Chicago. The millionaire pork packer was arrayed as became a millionaire pork packer. The old Civil War general looked almost shabby, and, when I said to my friend, the journalist, "Is it not rather strange that the general, who has rendered such distinguished service to his country, is so very modestly, not to say shabbily, attired, whereas Mr. Pork Packer, from Chicago, looks as if he really owned the earth?" the journalist replied: "Do you not understand, Dr. Wise, that this is only another illustration of the truth that the pen is mightier than the sword?" [Laughter]

Bryan followed with these opening remarks:

I have enjoyed listening to the address of Rabbi Wise, and I could not help wondering as he proceeded, as my interest increased, as my enthusiasm rose, I could not help wondering whether that lady in his church noticed the resemblance before he began speaking or while he was speaking [laughter]. I hope that it was while he was speaking, for while I should feel complimented to know that I resemble him, I would be even more proud to have my speech mistaken for his [applause]. He has embarrassed me a little. He has been so radical that I am afraid I shall seem conservative by contrast [laughter]. It is worth coming all the way from Nebraska to hear "the money power" get what was coming to it [laughter]. I thank him. If his ministerial duties do not occupy all of his time, we may be able to use him [laughter].

Gentlemen, I hope that I shall be always able to find someone to say for me what I would like to say as well as he has said what I would like to have said to you [applause]. But he, being a spiritual adviser, could do better than I could—that is, he could say it without being misunderstood [laughter]. It is mighty embarrassing to live under the restrictions that are imposed on a man in politics—for a man can be in politics without being in office [great laughter]. If I had said what he said, there are one hundred men around me who would have regarded it as a personal attack on them [laughter].

I have tried hard to keep my different speeches separate and distinct [laughter]. I have my Farmers' Picnic speeches, my Labor Day speeches, my Businessmen's Club speeches, my Commencement speeches, and yet,

William Jennings Bryan (1920)—
"Everybody knew he meant Broady."

try as hard as I could, I have found people so narrow, biased and prejudiced that they would get my speeches mixed up [laughter]. When I have made religious speeches, I have been accused of talking politics [laughter] and when I have made political speeches, I have been accused of preaching a sermon [laughter]. And I cannot explain it unless there is so little difference between a good Democratic speech and a good sermon that you will get them mixed [great laughter and applause].

We once had a civic federation in Lincoln, and the federation asked the various churches to hold meetings in the interests of good government on the Sunday night before the election. Our church held such a meeting, and they selected a Republican lawyer to speak for his party, and I was to speak as a Democrat. I liked his speech; he seemed pleased with mine, and the audience made no hostile demonstration [laughter]. But the next day a prominent Republican was denouncing me on the street for having desecrated the Presbyterian Church [laughter]. A friend of mine who was at the meeting assured him that I did not make a political speech, but, said he, "he told the people to vote for Judge Broady, the Democratic candidate for mayor." "No," said my friend, "he did not mention Judge Broady's name." "Ah," he said, "but he told them to vote for the best man, and everybody knew he meant Broady." [Laughter] You can see how a man in politics is misrepresented.

I came down here to New York a couple of months ago to make a speech, and knowing, as I do, how prone these New York papers are to jump onto me whenever they get a chance and "map" out my thoughts [laughter], I thought that this time I would be careful to avoid any possible cause for criticism, and I took as my subject "Thou shalt not steal," and I think I hurt more people's feelings than I ever did in New York before [laughter].

The ballroom in the old Waldorf-Astoria always was the scene. At that first joint banquet the room was not crowded, but it was filled to capacity when President Taft spoke in 1911.

President Taft (1911)—
He did the best he could.

*General   Charles   H.   Taylor
(1906)—"Just to decide a bet."*

With space at a premium, publishers nevertheless insisted upon bringing their New York advertising representatives and other guests. All were jovial and convivial. With cocktails and the serving of four wine courses, including a choice of nine brands of champagne, the function got quite noisy.

President Taft did the best he could to make himself heard by the vast audience. It was before the day of the microphone and the loudspeaker. Those in the rear, who couldn't hear him, tittered and joked or repaired to the Waldorf bar.

That noisy dinner of 1911 was the last one! At a Board meeting the next day, Victor Lawson, of the Chicago *News,* and William L. McLean, of the Philadelphia *Bulletin,* protested that the dinners had grown too large and too noisy. They and other members of the Board began to feel that the joint banquet of The Associated Press and the American Newspaper Publishers Association had infringed upon the dignity that should pervade an affair to which the great, sedate and conservative Associated Press had lent its name. Certainly it had contributed little or nothing to the standing of the organization or developed any loyalty whatever for The Associated Press among the members who attended.

In December, 1913, an anecdote recounted by General Taylor, of the Boston *Globe,* to The Associated Press Board gave the *coup de grâce* to the idea of the big joint AP-ANPA banquet. He said that President Theodore Roosevelt was a guest in Boston at a large dinner. The first idea was to give the banquet in a hotel dining room, but so many people wanted to come that it was decided to have the dinner served in an armory, where several thousand could be seated. Roosevelt had a good strong voice, General Taylor said, but he didn't have a strong enough voice to make himself heard at the tables farthest from the dais. Without a microphone and loud-speakers, he spoke as loudly as he could, showed his teeth and gestured in his usual manner, finished with a peroration and sat down to the applause of those down in front who had been able to hear him. As soon as quiet was restored, a diner at the last table in the back of the armory stood up on his chair and yelled: "Mr. Toastmaster, Mr. Toastmaster!"

The toastmaster yelled back to him: "The gentleman in the back of the hall—what does he want?"

Came the reply: "Mr. Toastmaster: Just to decide a bet back here, who was that last speaker?"

General Taylor's story was enough. It was decided that instead of a joint banquet, there would be an annual luncheon beginning in 1914 solely for Associated Press members. But when I went to work for the organization in 1910, it was clear to me that overcrowded joint banquets with another organization once every three years were doing nothing to advance AP welfare. In some other way new life and spirit had to be instilled in the attitude of members toward their own Associated Press to increase the essential element of loyalty that prospers a co-operative.

19

IT COULD HAVE
BEEN OTHERWISE

THERE NEVER had been an individual with the title of traveling inspector before I was so named in 1910. The ostensible reason for my employment, as I have related, was to install the telephone method of news delivery to small papers. But in going about the country to perform this function, I found good reason to assign myself to a duty that I thought should devolve upon one with the title of traveling inspector, namely, to travel and inspect! I had an unusual opportunity to gauge membership loyalty as well as employee loyalty.

Within a few years I had visited all The Associated Press bureaus, nearly 1,000 member newspaper offices, covered over 200,000 miles, and had slept in upper and lower berths or day coaches 136 nights out of 730. I was learning about The Associated Press and the degree of loyalty to it at its grass roots. I had no business card or letter of introduction. I needed none because I had made charts of every wire circuit The Associated Press had in the country. On each circuit the cities and names of newspapers served were marked. During the long, lonely train rides and nights in hotels, I amused myself by memorizing, not only the routings of all The Associated Press wires, but the names of the newspapers served on each circuit. Telling the members I visited that I knew on what wire they were served and all of the cities and newspapers with which they were grouped served as my credentials.

I asked the nearly 1,000 members and their employees if they had any criticisms of the news service. Many of them did! Since I had no executive authority, the only method I could then apply to gain corrections was through tactful discussions with the bureaus responsible for the service to such members. With the bureaus I tried to inculculate the idea that "the member is always right."

Yet to the bureau employees I was almost as much a stranger as I was to the members I visited. To the bureau employees the title of traveling inspector was an ominous one. It aroused both suspicion and fear, which in my contacts with them I tried to turn into confidence, even hope of better things to come.

The "better things" did not come, however, until 1928, when I completely nationalized the news administration as I did the traffic work sixteen years earlier.

The four news administrative divisions—eastern, southern, central and western, each presided over by a superintendent, were abolished. Thereafter, all forty chiefs of bureau who supervised the work of the newsmen in forty strategically located cities became responsible directly to the general manager in New York. Additionally, every employee in the service was told he could write directly to the general manager on any subject, but he was requested to give a copy of his letter to his local superior, who was responsible directly to the general manager.

I found that this centralization of authority in New York, where an individual personnel file of each employee was kept, paid The Associated Press handsomely by increasing the morale of all employees in the years that followed.

My contacts with members and their employees, to which I have referred, developed a close enough acquaintance that I could discuss without restraint the degree of their interest in The Associated Press. In this way I encountered personal antagonisms against the organization, especially on the part of Midwesterners who were members of The Associated Press when it was an Illinois corporation. When The Associated Press moved to New York, it seemed to have gone far, far away, so far that it practically moved out of their lives. No longer were they intimately interested in it. They always had attended the annual meetings when they were held in nearby Chicago. Few attended those held in New York, which to some of them might as well have been in a foreign city. Some seemed proud to say that they had not attended an AP annual meeting in New York for ten years.

Because the Midwest had given the re-organized AP its greatest strength, with a larger number of members than any other section of the country, I considered it important to overcome this feeling. I wanted to take the New York management right into their offices and create my own personal contacts with them as evidence that although The Associated Press management had moved to New York, I, a Midwesterner myself, was interested in their problems and would continue to be if they would let me.

It did not take long for me to realize I had assigned myself a large task. To organize it as well as I could, I kept a "membership loyalty file" in my office in New York. Following up my personal visits, I wrote countless letters telling the members that I was glad to have seen them in their own offices and detailing what I had done with bureau employees to create a more responsive attitude. I assured them that I always would be interested in hearing from them.

Though after two years my title had become chief of the Traffic Department, I still continued to write the letters and to make the visits. It seemed to be doing some good and I enjoyed it. No one interfered with me. As a result, I became an avenue of continuous contact between some members and the management in an effort to get the loyalty for which I hoped. It became noticeable that when some of the members I had visited came to New York and called at the general offices, they asked for me.

After becoming general manager, I continued this effort. It was anomalous that an employee like myself should undertake to make owners loyal to their own Associated Press, but I did not shrink from adding this as one of the responsibilities of my general managership.

Believing that The Associated Press news service could not rise to the new heights of efficiency that I planned for it without the militant co-operation of the membership, my effort to gain that co-operation during my administration increased to the point that it may have equalled the stress I was putting upon effecting radical changes in the news service. I did not have to worry about the two score AP members who had served or still were serving on the Board. Their interest was enduring.

I knew well enough it was this group of three or fourscore that had served as the hard corps of militancy that made The AP's high principled news service possible first with the Illinois corporation and afterward when The Associated Press moved to New York. But I wanted to enlarge this circle of interested members.

Though all members readily paid their assessments, that lone fact to my mind was not enough. I found that some of them had just come to feel that they were "buying" a service. The Associated Press had become an impersonal thing to them. Trying to get them to think their concern in supporting it should extend beyond that matter of merely paying their weekly assessments was difficult.

I tried to impress upon them that they should want their Associated Press constantly to improve, just as they wanted their own newspapers to improve and increasingly prosper. I would tell many of them that they were holders of memberships that originally were granted to founders of the organization. And I gained interest occasionally because I could tell some of them what I had learned from reading the correspondence between their predecessors and the management prior to the turn of the century.

I said that many who wrote those letters were stalwarts in a cause that was worth while. I stressed the fact that like the patriots of '76, they had their revolution against tyranny—a tyranny that might still prevail over every newspaper in the land even in a more aggravated form had they not forged the chain of co-operation which they named The Associated Press. For perhaps Scripps would not have founded the new United Press in 1907, nor Hearst his International News Service the same year, if the old United Press had been invulnerable to the attack that destroyed it.

I emphasized that membership in a strong Associated Press was a valuable insurance policy against a repetition of what confronted the newspapers in the nineties. I told them I was insisting that the entire AP staff plan for a greater Associated Press. And I reminded them that no plans could be successfully developed unless the members willed that they should; that without the co-operation of members in developing novel elements that would enhance the value of the service to them, The Associated Press would grow weaker in the face of competition, no matter how the staff might strive to make it stronger.

Because of the depression, the Board, in 1932, reduced assessments and allotted refunds of any excess still available. Salaries were cut 10 percent. The action was based on the belief that the reductions would be appreciated and would demonstrate to the members that a co-operative like The Associated Press can be truly responsive in helping its members meet adverse conditions. But the depth of the cut, I told the Board, was strikingly shown by these figures:

In 1929, the annual income was $9,660,000. Five years later, with the largest membership in its history, and the largest number of employees in its history and with more miles of leased wire than at any time in its history, the total income was only $8,087,000 annually. This was $1,573,000 per annum less than five years previously.

At a Board meeting in October three years later, I reported that the assessment reductions and the refunds to the members, not only had halted the progressive development of the general service for those three years, but that in my opinion they had brought about a retrogression.

I said that in continuous contacts with members, I had not found one who felt that the reduction to him had increased his interest in The Associated Press. The attitude was just that the reductions were welcomed. Some, however, did not know or had forgotten that any decreases in their assessments had been made.

Considering this, I told the Board I had reached the interesting conclusion that continuation of striking improvements in the service would have done more to enhance membership appreciation than was accomplished by reducing assessments and salaries. But regardless of speculation as to what might have been, the Board at that session approved my recommendation that fixing salaries above the level existing prior to the cuts in 1932 be left to my discretion. I acted accordingly and promptly aimed for new achievements.

In trying to promote Associated Press loyalty, what seemed to interest all members the most and gave them pause was whether they wanted the organization to be made strong enough to survive if the courts ever annulled their "franchises." If not, I asked, what better than a co-operative could they suggest which, after the loss of the "franchise" rights, would positively guarantee the integrity of the news and at the same time grant an insurance policy against inequitable costs. Contemplating the answer to that question always opened the avenue to the reminder that complete co-operative ownership did assure true and unbiased treatment of the news.

Most of them could be made to feel that this was worth while. But I knew well enough that if the news service was not strikingly efficient, support based alone upon ethical grounds surely would be badly shaken if and when the courts terminated the exclusive "franchises." For if the news service were not valuable, and the members supported it mainly because of the "franchise" element, they would find themselves hugging a delusion if and when the courts struck down their exclusive rights.

There had been considerable talk and even threats of court actions to destroy these "franchise" values as early as 1914. In New York in that year, the publisher of the *Sun*, then a nonmember newspaper, asked the United States Department of Justice to compel The Associated Press to admit the *Sun* to membership. The attorney general did not go to court to try to annul the exclusive rights, and the membership, which could have elected the *Sun* by a four-fifths vote, unanimously rejected its application. But as I read the plea of the *Sun* to the attorney general, and his conclusion, it seemed to me that eventually the "franchise" rights would be wiped out. I realized that loss of those valued rights of exclusivity could diminish or even end the loyalty of some AP members and the existence of The Associated Press itself.

By 1925, a definite trend that could lead to this became evident. Other corporations were being affected by court decisions based on the Sherman and Clayton anti-trust acts. I then reminded The Associated Press Board that these decrees warned of what could happen to The Associated Press "franchise" rights. I said that if for no other reason than this, my policy would be to project improvements and innovations in The Associated Press service to gain continued support for the co-operative.

For it was axiomatic that with their exclusive rights gone, efficiency of the service would be left as the only means to conserve the loyalty of all members. And I never let myself forget that the responsibility for designing plans to accomplish this rested solely upon me. That is why every road that possibly could lead to improvement was explored.

It was my hope that these improvements could be developed and perfected before a demand for service was made by a more determined applicant than the New York *Sun* proved to be—one who might get the courts to strike down the exclusive rights. My fear was that this might happen before the quality and scope of the service could be lifted to a plane that would increase membership appreciation enough that the loss of the "valuable" so-called franchise rights would not matter. Fortunately, a more determined applicant did not demand the service until 1942.

20

OCHS–MUNSEY– HEARST

IN PUBLISHER LOYALTY to The Associated Press, Adolph S. Ochs, Frank A. Munsey and William Randolph Hearst could be put down as representative of three classes that made up its membership.

I repeat that by loyalty I mean a sincere concern on the part of AP members that the organization's services be operated more efficiently than those of its competition, and a determination, as members, to contribute all that is necessary to maintain that predominance.

The group classically represented by Mr. Ochs had respect and devotion for The Associated Press because its ethical conception of unbiased news was guaranteed by the diversified beliefs of its owner members, who agreed that the news should be unbiased even though they might not have agreed on anything else. To them the monetary value of their AP membership was secondary.

The Munsey group was largely interested in the money value of what they liked to call their AP "franchises," by which they could prevent nonmember competitors from getting The Associated Press news service. This group was the smallest of the three, but there were enough of them that none was ever lonely.

All the rest composed the group in which I place Hearst. It was the largest numerically and occupied the middle ground between the

Munsey and Ochs classes. This group valued their "franchise" rights like Munsey; also, they felt that the news service was indispensable to their newspapers, as did Hearst.

Mr. Ochs once said:

I owe more loyalty to The Associated Press than I can express. For when I bought the *New York Times,* with its Associated Press membership, I had no money left with which to buy special correspondence. So the *New York Times* reached prosperity practically on The Associated Press news service alone. Though we now spend a great deal for our own specials, The Associated Press still remains our prime reliance. Therefore, for the property value the *New York Times* has now become, I owe most to The Associated Press, and I venture to say that scores of publishers who, like myself, struggled from modest beginnings would similarly express this loyalty to this mutual organization if they would take the time to think of it while today they enjoy their bountiful plenty.

The Columbia Encyclopedia says that Munsey "was· sometimes called the executioner of newspapers." In his purchases, consolidations and scrapping of newspapers, he had acquired James Gordon Bennett's New York *Herald* and *Telegram* in 1920. Previously he had bought the New York *Sun* and *Evening Sun.* Neither of these two had AP memberships. He bought the New York *Press* to gain the morning *Sun* a franchise, as he called it.

After his purchase of the morning *Herald* in 1920, he consolidated it with the morning *Sun,* but as both the *Evening Telegram* and *Evening Sun* were making money at the time, he did not consolidate the *Telegram* with the *Evening Sun* in order to give the latter The Associated Press service. However, to give the *Evening Sun* the service, he did buy the New York evening *Globe* in 1923.

The *Globe* had several valuable features which Munsey scrapped. When he was derided for this, Munsey publicly declared: "I paid nearly $2,000,000 for the *Globe* to get its Associated Press franchise for the *Sun* to make the *Sun* structurally sound. The *Globe* had nothing else that I wanted."

That was the highest amount anyone has ever claimed to have paid solely for an AP "franchise," though it was the newspaper with an Associated Press membership that was bought, not a "franchise." At any rate, the transaction gave me an opportunity to talk to Munsey about The Associated Press. We got on very well—well enough for me to ask him whether the story I had heard about the purchase of the New York *Herald* and *Telegram* by him in 1920 was true.

"What story?" he asked.

I replied: "The executor of the James Gordon Bennett estate, wishing to sell the *Herald* and the *Telegram,* and casting about for a purchaser, decided to approach you, Mr. Munsey. Accordingly, a representative of the executor was told to go to you and offer to sell both papers for a total of $2,000,000. If you started to bargain for a lower price, he was instructed to remind you that there was an advantageous $500,000 newsprint contract that went with the sale. The representative, having rehearsed his presentation, called on you. In the reception room to your office, he wrote on his card the nature of his business. You kept him waiting for some time. Then you granted him admission, looked at his card, and said:

'Oh, yes, you want to sell me the *Herald* and the *Telegram.* Well, I will give $4,000,000 for those properties if accepted immediately, and not one cent more.'

"Having been told to ask $2,000,000, the representative momentarily choked up with astonishment, but remembered there was something else he was supposed to say. 'You may not know it, Mr. Munsey,' he said, 'but there is an advantageous newsprint contract worth $500,000.'

"Thereupon you, Mr. Munsey, said: 'Yes, including that contract I will make it $4,500,000 if you accept right now.'

"The representative, having fully regained his composure, said: 'Yes, Mr. Munsey.'

"A memorandum agreement was promptly written and signed by both of you. Is all of that true, Mr. Munsey?"

Without a wink of an eyelash he said: "I got the properties."

I accepted that statement as confirmation of the story and, with a laugh, said so. He asked me why I was laughing, and I said: "I was only thinking of how much better you would have fared if you had asked what the price was instead of saying what you would pay."

He said: "There is an old adage about he who laughs last laughs best."

Fourteen months later, on March 18, 1924, I called on Munsey at his apartment in the Ritz-Carlton. He had wanted to see me because he was considering adopting a pension plan for his employees and wanted to know what sort of plan I had gotten The Associated Press to adopt.

"Do you remember," he said to me, "that last year you laughed at the story about me paying $4,500,000 for the *Herald* and the *Telegram* in 1920 when I might have gotten them for less?"

"Yes, Mr. Munsey," I said. "I remember that. Why?"

"At that time," he answered, "I told you that 'he who laughs last laughs best.' Today I sold the *Herald* to Mrs. Whitelaw Reid (of the New York *Tribune*) for $5,000,000 and I still have the *Telegram*, for which I hope to get $2,000,000."

As he amused himself by having the "best laugh," I asked if I might telephone the news of the sale to The Associated Press news desk. He said it would be all right if I did so.

From an authentic source came a detail of the story of that sale of the *Herald* to Mrs. Reid. It was that Munsey, desiring to buy the *Tribune,* approached Mrs. Reid with a "buy or sell" proposition. Mrs. Reid asked him what figure he had in mind on such a basis. Munsey said:

"I have in mind paying $5,000,000 for the *Tribune,* or you can have the *Herald* for $5,000,000."

Mrs. Reid told Munsey that her brother and others had stock in the *Tribune* and asked Munsey please to write a memorandum of his

Frank A. Munsey (1920)—
"I got the properties."

offer to sell the *Herald* at that figure, leaving out mention of buying the *Tribune*. Munsey did so then and there and signed it, whereupon Mrs. Reid made a holographic copy of Munsey's proposal, wrote the word "accepted" on it, signed her name on it, and handed it to Munsey to sign, which he did. Then she wrote "accepted" and signed her name on Munsey's original. This she kept.

Munsey died before I had a chance to ask him whether this story of the sale of the *Herald* was true. Nor had I been able to make any headway with him in discussing Associated Press loyalty.

I have known many who, like Munsey, thought of The Associated Press memberships primarily as something to buy or sell, with no idea that there was any necessity for AP loyalty. But Munsey was the only one who in his talks with me prided himself for having wiped out more AP memberships than anybody else, which he did by wiping out of existence newspapers that had the memberships. He once said to me when complaining about an AP story he did not like, that while he had paid nearly $2,000,000 for the New York *Globe* to get its AP membership for the New York *Sun,* he would not hesitate to resign the membership if The Associated Press displeased him.

After Munsey's death, Mrs. Ogden Reid, wife of the publisher of the *Herald Tribune,* invited me for a weekend with her husband and his mother, Mrs. Whitelaw Reid, at their summer home on St. Regis Lake in the Adirondacks. While there, I told Mrs. Whitelaw Reid the story I have here related about Munsey. She smiled and said:

"As a matter of fact, it was worth that and a great deal more to me to have the combined paper, which my son could direct. I could have sustained him in idleness, but I did not want his life to take that course, nor did he. We could have kept on publishing the *Tribune* without buying the *Herald.* But it would not have been the newspaper monument which I thought the *Tribune* plus the *Herald* could set up in honor of my husband, to say nothing of the future of my son. My only regret was that Munsey made a condition in the sale to the effect that the word *"Herald"* (the name of the James Gordon Bennett newspaper) must be hyphenated with that of the *Tribune,* the latter being the *Tribune* of Greeley and of my husband."

My memory of Mrs. Whitelaw Reid is that she was a woman of talent and competence, having a brilliant mind and worthy of the hopes all men have of the wives they leave behind them at death, with the burdens of great institutions to be disposed of or carried on. Such a woman, also, is Helen Rogers Reid, Ogden's widow.

In the matter of loyalty, the feeling of William Randolph Hearst was unusual even in the class in which I have placed him. He once owned more newspapers which were represented by membership in The Associated Press than any other individual, and the aggregate amount he paid for them while a member of The Associated Press for sixty years constituted an enormous sum. Over a period of sixty years, he paid a total of many millions of dollars in weekly assessments for Associated Press service to his newspapers.

Hearst felt that instead of being appreciated as The Associated Press' biggest financial supporter and catered to as such, there was deep antipathy toward him among some AP Board members whose newspapers were competitive with his. This strained relationship had started before the turn of the century. Twenty years later, when this was all but forgotten, litigation over the theft of Associated Press news by an employee of the Cleveland *News* on behalf of Hearst's International News Service rekindled a mutual ill feeling.

Nevertheless, after the legal battle over the theft of news had ended, I decided to do what I could to establish a truly cordial relationship with the publisher.

My first opportunity to meet Mr. Hearst came when David E. Town, who had been on The Associated Press Board of Directors, entered Hearst's employment. Town was sure there was ground for understanding between the Board and Hearst. I was assistant general manager at the time. Town wanted me to be the one to make the approach to Hearst.

That first meeting occurred in the Hearst apartment on Riverside Drive and Eighty-sixth Street in New York City in 1921. It lasted over an hour. I found the great publisher friendly. He seemed interested when I recounted that I had been a correpondent of his Chicago *American*.

"That," I said, "was when I lived in Indianapolis in 1903 and 1904. You remember that your friends in 1904 sought for you the Democratic nomination for the presidency. In their efforts to get the Indiana delegation to support you at the national convention, you issued a special Indiana edition of your Chicago *American*, which was distributed all over Indiana.

"Moses Koenigsberg, founder of King Features for you and president of the International News Service, was in charge of the edition, which was a newspaper restricted to boosting your candidacy and printing a lot of Indiana news. I was assigned the task of getting that Indiana news and undertook to do it at 'space rates.'

"As a result, a modest opulence noticed by my friends was due to the $400 to $600 a month I was receiving from you. Though my income at that rate did not last beyond the date of the convention, I was one of the very few in Indianapolis that year who cogitated whether to buy a horseless buggy or a horse and buggy. My choice fell upon the latter.

"Thus you were responsible, Mr. Hearst, for my becoming the owner for the first time of what we Hoosiers called in those days a 'courtin' rig.' Others of my friends had conveyances that belonged to their families, but I had the distinction of being the only Hoosier who owned a horse and buggy purchased with money I earned because of your candidacy for President."

Hearst chuckled just a little and congratulated me on getting more out of his ambition than he did. I brought up the reason for my visit. He said:

"I have never understood, Mr. Cooper, why apparently I have to

William Randolph Hearst (1925)—
"Because of the merger
my *Associated Press would have*
a much stronger competition."

be the only member who has to deal at law with The Associated Press, of which I am a member."

"A very important member," I interjected.

"I would be glad if that fact were appreciated," he continued. "The AP to me is a most important institution. I hold it to be my right to present my own views in my news columns if I want to. With me it is an obligation that I do so. But to be fair with our readers, I have· often insisted that AP dispatches on matters on which I am prejudiced be run in parallel columns with the specials that promote my views. I have always trusted the accuracy of The Associated Press news report. I wish I had the service for the several papers in our organization that do not have it. If they could get it, I would have no reason to operate the International News Service. You might tell that to the Board for me."

I told Hearst I would do so, as well as do all I could to create better mutual feeling.

"Tell them," he said, "that I have no personal ill feeling but that I am always going to insist upon my rights; that they cannot object that we have to operate a news service competitive with The Associated Press since we have newspapers that cannot get The AP. The trouble is that feeling a loyalty to The Associated Press and having newspapers in its membership, I am in competition with myself by having to operate another press association. Tell them I am not any happier about that than they are."

Hearst then referred to The Associated Press litigation with his International News Service over the theft of Associated Press news. He said no law suit would have been necessary to stop it; that all The Associated Press had to do was to tell him about it and he would have stopped it. He said that the Board would have done that with any other member.

"But Mr. Stone," he continued, "had obsessed himself with the conception that he must establish legally the principle that there is a property right in news. He wanted to use the courts to legislate by means of a decision that would construe news as property. Then, if one of my nonmember papers or my news service used Associated Press news, the offender could be sent to prison for theft of Associated Press property. Sometimes I have thought that they would like to put me there personally!"

I knew, of course, that it was Mr. Stone's idea to establish the principle of a property right in news; that he believed one way to keep competition at a disadvantage would be through the right legally to punish theft of news by a competing news agency or its use of the local news of an Associated Press member, the right to which, under the AP by-laws, is exclusively reserved for The Associated Press. I did not want to hide the role I played in the litigation at Mr. Stone's request.

"I may tell you, Mr. Hearst," I said, "that I am the one who first discovered the theft of news in Cleveland, and I went out there and exposed the fact to the publisher of the Cleveland *News*. Though I am not a lawyer, I dictated all the affidavits confessing the practice and had them notarized. On the evidence in these affidavits, the case reached the Supreme Court."

"And the Court," Hearst interjected, "did not accept Mr. Stone's contention that there was a property right in news. It just declared that to use another's news was an unfair trade practice and," Hearst smilingly added, "enjoined my International News Service and my Associated Press from doing such things to each other."

Though Hearst felt that he and not The Associated Press had won the case, Mr. Stone also claimed to be the victor, and to assure that his victory would prevent unauthorized use of AP news, the Board adopted a resolution requiring all members of The Associated Press to publish the following warning against piracy, which has appeared in every issue of every AP newspaper, including those of Mr. Hearst, for forty years:

The Associated Press is entitled exclusively to the use for republication of all news dispatches credited to it or not otherwise credited in this newspaper and all the local news published herein. Rights of republication of all other matter herein are also reserved.

When I left Hearst after that first visit, he was still in good humor. There was no upsurge of antagonism until 1924, when Paul Patterson's nonmember Baltimore *Evening Sun* and Frank E. Gannett's nonmember Rochester *Times-Union* sought admission to Associated Press membership. Both undertook to gain enough votes to override the exclusive rights of Hearst's Baltimore *News* and his Rochester *Journal* and *Post-Express*.

To accomplish this, the applicants had to receive the favorable vote of four-fifths of all of The Associated Press members present in person or by proxy at its annual meeting of 1924. In other words, that was the vote necessary to nullify Hearst's so-called franchise right to keep them out. Though both papers failed of election, Hearst felt aggrieved because he believed the Board of Directors had favored election of the applicants. He referred to this in 1927, when I sought his benediction for my efforts to establish The Associated Press news photo service.

"Well, Mr. Cooper, our papers won that fight against Baltimore and Rochester. You have talked to me about membership loyalty toward The Associated Press. What about loyalty of The Associated Press Board of Directors to its membership? We got enough votes to uphold my contention that members of a mutual organization should be loyal to each other.

"And, by the way, it has just been suggested to me that I could profitably sell the International News Service to the United Press. If I did so I could wipe out the International News Service annual losses of some $400,000 that my papers have had to meet, and because of the merger, *my* Associated Press would have a much stronger competition. It, however, would have been disloyal to The Associated Press if I had sold."

"If you had," I said, "your papers and all other International News Service clients would not have had for their exclusive use the distinctive kind of news service the International News Service affords. You would not have had what you wanted in the way of a news report but only what the United Press decided you would have."

"That," said Hearst, "is the first reason why I refused to sell. The other one about being loyal to The Associated Press is a good one, too; or am I wrong?"

If Hearst had not won the fight with Baltimore and Rochester, I am sure all I had done to create better mutual feeling would have availed nothing. As it was, the members of the Board who voted as individuals for the Baltimore and Rochester applications were generous in defeat, for later on they adopted my suggestion and made Hearst's son, William Randolph Hearst, Jr., a vice-president of The Associated Press.

Munsey and Hearst operated on a larger scale then any other publisher in spending money lavishly to obtain newspapers with Associated Press memberships in the largest cities. If Munsey ever had any idea of building a chain of newspapers in the fashion of others—

Hearst, for example—he failed completely. He bought enough news-papers to make a chain, most of them with Associated Press member-ships. Yet at his death he owned but one newspaper. Even that was sold and consolidated some years later with the New York *World Telegram.*

Thus, no newspaper owned by Munsey with or without Associated Press membership exists today as a separate entity. Either he scrapped them entirely or their separate identities were lost in consolidations with other newspapers.

21

THE AP'S LOYALTY

BRIGADE

FROM THE large number of acquaintances I made with Associated Press members in the first half of the century, many of whom became my personal friends, I can say that an imponderable, indefinable feeling akin to devotion for The Associated Press came into the hearts of some of them, as was the case with Mr. Ochs. They wanted The Associated Press to endure and to prosper because they felt its news standards to be the finest flower in the world's journalistic garden.

I quote three expressions made by Associated Press members who have this feeling of deep concern for their AP. I took what they were saying to mean, first, that their own Associated Press had been made stronger; and second, that they were grateful to me for having made it so.

For instance, in January, 1937, John Cowles, then an AP director representing the Des Moines *Register* and *Tribune,* wrote me:

As I told you following the last directors' meeting, every time when I leave one of those sessions I come away with even a higher estimate of your ability and force and qualifications to head The Associated Press than before. If The Associated Press had not been lucky enough to have you as general manager during the last ten years, but instead had a man

Louis A. Weil (1950)—
"I shall be forever grateful."

of less force and vision, even though he might have been competent and high grade, I think it is not only possible but probable that The Associated Press today would be moribund.

Although, as you know, I don't agree with you 100 percent in all details, I am, nevertheless, convinced that the more aggressively *you* shape The Associated Press' policies and determine its future course the better for the whole association.

It is an inspiration to see you in action, and although I may not be on the Board after the election this April, at least from the sidelines I hope to watch you running The Associated Press—the way *you* think it ought to be run—for a great many years to come.

Another letter, dated November 7, 1939, from Louis A. Weil, of the Port Huron *Times Herald,* reads in part:

I was thinking the other day about the development of the picture service, what a great job you did for The Associated Press under most trying circumstances. I shall never forget that New York fight and I shall be forever grateful that we had a man at the head of The Associated Press who had the vision, foresight and courage to stand up under it. It is the high spot in the history of The Associated Press. God bless you, my boy, and keep you in health and strength.

And here is a quotation of a statement by Edward E. Lindsay, of the Decatur *Herald,* who served as first vice-president of The Associated Press in 1947. In an address he made at a meeting of Associated. Press Illinois members in Chicago that year, he said:

There is a man in New York tonight who had more than anyone else to do with making The Associated Press what it is today. Years ago he visited most of you—or your fathers—and told you about the teletype replacing the old Morse wires. He is responsible for the development of Wirephoto. These are only a couple of the many improvements for which he is responsible. I know that on this approaching one hundredth anniversary of The Associated Press, all of us think of this man—the executive director and general manager of The Associated Press, Kent Cooper.

When I received comments like these, I accepted them as evidence that progress had been made in meeting a challenge which a New York publisher worded in 1900. Whitelaw Reid, who had conducted

Edward E. Lindsay (1955)—"There is a man in New York tonight . . ."

the New York *Tribune* during many changes and various vicissitudes of several news agency creations and reorganizations, said:

The life expectancy of an American news agency, as proved by what I have experienced, is brief. I can hope that this Associated Press as now re-organized will live and not grow old. I will hope in vain, however, if it lives until it does grow old, because if it grows old it will die like everything else.

When I heard in 1911 what Reid had said, it sounded like doom for The Associated Press because it already was dormant. Besides that, the frightening thing was the acceleration of the annual death rate of the men who brought The Associated Press successfully through the United Press fight. Unless convinced of the necessity of it, their successors could never have the feeling for the welfare of The Associated Press that their predecessors had because of that fight. Another and yet another generation would have to be imbued with appreciation of The Associated Press.

When appointed general manager in 1925, I intensified efforts to

Whitelaw Reid (1905)—
"I can hope . . ."

meet this challenge in one way by personally attending state meetings of members where AP loyalty as well as the news report could be discussed. The meetings of the state associations brought such good results that the advantage of a similar effort at the national level was apparent, since neither the news report nor concern for The Associated Press were ever discussed in the annual corporate meetings in New York.

Therefore, in 1928, I asked President Noyes for his support as a publisher of a proposal I first made to Mr. Stone in 1915, namely, that managing editors of member papers throughout the country be organized as a national group that would take an active interest in everything about The Associated Press, especially its news report. They and their telegraph and picture editors were the ones really in touch with what The Associated Press was delivering to their offices. I told Mr. Noyes that an effort to establish such an organization would have a better chance of success if undertaken directly and independently by the managing editors themselves rather than by me.

What I wanted was a national organization that would meet with the general manager and his executive staff in three or four-day annual meetings held in geographical locations rotated North, East, West and South. I was sure that because of the personal contacts between managing editors and AP executives a commendable, mutual interest would be aroused.

Mr. Noyes told Owen Kuhn, managing editor of the *Star,* of my idea and authorized Kuhn to become sponsor of a national organization. Kuhn did a magnificent job of organizing it and served as its first president.

There may be other organizations, big or little, that have done and are carrying on what the managing editors of Associated Press newspapers brought into being in 1933. If so, I never heard of one of them. In brief, it was and is a method by which representatives of all the "customers" who are the immediate users of a product meet in a large hall with the executives and representatives of the staff that turns out that product and with just one purpose in mind: to improve it!

The "customers" of The Associated Press took the name of The Associated Press Managing Editors Association (APME). At their meetings they discuss with AP men the news, picture and feature reports which their newspapers receive from The Associated Press. They condemn what they do not like and tell what they do like of what they get; also they tell what they would like to get if they could.

Nothing since those AP dinners in Chicago in the nineties has done as much to increase interest in The Associated Press as has this organization. It is a source of inspiration and drive for achievement. It has developed personal acquaintance and mutual friendships between managing editors and The AP staff. In importance it has gone beyond the fondest dreams I had for it when I first thought of it, or when it finally had its first meeting. Yet it didn't exactly start out as though it was going to be anything of the kind!

The meetings are extremely valuable, however, for the expression of requests, the decisions upon which are frequently made on the spot with the reasons therefor if the requests are denied. For instance, once in answer to a suggestion, I explained that whenever The Associated Press would follow that request and identify presidential candidate Alfred Landon as "budget-balancer," then for the same reason The Associated Press might be expected to comply with another request and identify the other candidate as "humanity's savior" Roosevelt, etc. There were at some meetings a few demands for this extreme sort of thing.

Oliver Owen Kuhn (1936)—
Did a magnificent job.

The first meeting in French Lick Springs in 1933 proved to be a good beginning. The managing editors fired away with their comments and we Associated Press employees listened. As was expected, the first opportunity the managing editors as a group ever had to let loose their comments face to face with AP executives brought out complaints on some incidents that were hoary with age and for which the then existing management had no responsibility whatever. To simplify matters, I made a suggestion that no reference be made to what had occurred before the change of management in 1925. The reaction of good-hearted, generous Paul Bellamy, of the Cleveland *Plain Dealer,* afterward an AP director, whose friendship I cherished, was consoling:

If we cannot refer to something prior to 1925, how are we going to prove to ourselves by comparison how much better we think The Associated Press news report is today than it was then?

Battered but unbowed, having taken it on the chin for all the references to what had occurred in the whole third of a century, we AP men showed our appreciation by countering with nothing at all specific in the way of blaming the managing editors in return for their derelictions toward The Associated Press. I had told my staff that we would do just that. So the first of the meetings of the APME came to an end, with the managing editors pleased at having had their say, and with no hard feelings on the part of The AP management.

Indeed, when I read what Malcolm Bingay, of the Detroit *Free Press,* wrote in his own paper on his return to Detroit, I could not believe my own memory of what occurred, so generous was he in his first-page, four-column head story of Sunday, November 5, 1933, excerpts of which follow:

There was something indefinably gripping about that long two-day session, a sense of the dramatic hard to explain. I think it came to most of us subconsciously—a realization that in some small way we were a part of an intangible something; that, through the power of the printed word, backed with the integrity and the solidarity of The Associated Press, all America, if not the whole human race, was tied into a common bond; the growing of a Galahadian tradition in the search for the Holy Grail of truth. . . .

After that the atmosphere quickly changed. Here was a gang of enthusiastic reporters indulging in their greatest pleasure: arguing news values. And how they argued! Editors my eye! They were reporters as ardent in their contentions as a bunch of youngsters around the press table at police headquarters. Tap the most dignified editor, and, if he is worthy of his title—no matter how gray his hair—he is at heart a reporter. . . .

Take The Associated Press bureau chiefs who were there. Though they headed bureaus they were still reporters. I could not find a gray hair among them. Virile, alert, keenly intelligent men, all in the prime of life and all who had won their spurs in the hard game of news gathering. And moving among them, smiling, urbane, was "the boss," Kent Cooper—still young enough to feel the thrill of action and yet old enough to dominate the most delicately balanced and complicated piece of intangible machinery ever conceived by mortal man.

The secret of it all?

Only men of proved character serve The Associated Press. Mr. Cooper determined long ago that a news service could be no better than the character of the men who write it and organize it.

"As these men are," he might have said, "so is the AP report."

And he could have paid them and it no higher compliment.

After our final meeting, I went for a walk over the hills with several of these younger executives. Mr. Cooper, by request, had closed the sessions with an address that turned out to be a quiet, informal, almost conversational talk.

It dawned on most of us that under his casual pleasantries he was, wholly unconsciously, delivering a message that throbbed with evangelical zeal for co-operation in the great search for truth. There was something stronger than oratory, stronger than the printed address could reveal—a quiet, deep-rooted passion to make still finer and stronger and purer this stream of life that is The Associated Press.

I commented on this to these young associates with whom I walked, and one of them answered, saying: "Yes, a man cannot be long associated with Mr. Cooper without absorbing something of him. No matter how divergent those personalities seem to be, if you talk to any one of them a while, you will find something in him that is Kent Cooper."

There is about the man an innate dignity, a gracious kindliness, if not courtliness. He has an amazing grasp of detail without ever letting himself become enmeshed in detail. He thinks a lot and talks little, but when he speaks he says much. He is the flowering of a journalistic culture and his personality sings its way over the thousands of miles of wires in the AP network. And he has implanted so firmly his ideals that a faithful staff will carry on long years after this generation has passed. . . .

To have attended that meeting was to be inspired afresh, to attain rebirth of confidence in the power and the glory of a free and untrammeled American press serving a free and independent people.

The next annual meeting was held in Chicago. In succeeding years the meetings convened in many cities, including Cleveland, New York, Detroit, New Orleans and again in Chicago in 1941. In none of the sessions had The Associated Press men been asked to make counter criticisms with bills of particulars against the managing editors. Neil Swanson, of the Baltimore *Sun,* chairman of the Chicago meeting of 1941, had a bright idea. He gave me the subject "Up and at 'em." He asked me to tell the managing editors what was wrong with *them.*

I tried to do so but smiled frequently as I let them have it! Perhaps the smile rather than what I said brought the standing ovation after I concluded. At any rate, back in my office in New York I received several letters in commendation. The shortest one was from W. W. Raynolds, of the Cleveland *Plain Dealer.* He wrote:

Malcolm W. Bingay (1948)—
"Something indefinably gripping."

I wanted to tell you in Chicago that I thought your talk was the sweetest most artistic ever. A record to be run at the state meetings would be wonderful.

Byron Price, executive news editor, spoke effectively itemizing his charges against the managing editors, as did Paul Mickelson, Brian Bell, J. M. Roberts, F. A. Resch and M. J. Wing. After that all of us still were welcomed at APME meetings!

Later I got The Associated Press Board of Directors to approve my proposal that the Associated Press Managing Editors be incorporated to give it permanent status. Also, at the meeting in Los Angeles in 1947, I suggested to the managing editors that they should not confine their consideration of The AP news report alone to what they could bring up for discussion at the annual meetings; that instead they should establish continuing study committees to work all year in cooperation with The AP management and watchfully endeavor to obtain corrections promptly as errors occur, rather than waiting to tell about them and to ask for action at their next annual meeting.

The promise of thorough work by these continuing study committees was so enthusiastically given that I arranged for their elaborate reports to be printed and mailed to the managing editors in advance of their annual meetings; also, that a full account of each year's meeting be issued in illustrated book form and sent to them as permanent records of their proceedings.

Alan Gould, executive editor, who was at the first meeting at French Lick as general sports editor, and who attended all meetings thereafter, proclaimed the work and standing of the APME in Associated Press affairs as follows in 1957:

It is vital to note that APME, as the best and most effectively organized voice of AP's membership, has broadened its range of influence and its contribution to our productive scheme of things. To a greater degree than ever before, it has put the Continuing Studies on a year-round co-ordinated basis. It has established closer working relations with AP bureaus and departments, and in the process built up increasing areas of mutual understanding. It has not only served essential watchdog purposes, in checking the shortcomings of both the staff and members, but has helped inject fresh ideas into our whole operation.

This militant interest on the part of APME members contributed to bringing to several of them the highest reward the entire AP membership can bestow, namely, their election to The Associated Press Board of Directors. Those who have been thus honored are: Paul Bellamy, Roy Roberts, E. P. Hoyt, Benjamin M. McKelway, N. R. Howard, Kenneth MacDonald and George W. Healy, Jr. One of these, Benjamin M. McKelway, later became president of The Associated Press. In an address to The Associated Press Managing Editors Association in New Orleans in 1957, he said:

Experience has shown that the APME is as natural, as workable and as component a part of The Associated Press as the telephone and telegraph wires which link AP members together.

To me the election of seven Associated Press Managing Editors Association members to The Associated Press Board, and one of them to The Associated Press presidency, strikingly evidences the results for which I hoped, namely, that the managing editors, in co-operation with The AP management, share responsibility for the betterment of The Associated Press news service, a membership obligation in which few publishers interest themselves.

Because the managing editors show an intense interest in The Associated Press—its news, photo and feature services; because they persistently demand improvements until they either get them or are convinced that what they ask for is impractical of achievement, and because they praise accomplishments with fervor, I feel they have earned the title of The Associated Press Loyalty Brigade.

It was this that I wanted. And it was the burden of my talks with managing editors for several years after I first formally disclosed my hopes to them in that address at their meeting in Chicago in 1941 when they let me tell them what was wrong with them. I then said:

Now there is one thing I shall disclose to you for the first time. It is that I wanted to have an Associated Press managing editors' association which would be the first front of an Associated Press loyalty brigade.

The Associated Press Managing Editors Association has indeed earned that title.

22

THE BIRTH OF

WIREPHOTO

I HAD TOLD The Associated Press Board of Directors in 1926 that I planned ultimately to send news photos by wire, but in 1930 I realized that my plans for this simultaneous transmission of news photos and the news in words throughout the country would have to be expedited.

For it was in that year that David Sarnoff told me of the coming of television. I realized then that television, when it came, would completely antiquate the printing by newspapers of news photos of events received by mail from one to several days after television had flashed pictures of those events on screens directly into American homes.

Moreover, since speed in delivering news in words by telegraph had drawn readers to patronize newspapers for decades, I wanted readers given the added attraction of pictures delivered with equal speed so that words and pictures could be printed simultaneously. But equally important, I did not want to contemplate the inferior position in which AP newspapers, with the advent of television, would find themselves because their own Associated Press had failed to offer them a practical way to obtain pictures by wire to print with the news in words. In other words, I wanted to give newspapers something as arrestingly attractive and practical in their field as I knew television would be for radio in its field.

With its establishment, Wirephoto became a symbol of a dramatic development in newspapering. It is a means by which pictures sent from anywhere can be instantaneously received by wire in every city of the United States at the same time, and on circuits that parallel those that transmit the news in words.

For The Associated Press to achieve perfection in picture transmission by wire before the advent of television, engineering difficulties had to be overcome. To finance the novel undertaking, contracts had to be secured with a minimum of thirty-five newspapers in key cities for an expenditure of $1,000,000 a year for a period of five years, while the country was in the throes of the depression of the 1930's.

There had been some unsuccessful experiments in picture transmission by wire. One was started by the American Telephone and Telegraph Company in 1920, when it installed receiving and sending equipment in its own offices in some half-dozen cities. This imperfect, impractical effort, geographically limited, was failing in 1930 for lack of patronage. The telephone company did not try to improve it.

Nevertheless, in that year I asked the A.T. & T. engineering staff if it could produce a new and simple type of equipment that would become standard in each subscribing newspaper office and that would send and receive pictures country-wide over telephone circuits for the exclusive use of The Associated Press. This was a challenge to the type of engineering talent that has convinced itself there is nothing of an electro-mechanical nature that cannot be created if it can earn a return on its cost. In 1933, the engineers said what I wanted could be supplied.

So that The Associated Press could be first with the newly developed equipment and have it exclusively for five years, some legal way had to be found to assure this priority from a public service corporation, which the A.T. & T. is.

In spite of the depression, I suggested to the telephone company that it send an identical letter to all four news photo services, including The Associated Press, saying that equipment for wire transmission of pictures into newspaper offices could be furnished. I also asked the company to state in the proposed letter that it would not be interested in proceeding without an order for twenty-five individual installations, which with the wires involved would incur an expense of not more than $1,000,000 a year. The general manager of the telephone company said:

"It is all your idea, Mr. Cooper. You write out what you want us to say to the four picture services and we will send the letters."

I did so. Attorneys of both the A.T. & T. and The AP said that this procedure to gain exclusivity for The Associated Press for five years could not be frustrated in court by any competitor. I didn't think any AP competitor would consider it.

Nevertheless, I hazarded my professional reputation and my position as general manager by accepting on behalf of The Associated Press. I waited for the A.T. & T. to hear from The AP's news picture competitors—Wide World, Acme and International News Photos. As soon as all of them had definitely declined, and without having a chance to discuss the matter with a single AP director, or without having mentioned the idea to a single AP newspaper, I orally accepted the terms of the A.T. & T.'s letter, the draft of which, as I have said, I had composed myself.

As the next step, tacit approval for what I had done was obtained from The AP Board, although several directors had grave misgivings.

As the quotations varied from three to fifty times what each subscriber was paying for AP news photos sent them by mail, only thirty-nine papers in twenty-four cities expressed any interest whatever in learning more about it. It seemed to me unwise that the proposal appear to take the form of an enterprise that members of the Board of Directors selfishly might be creating for the benefit of their individual newspapers. There was, therefore, no effort to pressure any of the Board members to lead the way by being the first to sign contracts. Nevertheless, the first to sign was Paul Patterson, an AP director. Patterson was president and publisher of the Baltimore *Sun*. For sentimental reasons, he wanted to be first because it was his newspaper that was the first to install another novelty, namely, the Mergenthaler typesetting machine. That was before the turn of the century.

The one thing that to me seemed important about establishment of the facility was that it be transcontinental in scope. By sending pictures back and forth from coast to coast across such a great distance, the novelty of the new enterprise would be dramatized in the public mind. I repeat that gaining public acclaim for a novel electrical achievement by newspapers in an electrical age was one thing I wanted to bring about. To make it a transcontinental system meant starting with subscribers in New York and California.

I had no trouble in gaining acceptance from Captain Patterson, of the New York *Daily News,* to finance the chief eastern terminal cost at a rate of $150,000 a year. The expense to a single Pacific coast paper, however, would have been exorbitant. At that, J. R. Knowland, a real friend of my administration and a director and member for the Oakland *Tribune,* probably would have underwritten the Pacific Coast connection if I had asked him to. He was, however, not the first Californian to be approached.

For twenty years I had been encouraged in my aspirations for AP accomplishments by an acquaintance I had made in California with one of the great publishers of the first half of this century. He was the only member of The Associated Press who invariably would make appointments for me to see him in his office after midnight. And when I called on him, he never seemed to be in a hurry to get the visit over with. Once, after spending two hours with him, it was 2:30 A.M. before I left his office. And it was I, not he, who broke it up. I was tired and said so. He didn't say if he was tired.

He had, in my several visits with him, extracted from me a rather full story of what I had done, was doing, and wanted to do with The Associated Press. He was inspiring to talk to. I wished that he were on the Board of Directors and told him so. He said he did not want to be. He was Harry Chandler, of the Los Angeles *Times,* father of Norman Chandler, the present successful publisher of that paper, who later served several terms on The Associated Press Board.

I had not been with Harry Chandler more than five minutes when he said I could count the Los Angeles *Times* in whether or not I could get another California paper. However, George Cameron, of the San Francisco *Chronicle,* also agreed to sign. Mr. Knowland, of the Oakland *Tribune,* was the third Californian.

All the newspaper and A.T. & T. contracts were signed before the new method of picture transmission had a name. The pictures were to be sent by wire. Why not, then, name the new service Wirephoto, which, of course, means a photo sent by wire? The coined word soon was in common usage, entering the dictionaries with this definition:

A method of sending photographs by wire; a trade name designating a service by The Associated Press.

It was the late Norris A. Huse, of The Associated Press executive staff, who suggested this name to me. He also was successful in getting several AP newspapers to sign contracts.

A year before the first Wirephoto was to be sent, the Hearst and Scripps organizations, both owners of news photo services, set out to prevent Wirephoto from being started. As both had representation in The Associated Press on behalf of their member newspapers, their first attack was made in The Associated Press annual meeting of 1934. Prior thereto I prepared a brief which the Board decided I should not read to the annual meeting of members. It felt the general

Harry Chandler (1935)—
Inspiring to talk to.

management should not involve itself in a controversy that had arisen in the membership. The brief follows in part:

Twenty-five years ago, when Melville E. Stone employed me, I told him it was my conviction that many constructive things had to be done if The Associated Press was to maintain its lead against newly inspired competition. I knew many scores of members, some still living, who had the same conviction. They were and are those who felt and feel deeply that The Associated Press is their AP, that it is in a way a department of their newspapers, that they want it to thrive and keep up to date. Because of their loyalty and the Board's backing, many of the constructive things I wanted to do have been done and are still being done. So it is gratifying to hear that The Associated Press, to use the words of a representative of one of its own competitors, "has grown stronger and greater in the last ten years."

Now historically, what were the opposition press associations doing twenty-five years ago? Such things pertinent to this presentation as these:

1. Pictures, mats, features and comics given free to newspapers that took the International News telegraph service. It was a so-called package rate. This may have been a good thing for the INS but it foreboded ill for The Associated Press. But if Mr. Hearst, the owner of INS, did not own a picture service, a mat service, comics and features, he could not have done this. With all of them rolled up in that one convenient package for an attractive price, valuable members of The Associated Press signed up with Mr. Hearst and resigned their Associated Press memberships, which availed them only a telegraphic news service.

2. Mr. Scripps, owner of the United Press, also owned picture, mat, feature and comic services but then as now operated them as separate entities, though in a benevolent co-operation. He did not, however, and has not thus far, authorized the United Press to make package rates. But at any time he feels it to be good policy to group these activities into one corporate existence and unified effort, it takes only the decision of one man to effect it.

Faced with that possibility, as insurance for the protection of its members, The Associated Press picture and feature services came into being upon my recommendation less than eight years ago, available alike to all members.

I personally express myself as believing that The Associated Press was just about twenty-seven years late in getting these services started. If, for instance, when newspapers first began printing news pictures The Associated Press had gone about furnishing them as it should have done, we would not then have faced any competition, and we would not now have this difference of opinion among the membership on the subject of Wirephoto.

And why did it not do so? Why should it have left the picture and feature field almost exclusively to the owners of its two competitors? Why should The Associated Press not be alive to a news picture of an event as well as to a news story of an event?

In actuality, what objectionable difference is there in performing the duty and obligation of getting a picture story of a news event from getting a word story of a news event, since member newspapers want them both? And finally, why should pictures go by mail while words go by wire?

Why in an electrical age that has brought to other industries wide public acceptance and acclaim should The Associated Press default to its members upon an opportunity to deliver pictures by wire when they are faced with the future of live pictures by television?

It should be remembered that advancing the welfare of a mutual non-profit press association offers discouragement to anyone who would like to develop improvements for member newspapers that want to give their readers better service. I have tried and I know. Private enterprise can plan in secrecy and, when ready, act openly and profit thereby. A cooperative cannot.

Thus, I cannot refrain from speculation upon what would now be said if a competitor of The Associated Press with good news photos had fully developed and successfully launched his own leased-wire, picture-transmitting equipment throughout the land as we have done, and The Associated Press had done nothing whatsoever in that direction! If that had occurred, the members justifiably now could be calling not only for my resignation but for the election of a whole new Board of Directors with vision.

Fortunately, our competitors are not objecting to the lack of such a startling achievement. They are deploring the fact that one has taken place successfully, fully available to all members as one of the services of their own Associated Press. Also, they are opposing it futilely, because legal five-year commitments have been made for the service. I suggest that all members be asked to wait until those five years have passed and then determine if they want to kill Wirephoto solely because The AP's competitors want that to happen!

The points I thus made were used by individual members of the Board in speeches at the 1934 annual meeting and successfully met the challenge of the opposition. At the annual meeting in 1935, four months after Wirephoto had been operating, Board members successfully met it again when the attack was repeated.

The taut expectancy of that New Year's Eve of 1934, when Wirephoto operation was to start after midnight, is unforgettable. Tired engineers in the New York AP office, sleeves rolled up, made final tests and adjustments on a neatly arranged panel of mysterious-looking bulbs, wires and indicators with wavering needles.

On a table near by was a machine holding a news picture wrapped around a horizontal cylinder. Within easy reach were a telephone and loudspeaker.

AP Wirephoto was ready for inauguration after months of work, after years of search for a system that would transmit news pictures by wire to newspapers hundreds or thousands of miles away. If it worked, news in words and pictures would ride the wires side by side for simultaneous publication throughout the country.

If it worked. . . .

The time approached for the start—one A.M., January 1, 1935. AP engineers and technicians crowded around the equipment. Onlookers talked in whispers. And in twenty-four other cities—Atlanta, Baltimore, Boston, Buffalo, Chicago, Cleveland, Dallas, Dayton, Denver, Des Moines, Detroit, Kansas City, Los Angeles, Miami, Milwaukee, Minneapolis, Oakland, Oklahoma City, Omaha, Philadelphia, St. Louis, San Francisco, Syracuse, Washington—experts made ready their receiving equipment. All were connected to one high-fidelity telephone line comprising one vast circuit.

In New York an engineer lifted the telephone: "New York calling all points. Are you ready?"

One by one, the receiving points said Yes.

A switch was thrown on the sending machine. The cylinder and the photograph began to turn.

In the twenty-four receiving cities, the units likewise began to turn in even, synchronized revolutions.

If everything worked, the picture on the cylinder in New York would soon be in the hands of newspaper editors all along the widespread network.

If it worked. . . .

It worked.

That 1935 beginning brought a new era to American journalism, and The Associated Press was elevated to a new summit of achievement. Thereafter, it had news in pictures from afar as well as near to be published simultaneously with word records of the same events.

Before the half-century mark was reached, both the Scripps and Hearst interests had found it necessary to follow The Associated

Press by establishing their own methods of photo transmission by wire. But Wirephoto had been first by several years and dramatically led the field. It still does.

In less than two decades, AP changed the face of modern journalism as Wirephotos began to be delivered regularly to more than 500 newspapers and television stations in the United States. Other hundreds abroad receive them.

The sponsors of Wirephoto reveal an imposing list of newspaper publishers who pinned their faith on my personal assurances that "Wirephoto would work" and risked a total of $5,000,000 to see the novelty established for the benefit of all AP members. I have frequently referred to membership loyalty. What they did in financing Wirephoto is an example of the type of loyalty I mean. In giving their names, I also acclaim them with deep appreciation of their confidence in me:

Paul Bellamy—Cleveland *Plain Dealer*
Edward H. Butler—Buffalo *News*
George T. Cameron—San Francisco *Chronicle*
Harry Chandler—Los Angeles *Times*
John S. Cohen—Atlanta *Journal*
W. J. Conners, Jr.—Buffalo *Courier-Express*
John Cowles—Des Moines *Register*
Gardner Cowles, Jr.—Des Moines *Tribune*
James M. Cox—Dayton *News* and Miami *News*
George B. Dealey—Dallas *News*
Henry Doorly—Omaha World *Herald*
Richard Finnegan—Chicago *Times*
E. K. Gaylord—Oklahoma City *Oklahoman*
Harry J. Grant—Milwaukee *Journal*
D. R. Hanna, Jr.—Cleveland *News*
E. J. Kiest—Dallas *Times-Herald*
J. R. Knowland—Oakland *Tribune*
Frank Knox—Chicago *News*
George B. Logan—Kansas *City-Star*
John C. Martin—Philadelphia *Ledger*
Robert R. McCormick—Chicago *Tribune*
Robert McLean—Philadelphia *Bulletin*
Eugene F. Meyer—Washington *Post*
F. E. Murphy—Minneapolis *Tribune*

Frank B. Noyes—Washington *Star*
E. H. O'Hara—Syracuse *Herald*
Joseph M. Patterson—New York *News*
Paul Patterson—Baltimore *Sun*
Joseph Pulitzer—St. Louis *Post-Dispatch*
E. Lansing Ray—St. Louis *Globe-Democrat*
Roy A. Roberts—Kansas City *Times*
W. E. Scripps—Detroit *News*
W. C. Shepherd—Denver *Post*
E. D. Stair—Detroit *Free Press*

The twentieth anniversary of Wirephoto's creation brought a wholly unexpected salute from a Dallas AP careerman, Richard McMurray, whom I had not heard from nor seen for years. It is the only letter I shall quote of many I received from still active AP employees, after my retirement from authority:

January 7, 1955

Dear KC:

We distributed last month the story of Wirephoto, and I cannot resist telling you how great a mark you have made on the newspaper business.

Wirephoto, a great achievement, alone is enough to make you remembered forever with gratitude by the profession.

But to me—an AP private in the rear ranks—two other things you accomplished rank even higher. First is the way you humanized the news report and made it readable and interesting. That alone was a revolution. I remember the story you once told me of Washington copy in which a twenty-fourth add Congress said, "At this point, Senator Jones hurled a bottle of ink at Senator Smith."

The other great achievement is your long, continuing battle for AP men—which resulted in making The Associated Press the best place in the newspaper business in which to work. I think of our salaries, higher on average than paid anywhere; of the five instead of seven-day week; pensions; paid vacations; and sick benefits. All resulted from your efforts, and all these benefits came years before they came to other places.

To me AP always will mean KC, too, and I just wanted you to know that.

Please don't bother to reply. My good wishes for this and many more years to come.

23

DEDICATED MEN

A DEEP SENTIMENT of appreciation and thankfulness moves me as I undertake to write of employee devotion to The Associated Press during my long service. There is a human side of The Associated Press in the minds and hearts of its employees, of which the public knows nothing. Starting as I did at an average level of opportunity, I could not have found myself with any band of men and women more loyal to their duties, to themselves and to each other.

I cherished this as I cherished the reality that this was due to a consciousness that they were engaged in a common mission that transcended any other secular profession. If they had not been of good character, with a wholesome outlook on life, they would not have been interested in the work they were doing. For it was not markedly rewarding.

In no group would one find opportunity for more enduring and more satisfying friendships. Fifty years later this still was true. When I started with The Associated Press, I made friendships that led to companionship at work and at play. With this the atmosphere in which I found myself in 1910 and continuing thereafter, it is with a profound feeling of gratitude that I appreciatively attest to the fact that as I went onward and upward in the work, my administrative efforts were the beneficiary of unusual employee co-operation.

In later years I frequently referred to this with gratification. Once I told of it to a younger man who later was to be president of The Associated Press. In our separate fields of responsibility, we both carried on the work of The Associated Press as it went toward its destiny. He is Robert McLean, publisher of the Philadelphia Bulletin, long an AP director, who succeeded Mr. Noyes as president in 1938. In a tribute expressed in 1950 at the conclusion of my twenty-five years as chief executive, he generously referred to my relationship with the employees, saying:

"Kent Cooper's understanding, his dedication to certain ideals and his quick sympathy in his contacts with the staff are the unusual qualities which have been mainly responsible for his great success. Certain it is that he has inspired men all his life."

In many, very many instances, I observed with reverent satis-

*President Robert McLean and AP executives of 1950 at dinner in K.C.'s honor—*Left to right: (standing) *President McLean; Executive Director Kent Cooper; Assistant General Manager Charles E. Honce* (seated, clockwise) *General Manager Frank J. Starzel; Assistant General Managers Oliver S. Gramling and Lloyd Stratton; Executive Editor Alan J. Gould; Director Robert Choate.*

faction, as the years went by, how the feeling for The Associated Press was ripening into remarkable devotion among those employees who had decided to make a career of their Associated Press work as I had done.

Scattered throughout the country and the world, as is The Associated Press staff, intimate acquaintance with employees was possible only through my extensive travels. Without travel, however, it was not difficult to spot ability, so effectively did the written word in AP news dispatches reveal talent. Besides, with the complete nationalization of the service, to which I have referred, there were annual conferences between the general manager, his executive assistants and all of the chiefs of the domestic bureaus.

At these meetings I always tried to instill deeper interest in The Associated Press work, expressing in various ways how better results could be attained by arousing loyalty and ambition in each employee under the bureau chiefs.

Conference with bureau chiefs, Chicago (1943)—Left to right: (seated, first row) *Glenn Babb, foreign editor; W. F. Caldwell, Atlanta; Robert Cavagnaro, sports; Paul Cochrane, New Haven; Ben Conner, Newark; K.C.; W. Crawford, Louisville* (second row) *Cy Douglas, Oklahoma City; Frank Fuller, Richmond; Max Fullerton, Charleston; Frank Gorrie, Seattle; Alan J. Gould, assistant general manager; Dillon Graham* (partly hidden), *Charlotte; Kenneth E. Hopping, Little Rock* (third row) *Claude A. Jagger, assistant general manager; B. T. Johns, Columbus; Hubbard Keavy, Los Angeles; H. V. Kelly; Loudon Kelly, Salt Lake City; Frank H. King, Dallas; Floyd Lansdon, Portland; W. J. McCambridge, radio* (fourth row) *George McConville* (partly hidden), *Minneapolis; Warren McNeill, Nashville; Paul Mickelson, Kansas City; Paul Miller, assistant general manager; Ted Metzger, Denver; Harry Montgomery* (partly hidden), *Phoenix; Oliver S. Morton, Jacksonville; Alvin Orton, Indianapolis* (standing) *W. N. Paxton, Albany; Milo Thompson, New Orleans; Harold Turnblad, San Francisco; Glenn Ramsey, New York; William O. Varn, Baltimore; F. A. Resch, news photos; Hugh Wagnon, Philadelphia; Marion J. Sheen, Chicago; W. A. Weekes, Milwaukee; Ted Smits, Detroit; Al West, Albuquerque; Murlin Spencer, war correspondent; Ben Wickersham, Boston; M. J. Wing, features; Frank J. Starzel, assistant general manager; L. P. Yale, Des Moines; Lloyd Stratton, assistant general manager.*

Among those in the Traffic Department, there was an unusual type of loyalty from the time the department was inaugurated in 1912. They gave unstinted effort in attempting to solve the problems and perfect delivery of news in words and pictures.

From Morse telegraphy they went to teletype transmission both by wire and radio, and they mastered the eerie thing we named Wirephoto. Their genius and adaptability in efficiently engineering and operating Wirephoto was a prime contribution to its success.

It is a heavy responsibility to see that news in words is accurately and speedily dispatched, and that news in photographic form is delivered as speedily and flawlessly as possible. This duty was nobly and loyally discharged. It being my own child, grown to nearly fifty years of age, I naturally glowed when I took note of Traffic Department accomplishments.

Long ago I said that men release themselves from thralldom only when they find the great highway of truth. The development of a spirit of service well performed by newsmen can guide the people on that highway like the priesthood serves them in religion.

As an element that makes this service of truth possible, employees in The Associated Press News Department develop an isolation of the mind from bias toward any cause no matter how worthy. In appreciation of this, there were limitations to what I could do for them financially. To exceed those limitations would not have been profitable for them in the long run. That they appreciated this may have been evidenced by the fact that in my forty years of executive responsibility, the word "strike" was never mentioned either among the newsmen or traffic employees.

That surely indicated contentment. Perhaps one reason for it was that professionally they enjoyed their acquired, detached viewpoint so they could write and edit the news accurately and without bias. Yet superficial observers have said that such an unbiased attitude smacks of the cynical—even that good writing talents are spent uselessly by failing to seize such wonderful opportunities to inject personal prejudices on controversial subjects.

But Associated Press men are not spending their talents uselessly. They are performing an important function honorably. They have views, probably, but they do not inject them in what they write for The Associated Press. As reporters, they put down what others say for publication. I doubt, however, if there has ever been one mature AP man who has either formed an opinion or changed any opinion he may have had because of what he heard as a reporter or from reading what he edited for publication. With them it is one chore done, forget it and on with the next! In that way an unbiased, accurate historical record is made for simultaneous reading by millions. It forms the basis of mass thinking.

This writing and editing the truth without bias, therefore, becomes a newsman's ideal employment—that he never has to do anything he would be ashamed of. For he is never instructed to, he does not and must not degrade himself by tainting the news to please the boss or anybody else. Indeed, he knows that if his AP superior tells him to do any such thing he can completely disregard the order and no punishment will be imposed.

Moreover, no superior would ever dare to give any such instruction. Being, in that supposititious case, the offender, he would know that such an order could bring exposure that would end his usefulness, even though he holds the highest position in The Associated Press.

It is no wonder that the enterprise and distinct styles of AP news writers have constantly been proclaimed by the profession. The most appreciated prizes in newspaper work are those awarded by the Pulitzer board, upon which I had the honor to serve for more than twenty-five years as successor to Melville E. Stone, who was one of the original board members named by Joseph Pulitzer himself.

The following eight Associated Press reporters were given Pulitzer prizes after Kirke Simpson's story of the honors accorded the Unknown Soldier in 1921: Frank A. Jamison, 1932; Howard W. Blakeslee, 1937; Louis P. Lochner, 1939; Larry Allen, 1942; Dan DeLuce, 1944; Harold V. Boyle, 1945; Eddy Gilmore, 1947; Don Whitehead, 1951; Relman Morin, 1951; John M. Hightower, 1952; Don Whitehead (second time), 1953; Relman Morin (second time) 1958.

There is another kind of devotion that goes far beyond the feeling any newsman—writer or photographer—has for any newspaper or press association that may be the beneficiary of his work. It is a characteristic of all of them and I salute them for it. It is devotion to duty even when faced with physical peril wherever and whatever the news may be in peace or war. To get the story or photo in time of peace could mean to battle the elements of nature—storm on land or sea, fire or flood. It means not only to get the story but to live to get it back to transmission facilities usually not easily available in such times. That constitutes the heroic job of covering the news of terrors that nature has wrought.

To get the story of war means to risk their lives for what "great" men in authority impose upon those who have to fight because the minds of the "great" men on one side or both are not great enough

Pulitzer Board (1941)—
The last meeting attended by
Dr. Butler. Left to right:
(standing) *Sevellon W. Brown;*
Frank Kent; Arthur Krock;
Dean Carl Ackerman; Robert
Choate; Roy Roberts; W. R.
Mathews (seated) *Harold S.*
Pollard; Arthur Howe; Joseph
Pulitzer; Dr. Nicholas Murray
Butler; Stuart H. Perry;
and K.C.

to solve disagreements in any other way. That constitutes the heroic job of covering the news in words and photos of terrors for which men, not nature, are responsible.

When, with the outbreak of World War II, I was compelled to select AP reporters who volunteered to cover it, I was well aware that the type of war correspondent the papers wanted was characterized by hazy memories of the then legendary Richard Harding Davis. I understood why Davis' fame in his era was justified. He was the first reporter to write human interest stories about men at war. His personality was charming. He was handsome, dashing and generous. He visited army headquarters and turned what he learned there into news stories of the Greco-Turkish, Spanish-American, Boer, Russo-Japanese wars.

Davis was also in Belgium in World War I. He died in 1916, before America became involved. Having talent, he assigned himself as a

war correspondent to do just what he wanted to do when and if he wanted to do it. In other words, he was considered so competent in fulfilling what was admired in his day that he could select his assignments, even select for whom he would write. Except for the little affray in Cuba in 1898, however, the wars he reported were far away from America. He could and did make war news romantic—even dramatic.

But there were several Associated Press men in World War I whose work was, from AP standards at the time, magnificent. They never obtained personal fame, however, because their names were not allowed to appear over their stories. Nor did they write human interest stories, which were then taboo in The Associated Press service. They wrote factually. Some of them wrote expertly in the code-of-war reporting of that era.

Charles Stephenson Smith's stories, written as he worked his way from Ostend to Brussels and back again to London within two weeks through the onrushing German lines, gave word-pictures of the dead, dying and the destruction that he saw. That was in the fall of 1914. From London he then went halfway around the world via New York to China, where that nation was still smarting under the thirty-one demands that had been made by Japan.

Charles Stephenson Smith (1916)—Comrade Sverdlov had an announcement to make.

Richard Harding Davis (1902)— "His personality was charming."

Eventually he made the twelve-day railroad trip across Siberia from Vladivostok to St. Petersburg, arriving in the Russian capital in time to report the wild confusion during the Bolsheviks' displacement of the Kerensky Government. The next year, he went with Lenin, Trotsky and Stalin to Moscow, which became a hot center of intrigue and wanton slaughter. He was in the Moscow opera house the night Lenin got thunderous applause in support of his having accepted the humiliating terms of the Brest-Litovsk Treaty, after which Lenin introduced Comrade Sverdlov, who made an announcement which stunned the crowded opera house into a deadly silence. Sverdlov said:

"We have received a report that in Ekaterinburg, in accordance with the decision of the local soviet there, Nicholas has been shot. Nicholas wanted to escape. The Czechoslovaks were approaching the city. The presidium of the Central Executive Committee has decided to approve this act."

Nothing was said about the shooting of the czarina and her children, as well as her physician and the royal family servants. Sverdlov stood motionless for a short time and then broke the silence with an announcement that routine business would be resumed.

Ever since he had been in Russia, Smith had gotten his stories to The Associated Press in New York via the Siberian telegraph. But the Czech occupation of Siberia interrupted that route. He sent Sverdlov's announcement by the British wireless from Murmansk. Thereafter, that route was closed, and as there was no way left to send his news, Smith completed his four-year, eventful, round-the-world trip on his arrival in London via Finland and Norway.

Great stories throughout World War I also were sent from the western front by James P. Howe, DeWitt Mackenzie, Robert T. Small and other AP careermen, but none of whom, in spite of their meritorious work in times of stress and danger, ever got a by-line.

Even before World War II, with the coverage of the Italian attacks in Eritrea and Ethiopia and the Spanish Revolution, new concepts of AP war news writing were developed. One of the war reporters of that period was Edward J. Neil, who literally was born into The Associated Press. Neither he nor his father ever had any other employer. His father was an AP telegrapher.

As a boy, Eddie was fascinated as he watched the news dispatches from everywhere roll out of his father's typewriter. As he grew up, he read many of them, hot off the wire. They fired a desire in him to be an AP reporter. He thought of doing nothing else. Because it was constantly a matter of reporting contests of men in action, he took to sports writing. For his years and experience none was better. He had the advantage of working under Alan J. Gould, who was, in my estimation, the peer of sports reporters and whom I later named executive editor of The Associated Press, the position he still fills with distinction.

Adventure to get the news while exposed to danger must have been in Neil's blood. He talked to me about this, saying he wished he had been old enough to report World War I. I asked him where he got the idea of wanting to be a war reporter. Sure enough he replied: "Richard Harding Davis was."

And then I saw in him a handsome, dashing and brilliant possibility as a war correspondent. So I was not astonished that, when Mussolini sent his troops to attack Ethiopia, Neil came to me and said: "Well, boss, this looks like it's it."

"What do you mean?" I asked.

"Ethiopia," was his one-word answer. And off he went, with a glow of hopeful adventure, and making as striking a picture as ever I had seen.

After a spell of it he came home. The change I saw in him was noticeable. I knew what it was without asking. He had seen men die—many of them. He also had suffered privations and illness. Yet while the Spanish Revolution was on, he wanted to go again. Laughing, he told me that in Africa he had risked danger to get a story for which I had commended him. The last thing I said to him before he went to Spain was:

"Eddie, promise me that you want to live, for if you will promise me that, you won't needlessly expose yourself again. There is no story you can go after that is worth your courting death. The crucifixion would have been worth it but you were not living then!"

He promised. I am sure he didn't think he was facing danger that morning in Spain. I knew he didn't mean to break his promise. So I think it must have been a stray shell that sought him out and made him The AP's first casualty in the line of reportorial duty under fire. When that shell got him, it killed an AP man that no one who ever saw him will forget. We brought him home to his wife and child, Eddie, Jr.

He didn't know, his wife didn't know, nor did his sports-writer buddies of New York City know that provision had been made for his baby boy if he never returned. So his sports-writer pals in New York took up a collection of all they could afford to contribute to take care of the boy. That was the generous custom of the craft. Perhaps no collection was ever as big as the one in memory of Eddie Neil. I heard about it and was touched, but sent word that I had heavily insured Eddie's life in Lloyd's for just the emergency they wanted to meet, and Eddie's widow seemed to think it was enough. But they loved Eddie, too, and they wanted to do something worth while with the money. So with it they financed an award and announced it as:

The Edward J. Neil Memorial Trophy awarded annually by the Boxing Writers' Association of New York to the one who has done the most for boxing in the preceding year. The plaque is dedicated to the memory of Edward J. Neil, Associated Press sports writer, killed in the line of duty in 1938 while covering the Spanish Revolution.

The first award went to Neil's old friend, Jack Dempsey. The ones that followed, whom Neil knew, were: 1940, Henry Armstrong; 1941, Joe Louis; 1942, Barney Ross. What would have pleased Neil im-

Edward J. Neil (1936)—
To Ethiopia, then
to his death in Spain.

mensely then occurred. In 1943, "4,019 boxers in the armed services and those yet to take up arms" got the award.

Eddie's boy, Edward J. Neil III, when he reached twenty-one, went to work for The Associated Press.

The depth of feeling about The Associated Press that Eddie Neil shared with other AP men was revealed to me yet again in a letter written June 21, 1938, by James B. Reston, then a member of The Associated Press London staff. Afterward, Reston went to the *New York Times* and became chief of its Washington bureau. I had written Reston at London commending him. His letter in reply said:

Dear Mr. Cooper:

This generous letter from you gives me a chance to say one or two things I have had in mind for some time.

Without a single exception, I have had an opportunity to do every job in The Associated Press I have seriously coveted. Nobody has tried to talk me into anything or out of anything. I have never even heard the word "seniority" used in an AP office.

Paul Miller (1955)—
To high position
in the newspaper field.

Seven weeks before Eddie Neil died, he spent a night at my house and we talked about this. Neil said:

"I've come to think about my mind as if it were a field. When I was in Boston I cultivated only a corner of it. When I moved down to Baltimore and then on to New York, I cultivated a great deal more. But not until I went to Ethiopia and Spain did I realize how much ground there was left. . . . When people ask me why I don't do this or that, I ask them where I can do this main job better than in The AP."

There's just one other thing. You will remember Lee Horton, who used to be in the Photo Service. I saw him in New York the day he came back from the doctor's office and after Hicks had told him he didn't think The AP could use him. I also saw him after he came out of your office. You had assigned him to the Phoenix bureau. I am convinced the boy now thinks of you as bread and life.

The only point I want to make is that I believe there is something indivisible between a man's job and his life, and thus between your job and our lives.

I also feel that you believe this. These touches—this noble act for Horton, this simile of Neil's, this note of yours to me this week—have convinced me.

> Sincerely and gratefully yours,
> James B. Reston

Reston is one of several AP alumni who went to the *New York Times* as by-line reporters at home and abroad. But since nearly all the members of The Associated Press news staff have been recruited from member newspapers, it is perfectly natural that some of them should go back directly into newspaper work. In going to AP member newspapers, I have never felt that they separated themselves from The AP family. In fact, The Associated Press, being a co-operative dependent primarily upon the strength and success of its member newspapers, continues to benefit from the talent of former AP men in high positions in the newspaper world.

I may not recall all of the former AP men now in high position on newspapers, but I begin with the name of the only one who left a high AP executive position and a promising future for an unusual opportunity in the newspaper field. He is Paul Miller, now president of the large group of Gannett Newspapers, of which the late Frank E. Gannett was founder and president.

Miller was at one time an assistant general manager of The Associated Press and was serving as head of the Washington Bureau, where the largest reportorial staff in any one office in the world was maintained at the time of his resignation. Fortunately for The Associated Press, however, he has continued his lively interest in it as a member of the Board of Directors and as first vice-president.

Two other successful newspapermen who once were AP employees also became directors. They are Mark Ethridge, publisher, Louisville (Kentucky) *Courier Journal* and the Louisville *Times;* and Dolph Simons, publisher, Lawrence (Kansas) *Journal World.* Other former Associated Press men who are now editors or executives of newspapers are:

Milburn P. Akers, Executive Editor, Chicago (Ill.) *Sun-Times*
Robert B. Beith, Executive Editor, Portland (Maine) *Press-Herald*
Fred Burgner, Managing Editor, Trenton (N.J.) *Times*
Norman Bradley, Executive News Editor, Chattanooga (Tenn.) *Times*
Robert Bunnelle, Publisher, Asheville (N.C.) *Citizen-Times*
James A. Best, Managing Editor, Charleston (S.C.) *News & Courier*
R. W. Barry, Managing Editor, Phoenix (Arizona) *Gazette*
Paul R. Bumbarger, Publisher, Charles City (Iowa) *Press*
Aleyn Burtis, Publisher, La Junta (Colorado) *Tribune-Democrat*
John H. Colburn, Managing Editor, Richmond (Va.) *Times-Dispatch*
Hodding Carter, Publisher-Editor, Greenville (Miss.) *Delta Democrat-Times*
Gail W. Churchill, Managing Editor, Nashville (Tenn.) *Tennessean*
Ken Dixon, Managing Editor, Lake Charles (La.) *American Press*
William H. Ewing, Managing Editor, Honolulu (Hawaii) *Star-Bulletin*
Herndon Evans, Editor, Lexington (Ky.) *Herald*
Orin Fifer, Managing Editor, Phoenix (Arizona) *Republic*
William E. Folsom, Jr., Editor, McAlester (Okla.) *News-Capital*
Ed Field, Editor, Selma (Alabama) *Times-Journal*
Frank Gilbreath, Assistant Publisher, Charleston (S.C.) *News & Courier* and *Post*
James H. Hutcheson, Executive News Editor, Walla Walla (Wash.) *Union-Bulletin*
Malcom B. Johnson, Executive Editor, Tallahassee (Fla.) *Democrat*
William F. Johnston, Managing Editor, Lewiston (Idaho) *Morning Tribune*
Henry B. Jameson, Publisher, Abilene (Kansas) *Reflector-Chronicle*

Edward Kennedy, Asst. Publisher, Monterey (Cal.) *Peninsula Herald*
Jack B. Krueger, Managing Editor, Dallas (Tex.) *Morning News*
Henry Leader, Editor, Plainfield (N.J.) *Courier News*
William Macklin, Managing Editor, New Ulm (Minn.) *Journal*
John W. Moran, Managing Editor, Bangor (Maine) *Daily News*
E. V. Mitchell, Managing Editor, Gastonia (N.C.) *Gazette*
James H. McKinney, Managing Editor, Greenville (S.C.) *Piedmont*
Latham Mims, General Manager, Harrisonburg (Va.) *Daily News-Record*
Felix R. McKnight, Executive Editor and Vice-President, Dallas (Tex.)
    Times-Herald
Harry Montgomery, Asst. Publisher, Phoenix (Ariz.) Arizona *Republic*
    and Phoenix *Gazette*
Jay Milner, Managing Editor, Greenville (Miss.) *Delta Democrat-Times*
Stewart Newlin, Publisher, Wellington (Kansas) *News*
Herb O'Keef, Editor, Raleigh (N.C.) *Times*
M. M. Oppegard, Publisher, Grand Forks (N.D.) *Herald*
William M. Pepper, Jr., Editor, Gainesville (Fla.) *Sun*
Woodrow Price, Managing Editor, Raleigh (N.C.) *News & Observer*
R. V. Peterson, Publisher, Durant (Okla.) *Democrat*
Dale Stafford, Publisher, Greenfield (Mich.) *News*
William R. Spear, Editor, Fort Myers (Fla.) *News-Press*
James H. Shumaker, Managing Editor, Durham (N.C.) *Herald*
George Scott, Editor, Clearfield (Penn.) *Progress*
Wendell Webb, Managing Editor, Salem (Oregon) *Statesman*
Nelson R. Wilson, Managing Editor, Red Bluff (Cal.) *News*
Miles H. Wolff, Executive Editor, Greensboro (N.C.) *Daily News*
Charles J. Wellner, Editor, Auburn (N.Y.) *Citizen-Advertiser*
Jerome Weinstein, Editor, State College (Penn.) *Centre Daily Times*
Hugh Wagnon, Publisher, Pocatello (Idaho) Idaho *State Journal*

24

AN AP REPORTORIAL

HALL OF FAME

AT ITS START, it was apparent that reporting the news about World War II meant that the best stories were not going to come out of army headquarters. Associated Press men were going to have to go to the field to report dramatic events. It could not have been otherwise. The war was a massive thing! It was fought on many fronts. New devices to kill, finally the atomic bomb, were used. Battles were fought at times when opposing forces could not even see each other.

One man could write all that Americans wanted to read about the Boer War, for example, or the Russo-Japanese War, which were so far away, so very far away, with Americans not involved.

Although I assigned 100 Associated Press men to write and photograph World War II on its various fronts, ten times 100 could have been assigned, and not one would have had to encroach upon what another witnessed. It was just that big an affray with its Atlantic, African, Eurasian and Pacific theaters of military, air and naval conflicts.

The Associated Press men who wrote the news and photographed the scenes of that global war hailed from all parts of the country. Not only were they crack cameramen and experienced reporters who were able writers, but they had the youth and vigor to sustain themselves

Iwo Jima (1945)—The American flag goes up on Mount Suribachi. An AP photo which was the most inspiring war picture ever taken.

in whatever area they were. Noncombatant and, therefore, unarmed and defenseless, they suffered hardships, were taken prisoner and met death with fortitude equal to that of the bravest of the armed and armored troops of whose deeds they were telling in pictures and words.

Their photos memorably recorded tragic scenes in permanent form. Some of them inspired patriotism—Joe Rosenthal's photo of the Marines raising the American flag on Mount Suribachi on Iwo Jima is an example. For it Rosenthal was given a Pulitzer prize. The right to use the picture in figurines, wall decorations and monuments produced several thousand dollars in revenue, all of which was turned over to the United States Marine Corps, as a gift from The Associated Press, for its hospital in Washington.

The news stories the men wrote had personality—so much personality that the appearance of their names over their dispatches enhanced reader interest.

Before they went, after they came back, and before they went again, I wanted to see and talk with all of them. I had a twofold appreciation of them: First was an older man's feeling of admiration and affection for the clear-eyed, determined younger men who were going to do the job they were undertaking regardless of danger; second, I enjoyed sharing their anticipation for adventure.

Like the army, naval and air men whose deeds they would report, they, too, were leaving loved ones behind. I talked to many of them about their responsibilities and cautioned them to avoid needlessly endangering themselves. I can confess now that as they left my office, I hoped they would be out of sight before I choked up. I never wanted them to know that I did, and they never did know. Many who covered the war in the Western Pacific went directly from California. I did not see them before their departure, but many of them I was personally able to thank and congratulate for their work upon their return.

Tragically, in all war theaters and later in the Korean affair a total of six lost their lives. Several were badly injured or suffered illnesses constituting a casualty percentage of a higher proportion than that of the armed forces. On behalf of The Associated Press, I had heavily insured the lives of all of them. Dependents of those who died were the beneficiaries of this policy. These never returned:

Daniel Witt Hancock—lost his life in the Japanese bombing and sinking of a Dutch refugee ship on March 7, 1942, in the Indian Ocean while enroute from Java to Colombo, Ceylon, following the fall of Java to the Japanese.

Edward H. Crockett—died of wounds received in the torpedoing of a British warship of the Mediterranean Fleet, February 5, 1943, while covering British Fleet operations. Buried at sea.

George Bede Irvin—killed in action July 25, 1944, by explosion of a bomb from "one of our own bombardment aircraft" while photographing activities of air and ground forces at the St. Lo battlefront.

Asahel Bush—killed outright by a Japanese bomb on October 24, 1944, at Tacloban, Leyte, Philippines, just after giving first report on the Leyte naval battle.

Joseph Morton, Jr.—executed by the Germans on January 24, 1945, at the Nazi concentration camp in Mau Mausen, a small Austrian town on the Danube, ten miles southeast of Linz. Taken prisoner at Banska Bystrica in Central Slovakia, 125 miles north of Budapest when he accompanied "a military mission of seventeen Americans and British to join Slovak patriots."

William Russell Moore—reported killed in action in Korea on July 30, 1950. Disappeared between Masan and Chinju enroute to the Chinju battlefront in southern Korea with an element of the 24th Division.

For World War II, I wanted the names of commanders of both sides in all battles in order to designate the army groups involved, but unless they were heroically involved in battle that could be all. What I did want and got were stories with the names of boys in the front-line trenches. Not only that, but I wanted and got their pictures, since The Associated Press had been the first press association in any war to have news cameramen sharing coverage at the front with news writers. Among the cameramen who, besides Joe Rosenthal, did wonderful work and, unlike Irvin, escaped death were Frank Noel, a Pulitzer prize-winner, Frank Filan, Pete Carroll, Harry Harris and Charles Goring.

Of them all I asked, too, that occasional pictures of officers be sent home if they were newsworthy, not just posed "shots," which I did not want. However, we got hundreds that were excellent, though not one of General Patton slapping the young soldier in the hospital.

As I saw these remarkable evidences of expert photography speed-

Daniel Witt Hancock

*Tragically they met death—
constituting a higher casualty
percentage than that of
the armed forces.*

Asahel Bush

Edward H. Crockett

George B. Irvin

Joseph Morton, Jr.

William R. Moore

ing to America by radio and out over the Wirephoto network to member papers all over the country, I could not help but contemplate how it would have been had I not been allowed to establish The Associated Press news photo service and its great Wirephoto method of instantaneous distribution, especially if either the United Press or the International News Service or both had first been alive to the possibilities and had beaten The Associated Press into that field.

The idea in spreading the news coverage to the trenches was to bring the war in words and pictures to the homes of America through personal interviews and news stories with photos if possible. The assignments given were that Associated Press men write about and photograph subjects when on the alert for an impending attack, when in action during the attack, or when in restful relief afterward. I asked for and hoped we could get at least one such story and picture from someplace in some war area about a boy from each home town where The Associated Press had a member paper.

That was a big order, but as a result it was not uncommon for AP newsmen or AP photographers with AP lists of members in their pockets to be heard calling out to this company or that company, always in the front lines: "Is there anybody here from so and so?" If a boy from an AP member paper town could be found—and scores upon scores of them were found sooner or later—stories and photos were sent back for the folks at home to read, to see and to talk about.

For this war I wanted all of the human interest stories about the soldiers, sailors and airmen we could get. Army, Air Force and Navy headquarters staffs engaged in no dramatic conflicts. I wanted it to be the day of the common soldier, the "jack-tar" or the combat pilot. For it interested me that the history books of all previous wars were written as if the commanding officers themselves were doing the fighting. With the Revolutionary War it was Washington. In 1815 it was Jackson at New Orleans. In 1846 it was Taylor and Scott. In 1861-1865 it was Grant against Lee. In 1898 it was Admirals Dewey, Schley, General Shafter and Colonel Theodore Roosevelt. In World War I it was Pershing and Foch. In none of the histories were the deeds of the common soldier celebrated by human interest reporting.

What flashing homeward good stories and pictures of privates in action meant, besides pleasing The Associated Press members in this town and that city, was that for the first time in history many without rank from somewhere in America who fought on land, at sea or in the air, got the big headlines in their home-town newspapers and were the talk of their fellow townsmen at least once during the war. They were not in their own localities unknown, even if fate decreed that they could never return. And that brought the war right into American homes.

When, in what follows, I mention individuals, I hope they will be taken as representative. For I cannot write of all those similarly assigned nor quote the stories that were written. But for those who still think of Richard Harding Davis as the best ever, I can only say that if Davis, competent as he was, could read the following brief sketches about how AP war reporters risked their lives, and could read their dispatches, as I did, he would at least say: "Come alongside me, buddies. You were great!" Indeed, if he knew what I know of their work, he would say they equalled or excelled his own.

Larry Allen was the first American war correspondent ever allowed aboard warships of the British Fleet during wartime. He personally witnessed and wrote of every major action against the Italians and

Larry Allen—He was "rescued" by the enemy.

Germans in the Mediterranean from the summer of 1940 into the fall of 1942.

He was aboard eight warships that were sunk by enemy torpedoes or bombs, and each time was miraculously saved although he did not know how to swim. He was sunk for the first time on December 15, 1941, while aboard the 5,600-ton British cruiser *Galatea* off the coast of North Africa. He dog-paddled until picked up by a British destroyer after fighting off attempts of drowning sailors to tear from his chest a partially inflated "Mae West" lifebelt.

He also was aboard the giant British aircraft carrier *Illustrious* when it was savagely attacked and almost sunk by swarms of German divebombers on January 10, 1941, off Malta. On September 14, 1942, he was aboard the British destroyer *Sikh* when sunk by German-Italian coastal batteries off Tobruk in Libya.

"Rescued" by the enemy, he was a prisoner of war for twenty months. He escaped three times from the Italians. The last time he got within five miles of the Swiss frontier. Starved and exhausted, he sought the aid of peasants. They betrayed him and "sold" him to a nearby German patrol for 2,000 lire.

The Germans finally took him into northern Poland to a prisoner-of-war camp near Poznan, there to endure intense cold and hunger for eight months. On May 4, 1944, he was transported to Barcelona, Spain and home.

A rough and troubled voyage aboard a banana boat loaded with beef for Britain which started from New York on Christmas Eve, 1942, conditioned Ed Ball for the next eighteen months in wartime London, D-Day and the drive by General George S. Patton's Third Army across Europe. With awe and apprehension he saw London hit by the buzz bombs and the first of the V-2s, the creation of a young German scientist by the name of Werhner von Braun. Fifteen years later, Ball, at Redstone Arsenal, watched with awe—and this time with admiration—the static firing of a Jupiter-C, brainchild of a middle-aged scientist by the name of Werhner von Braun, naturalized American.

On D-Day, Ball rode a PT boat in the squadron led by Commander John D. (*They Were Expendable*) Bulkeley.

Then he received orders from General Patton:

"Tell about Third Army but NOTHING about what George Patton

Ed Ball—Once again "Georgie" Patton talked too much.

does, says or thinks." The swashbuckling Patton, who'd been in a lot of hot water for talking too much, was taking no chances. "Here's your army and there's your war," Patton added, waving toward the front with his needle-pointed French hand sword. "Get hurt and we'll doctor you. Get killed and we'll bury you."

By being in the right place at the right time, Ball was the only correspondent to jump the Rhine with the Third Army. Afterward, in Berlin, it was Ball who broke the story of Eisenhower's firing of Patton from his Third Army command.

"Georgie" Patton once again had talked too much!

"The Japanese are attacking Pearl Harbor."

That fateful and drama-packed message of six words to Ray Cronin, chief of The AP Manila bureau, was his introduction to the Pacific War, which proved to be a nightmare of flaming, devastating, massed air raids by the Japanese and a ground war front that was hard to find.

For three weeks the raids kept coming at Manila day and night, taking uncounted thousands of civilian lives besides the terrible losses suffered by U. S. military forces. Cronin and his photographer, Honesto

Vitug, were all but caught up with several times. Drainage ditches and bomb craters became their havens.

The military authorities were quite vague about the ground war fronts. Despite a threat of military authorities to arrest any correspondent poking into the south, Cronin took off in that direction. About thirty miles south of Manila, he saw well-scattered Japanese troops slogging through open fields, headed north. Manila was declared an open city, and on January 2, 1942, the Japanese marched in and threw all Americans into a concentration camp.

There was a crying need for medicines and money in the military prison camps where hundreds of American soldiers were dying daily.

Ray Cronin—He filled a crying need for medicine.

Dan DeLuce—To Rumania, Greece, Southeast Asia, Africa and Europe.

The Japanese made it a death penalty to send anything to a military prison camp. So Cronin and a few others set up a smuggling ring that worked effectively until his aide, living outside because of his Filipino citizenship, was captured and beheaded.

Forty-eight hours before the Ribbentrop-Molotov pact fixed the terms for carving up Poland, Dan DeLuce went on a taxi ride in a beat-up Skoda from Zilina, Slovakia over backroads in the High Tatra.

Seeing German 14th Army units assembling ominously close to the Polish frontier, DeLuce phoned his eyewitness report to the west.

Two weeks later, World War II having started, DeLuce entered Poland. When German tanks were thirty-five miles distant, he hitch-hiked to Rumania and joined the Greek Army fighting the Italians in Albania; then to Athens, where the Greek king was preparing to flee by warship.

After the collapse of Greece, which he reported after having fled to Turkey, DeLuce went to Teheran, then to Southeast Asia, where he accompanied British forces in a retreat all the way from Rangoon to India.

In 1943, he covered the fall of Tunis and the capture of the Afrika Korps at Cape Bon. He went with British forces across the Messina Straits from Sicily when the Italian mainland was invaded. At Bari he crossed the Adriatic to Yugoslavia on an Italian fishing boat sent by the Italian admiralty, with British consent, to evacuate Italian troops.

The boat reached Yugoslav territory controlled by a brigade of Tito partisans. Formerly this territory had been under Italian occupation. The Germans were attempting to seize it. DeLuce's dispatches from the partisan brigade headquarters won him a Pulitzer prize.

In 1944, he covered the breakout offensive from the Anzio beach-head and the liberation of Rome.

When the Marines struck at the heart of the Japanese—their strong-hold in the Marshall Islands—Al Dopking, on his first assignment as a war correspondent, was with them on the main road to Tokyo.

From the bridge of a troop transport, Dopking watched the deadly naval bombardment of Roi-Namur, two little islands joined by a

Al Dopking—He hit the beaches, stumbling over bodies.

causeway and shaped like a butterfly. The night sky was aglow with the fireworks but it was no celebration, as Dopking was to learn the next morning. Hardly had he hit the beach in a light drizzle before he heard a marine scream hysterically: "The dirty, yellow bastards, they've shot my arm off!"

Dopking began stumbling over bodies, Japanese and American. The next two weeks he hit three more beaches in the Marshalls. Then there was the escort carrier and a Japanese sea hunt into the Solomons. There Dopking took a night flier with the 13th Airforce for a strike on Truk, mightiest of Japanese bastions. He was in the second bomber. The first had hit an ammunition dump and the sky was full of anti-aircraft fire.

"You could see those flower pots (shell bursts) breaking all around and you kept wishing you could get the hell out of there," Al recalled later.

Next came Hollandia in New Guinea, Guam, Leyte and Luzon in the Philippines, the Iwo Jima campaign and at last Okinawa, where the Japanese were to make their last land stand.

Dopking had been a man who hit the beaches, but at the war's end he was with "Bull" Halsey's Third Fleet off Japan. He helped cover the surrender aboard the *U.S.S. Missouri* and was one of the first correspondents to reach Tokyo.

To Dopking, his big Tokyo moment was when General Homma walked into his hands at a suburban Toyko railway station one morning while the army was still searching for him. A friendly Japanese general had tipped Dopking off, and The Associated Press had Homma for twenty-four hours before he turned himself over to the Americans, later to be hanged in the Philippines for the death march there.

On the morning of December 15, 1943, Robert Eunson, assigned to the South Pacific, was in the first wave of an attempted surprise landing by the 112th Cavalry Regiment on the south coast of New Britain. Across the island was the mighty Japanese fortress of Rabaul.

Just thirty-five yards from the beach, the air was split with red and white tracer bullets as Japanese machinegunners cut down on the attacking force. The fire was so intense that all but five of the seventeen American boats were sunk in the first twenty minutes.

At that point the *U.S.S. Shaw,* which at first was just a sleek gray line of a destroyer on the horizon, raced in at 1,200 yards and, shooting five-inch shells over the attackers, silenced the Japanese guns.

Another two hours passed before Eunson and other survivors were

Robert Eunson—Five of the 17 boats were sunk in 20 minutes.

pulled out of the water, and two days went by before Eunson got back to Port Moresby and wrote his story.

Later, Eunson was with the Fifth Air Force in New Guinea. During the Hollandia landings in Dutch New Guinea in April, 1944, he got malaria, and the doctors sent him home. When he recovered, he was assigned to Europe to cover first the Canadian Army and then the American Ninth, and was with the latter practically until the end.

Wes Gallagher was in early and stayed to the end. He was overrun by the Germans and arrested by the Gestapo before he finally landed on the winning side in World War II. In 1940, in Copenhagen, Gallagher found himself in the middle of an invasion when German soldiers literally came out of the sewers the morning of April 9. Later, Gallagher was transferred to the Balkans. The day after the Italians invaded Greece, he hiked across the border from Yugoslavia to spend a rough winter on the Albanian front. Gallagher stayed in Greece when the Germans finally swarmed into Athens in the spring of 1941. Held for some weeks, he was given permission by the German Army to leave Athens for Vienna—the morning the Germans marched on Russia.

Wes Gallagher—Headed The AP's African forces and the field staff on D-day.

He was immediately arrested by the Gestapo in Vienna, questioned, imprisoned in a hotel with the Russian Embassy group, whisked to Berlin under guard, and then released through the efforts of Louis Lochner, the Berlin Associated Press' chief of bureau.

Leaving Berlin, he headed the AP's group covering the North African invasion forces in November, 1942. As the North African campaign drew to a close, Gallagher's back was broken when he was pinned under a jeep coming out of Bizerte the day that town was captured in the spring of 1943. He got back to the war fronts in Italy in the fall of 1943.

From there he was sent to buzz-bombed London to lead The AP's field staff accompanying the Allied invasion force in Europe in June, 1944. He followed the First, Third and Ninth U. S. Armies across France, Belgium, Holland and finally Germany. Included were assignments with General Patton in the armored race across France with the First Army in the bitter Battle of the Bulge and finally with the 9th Army's dash to the Elbe River to meet the Russians.

Vern Haugland covered World War II in the southwest Pacific almost from beginning to end. He watched the arrival of General Douglas MacArthur at the railroad station in Melbourne, Australia, March 17, 1942, after MacArthur's escape from Corregidor. On August 30, 1945, he was waiting at Atsugi airfield near Tokyo when the shiny C-54 airplane, *Bataan,* landed, and a victorious MacArthur emerged, looked about him and said, with quiet drama: "From Melbourne to Tokyo. It has been a long road, but we made it."

Haugland in succession covered ground and air operations against the Japanese in New Guinea; sea, ground and air operations in the Solomons from Guadalcanal northward; naval headquarters at Pearl Harbor; B-29 strategic bombing from the Marianas; the Okinawa invasion from D-Day until resistance ended.

He covered carrier strikes against the Japanese mainland, and was aboard the battleship *Missouri* on the first shore bombardment of the main island of Japan. He made an exciting night mission "up the Slot" in the Solomons on a destroyer which sank several Japanese ships—and saw surviving crew members stab themselves in the water rather than be taken prisoners.

Haugland became The Associated Press representative on a new team of "air correspondents," toured bombed-out Europe and the

Vern Haugland—Forty-two days of starvation, exposure and exhaustion.

China-Burma-India theater. With their own B-17-flying pressroom, these were the first newsmen to get into Shanghai, into atom-bombed Hiroshima and Nagasaki, into a number of prisoner-of-war camps in Japan and China.

Haugland's most memorable experience was that of parachuting in a storm at night into the New Guinea jungle and of surviving forty-two days of starvation, exposure and exhaustion. But at least two other experiences were more terrifying, and closer to death.

On a lonely road in Okinawa, a Japanese sniper pinned him down with gunfire for half an hour in approaching darkness, until an American tank came rumbling along unexpectedly and served as a screen.

At Nissan, or Green Island, north of Bougainville in the northern Solomons, he was one of about twenty persons aboard a small landing craft which, just as it touched a beach, came under the direct fire of Japanese machine guns hidden in jungle growth on a high bank not more than thirty feet away. Four men were killed and half of the remainder injured before a heroic crew member managed to back the boat off the beach and out of enemy range.

In the Mediterranean Fleet they called The AP's Paul Kern Lee "Lucky." Night after bomb-blasted night, and day after shell-filled day, he sailed aboard British destroyers and cruisers out of the hungry rock of Malta, looking for action, finding it, and writing of it.

There were nightly destroyer sweeps through the Sicilian Narrows, the squeeze play against the Nazi army on the Tunisian peninsula, the storming of central Mediterranean islands, the invasion and conquest of Sicily, the fiery leap across the Straits of Messina and up the Italian boot, Salerno of bloody memory, assorted commando operations.

There were mornings when the bomb splinters from attack by 50-plus Junkers-88 dive bombers could be kicked along the decks like cinders on a garden path; days when shell fragments burned the paint. Yet no ship in which Lee sailed ever suffered a hit or a casualty while he was aboard.

Lee was sent out to the Mediterranean after Larry Allen had been captured at Tobruk. Travel took too long, and when he arrived, the fleet assignment had been filled by E. H. Crockett, already on the scene.

Lee covered British Eighth Army headquarters in Egypt, Palestine at Christmastime, Syria, and the snake pit of intrigue that was neutral Turkey. Then he was suddenly called back to the central Mediterranean. Harry Crockett was dead—victim of a torpedo. The man who had filled Lee's shoes was gone. One was in prison, one dead, and the third time had to be the charm. Lee must go on every mission, great and small.

Paul Kern Lee—Night after bomb-blasted night he found and reported action.

"Lucky?" Yes. And lucky for The Associated Press that he got home safely.

Relman Morin was chief of the Tokyo bureau when World War II began. Almost overnight, Southeast Asia became a region of vital concern. In December, 1940, I sent him to Indonesia, Malaya, Burma, Siam, and finally Indo-China.

One year later, Pearl Harbor had been attacked. Morin, in Saigon, was promptly taken into custody and remained a prisoner there for eight months, then he was repatriated and came home on the "exchange ship" *Gripsholm*.

Once home, he asked reassignment to the western Pacific. I said: "If the Japanese catch you again, it will be curtains. How about Europe?"

Morin joined the Mediterranean staff and in September, 1943, was with the U. S. 5th Army in what was supposed to have been an unopposed landing in Italy because Italy had formally surrendered the night before.

Two German divisions, strung out along the beaches south of

Relman Morin—Eight months a Japanese prisoner and then to Europe to finish the war.

Salerno, had by no means surrendered, however. Artillery and machinegun fire churned the ocean to a white froth as the landing craft came in. Morin spent the first hour on shore pinned down in an abandoned gun position. Then he found himself in the path of German tanks that were counterattacking, and dove into a sewer. Soon after dark the bombs began to fall. This was Morin's first time under fire. It took place on his thirty-sixth birthday.

He saw the fall of Naples, and the savage fighting along the Volturno and Rapido Rivers, battles that have gone into the records as among the bloodiest ever fought by the Americans. The landings at Anzio, designed to outflank German positions at Cassino, were made early in 1944. Morin covered the landings from aboard a destroyer and then went ashore.

Next he was assigned to India. He rode "the Hump," the air route over the mountains to China, and the Ledo Road through the eerie, steaming jungles of Burma, and covered the attack on the Japanese base at Hyitkina by a celebrated unit, "Merrill's Maurauders." An even better story developed as an aftermath to that operation. Some of the "marauders" staged a near mutiny. Morin got the story from the late General Frank Merrill himself, then went to North Africa and Central Europe.

During his year and a half in London starting in March, 1941, Noland (Boots) Norgaard covered what he considered the most incredible story of the war—the flight of Rudolph Hess, Hitler's chief aide, to Scotland.

On November 8, 1942, Norgaard landed in North Africa with invading Allied troops, and followed the fighting across Algeria and Tunisia.

In Tunisia an associate termed Norgaard a "bomb magnet" and cautioned others against traveling with him. On one occasion a German bomb riddled his jeep, which he had momentarily left in order to walk forward to see a tank battle in the beginning of the German drive at Kasserine Pass.

Near Maknassy, Norgaard found all holes occupied when enemy dive bombers swept in. He hugged the ground while three bombs crashed only forty feet from him.

During a period in Algiers at Allied Force Headquarters, Norgaard covered the dramatic story of Italy's surrender and the flight

Noland Norgaard—To Pantelleria and to Sicily with Field Marshal Montgomery.

of the Italian navy, under bombardment by German planes, to Allied-held ports.

After the African campaign, Norgaard accompanied British troops on the capture of the Mediterranean island of Pantellaria and covered the British Eighth Army of Field Marshal Montgomery—with which he had spent the closing month of the fighting in Tunisia—in the conquest of Sicily.

In the spring of 1944 an attack of pleurisy, followed by pneumonia, sent Norgaard into an army hospital in Algiers, then into another in Naples. He emerged with a doctor's warning that "you stay out of the field or we'll ship you home in a bed."

Heeding the warning, Norgaard spent the last year and a half of the war in the Naples and Rome bureaus, and was transferred in September, 1945, to Germany to assist in coverage of the first war-crimes trial in history, which ended in conviction of Goering, Hess, von Ribbentrop and other top Nazis.

Murlin Spencer boarded a transport in San Francisco in May, 1942, headed for General MacArthur's headquarters in Melbourne, Australia. His first, longest and most arduous front-line assignment was with the 32nd Division at Buna, a fever-ridden, swampy battleground on the southeast coast of New Guinea. Fifty-five days later, suffering from dysentery and thirty pounds lighter than when he started, he wrote his story of the fall of Buna Mission, plodded five miles to a field hospital and asked for treatment.

On Christmas Day of 1943, nearly a year later, he was back aboard another ship, fighting pre-landing nerves with the Marines, who were to land the next day on Cape Gloucester. Interspersed with coverage of headquarters, there were three more landings at Hollandia, in New Guinea, near Tacloban on the island of Leyte and at Ormoc, also on Leyte.

Spencer was on the cruiser *Nashville* when a lone Japanese Kamikaze, just skimming the water, crashed into the ship and set it on fire. Spencer, lying in the shade of a gun turret on the open deck, was saved from the blast by the intervening bridge.

A change in assignments took him to Admiral Nimitz' headquarters on Guam in time to interview the crew members of the B-29 who had dropped the first atomic bomb on Hiroshima.

As chief of bureau in the Central Pacific, Spencer covered the surrender ceremony aboard the battleship *Missouri*. In the hectic news

Murlin B. Spencer—From fever-ridden, swampy New Guinea to Japanese surrender aboard the Missouri.

days that followed, he learned the whereabouts of former Premier Hideki Tojo. Spencer and Russell Brines, an AP buddy, obtained the first interview with him. Counter Intelligence officers, ordered by MacArthur to bring Tojo in for questioning, asked Spencer to lead them to Tojo's modest home on the outskirts of Tokyo.

He went with the officers and a group of correspondents, but Tojo, instead of submitting, shot himself. Spencer watched the unconscious former war lord, waiting to see whether he would live or die. At his first movement, Spencer used Tojo's own telephone to dictate the story of the suicide attempt that failed. He returned to the United States in April, 1946, after four years of war duty.

Don Whitehead went to the Middle East war front in 1942, where he joined General Bernard Montgomery's British Eighth Army in its great drive against Nazi General Rommel's Afrika Korps.

From the day he joined the British, Whitehead was a combat reporter. "You can't write about war," he once confided to a friend, "unless you share with the troops the fear, suffering and cruelties— and the glories—that are war."

When Rommel's Afrika Korps was destroyed in Tunisia, Whitehead shifted to the American Army. He was with the assault troops when they attacked the beaches of Sicily at Gela, and when they broke the German stronghold at Troina in central Sicily. He landed behind the enemy's lines at Brolo on the northern coast of Sicily to report how an American battalion gambled its life to halt the German retreat toward Messina—and he was among the survivors of the battalion who walked off the ridge when a rescue regiment lifted the German siege. From Brolo he moved up with the first troops to enter Messina.

At the invasion of Salerno, Italy, Whitehead was on the beach with the Navy's beach squads, who had been sent ashore to help the army get men and equipment across the beaches and into action. He volunteered to land with the assault troops at Anzio, and he got out the first dispatch telling how the American and British forces had succeeded in their initial thrust. His later dispatches reflected the story of how the Allied strategy at Anzio had failed.

From Anzio, Whitehead went to England. He was with the assault troops of the U. S. First Infantry Division when they stormed the beaches on the coast of Normandy on June 6, 1944. He was with the

Don Whitehead—He saw more actual fighting than most combat soldiers.

spearhead troops who captured Cherbourg and he was on the ground to report the Allied breakthrough at St. Lo. He was among the first correspondents into Paris and his 4500-word description of the liberation was the only story to get through before communications broke down.

He was with the first American troops when they marched into Belgium and then into Germany, and he reported the capture of the Remagen Bridge, the breakthrough at Remagen, the discovery of the horror camp at Buchenwald, and, finally, the link-up of the Americans and the Russians on the Elbe River.

Whitehead saw as much or more actual fighting in World War II than most combat soldiers—but he came out of the war without a scratch.

In concluding these references to the work of Associated Press men, I quote the last two paragraphs of an address I made just before World War II ended in 1945:

"But let me end on a sentimental note. Associated Press men are the best in the world. For many, many years I have directed their work, but of all the thousands not one have I personally employed. I have seen them begin at the bottom of the ladder and I have seen many of them constantly going higher and higher, propelled upward by their own great work. I have seen them go away to cover wars the like of which no previous war correspondent ever had dreamed of. I have seen them show bravery and I know they have suffered privations equal to what the soldiers of any war have suffered. Lives have been lost. Some are captives. Yet I constantly have been pressed to find ways to say No to all those who want to go—to go anywhere, face any danger, to go to the four corners of the earth.

"I have grasped the hands of AP men who have miraculously escaped death in torpedoed warships and who have been lost for weeks in jungle warfare. And right now they may be giving their lives, for what? For you to know the day-by-day history of the world. And The Associated Press never sought a one of them to get him to work for it. Each of them sought The Associated Press. Know these thousands of men as I have known them and you will know why The Associated Press news service is what it is.

"And remember this: that since The Associated Press attracted them, that since each of them sought the connection, and since each of them is the news hero that he is—well, The Associated Press, whatever its faults, can't only not be very bad, it can be, and I say it is, very, very good—thanks to them—all of them, wherever they are!"

For those living and dead who reported in news and pictures from the areas of World War I, World War II and the fighting in Korea, whether or not they have been mentioned here, this is acclaim on behalf of their associates who hold them eligible to enter an Associated Press hall of fame!

25

INTO THE WORLD

AT LARGE

THE SWAY the European news agency cartel had held for forty-one years over the destiny of The Associated Press as a world news service came to an end, and The Associated Press got its freedom from the cartel's repression of its activities on February 12, 1934, the birthday of America's great emancipator. Not since England lost this land of ours did the old world ever give up anything to the new world more grudgingly.

Tragically for our country until then, the restraint that The Associated Press so willingly accepted had placed the United States, as a nation, in an inferior position abroad, and the cartel knew it. Each member of it except The Associated Press was more or less responsible to and motivated by the government of its own country.

England had its empire. Reuters was the instrument that, through its news reports, undertook to weld Britain's dependencies exclusively to the mother country. With the same restraint, it kept all other members of the cartel from sending news to the heavily populated areas of the western Pacific, including China and Japan. England's dominance in trade and influence of all of these vast territories was supported by the pro-British news delivered to them by Reuters. Reuters had done more for England in that respect than either

England's great navy, which ruled the seas, or its shipping, which then led in carrying on the commerce of the world.

France had built a smaller empire. Its Havas News Agency played the same role as did Reuters for the British.

Germany, after the accession of Wilhelm II, sought its empire and girded for war to obtain it. Its Wolff News Agency served as well as it could in fulfilling that ambition.

Not only did these three news agencies prevent The Associated Press from sending its news abroad, but correspondents of Reuters, Havas and Wolff, stationed in The Associated Press office in New York, could and did pervert AP news into dispatches that misrepresented and disparaged America before the rest of the world. This was the worst feature of The Associated Press contract with the cartel.

The fifteen years I had spent before Melville Stone's death in 1929 stressing the urgency of breaking the fetters by which the cartel bound The Associated Press had availed nothing but the right to take South American newspapers into Associated Press membership. After Mr. Stone's death, President Noyes held as firmly as did Mr. Stone against a break with Reuters. His reason was unswerving loyalty, not only to the wishes of Mr. Stone while Mr. Stone lived, but also to the memory of Victor F. Lawson of the Chicago *Daily News,* who died in 1925. It was Lawson who, as president of the first national Associated Press, approved the contract with Reuters in 1893, and it was Lawson who made Noyes his successor as Associated Press president in 1900.

Though all other Board members were willing to risk a break with Reuters, Mr. Noyes continued to remain adamant, and the Board deferred to him. He was willing, however, for the Board to give me permission to negotiate with the cartel for a free hand to disseminate Associated Press news anywhere provided it could be done within the framework of the existing relationship; that is, I could try to get what I wanted if the cartel contract remained in force in all other respects.

I was sure that what he wanted done presented an insurmountable barrier. Nevertheless, I tried to hurdle it. Three months after Mr. Stone's death, I was in London pleading with Reuters. No success. In 1930 I was there again. No success. In February, 1932, once more in London, I got a letter from Reuters giving The Associated Press a free hand in Japan.

This letter gave me what I needed for my immediate plans. Tension, which later led to the Pearl Harbor tragedy, had already risen in

Japan against America, its transpacific neighbor. It had been increased by the distorted news Reuters was sending to that country from the United States. I was made aware of this by The AP's Tokyo staff and promptly notified Rengo, a Japanese co-operative news agency similar to The Associated Press, that The AP was prepared to make a contract with it for the exchange of news. Rengo was headed by Yukichi Iwanaga, a friend of America. He eagerly and earnestly desired a contract with The Associated Press. He also wanted to continue Rengo's contract with Reuters.

At Iwanaga's earnest invitation, I spent the month of May, 1933, in Japan. Between rounds of Japanese hospitality a firm contract on a nonexclusive basis was made between Rengo and The Associated Press. Upon learning of it, Sir Roderick Jones, managing director of Reuters, was incensed and promptly marked Rengo for Reuters' discipline. Mr. Iwanaga showed distress when he told me Jones had notified him that Reuters would refuse to have any further relations with Rengo unless the contract with The Associated Press was annulled.

I considered this a negation of the letter in which Jones conceded a free hand to The Associated Press in Japan. I thought it a justifiable cause for open warfare unless Jones withdrew the notice he sent to Rengo. Instead of returning directly to the United States, I decided to proceed to London via the Suez Canal to make a demand personally for an explanation, and notified Jones I was coming.

While I was still on the high seas enroute to see him, he sent a coldly formal notice to The Associated Press in New York terminating Reuters' contract with The AP. I thought this a shameful procedure for an ally of forty years to take. When I got to London I told Jones so. He replied that I had "gotten out of bounds." He refused to give me any explanation of that remark.

Resenting this, I wondered how long it would be before this bubble of Reuters' world domination of the news would burst, but all I said was that I believed the press of every country should be free to act as it chose and that no news agency should have exclusive contract rights in any country, including its own.

I told Jones what I had wanted to tell him when I first met him in 1919, namely, that I was interested in a better acquaintance among the peoples of all nations, which truthful international news exchange could bring about.

His attitude was no more responsive in 1933 than it was fourteen years earlier. He merely said that in due course a letter would be sent to me in New York stating the conditions upon which The Associated Press relationship with Reuters could continue.

When the letter came, it contained an exorbitant demand for a cash differential from The Associated Press.

The Associated Press answer was even more sensational than the demand. It was that The AP Board of Directors had reached the conclusion that the points of view were so divergent that the two could not be reconciled. Reuters' denunciation of the four-party treaty was, therefore, accepted. President Noyes wrote Jones that "the break is a great if not the greatest disappointment of my life." Jones replied that he would come to New York at once.

With an idea that it would be well for the two large news agencies of the United States—The Associated Press and the United Press— to stand together against Jones in any maneuver by him to play one of them against the other, I asked Karl Bickel, president of the United Press, to join The Associated Press in a most unusual contract. Highly competitive as the two agencies were and always had been, Bickel and I personally were the best of friends, and after forty years

Karl A. Bickel (1935)—
Agreed to a meeting in Moscow.

we remain so. We had the same feeling about the cartel. The contract we made provided that neither The Associated Press nor the United Press would make an exclusive contract with any European news agency. I was deeply grateful to Karl Bickel for joining me in this action, just as I deeply regretted his retirement from the United Press presidency shortly thereafter.

As the members of The Associated Press Board knew, I never had wanted an exclusive contract with any foreign news agency that was subservient to the will of the government of its country, as were Havas and Wolff, and as Reuters had been. I disliked the idea of The Associated Press having exclusive access to and being an outlet for the propaganda-tainted announcements of foreign governments, which in effect set The Associated Press up as the exclusive mouthpiece in America for those governments. Since the exclusive cartel contracts had been nullified by Jones, the only exclusive European agency contract The Associated Press still had was with the Soviet Government's news agency, Tass.

Bickel knew that besides the cartel contract, The Associated Press also had this exclusive agreement with Tass. I told him that I would go to Moscow as soon as possible with a request to Tass that its exclusive contract with The Associated Press be modified to permit the United Press also to have the Tass service. Bickel and I agreed to meet in Moscow. By the end of March, 1934, both The Associated Press and the United Press had contracts with Tass.

When Jones arrived in New York, I composed a form of contract with Reuters giving The Associated Press absolute freedom to distribute news throughout the world. It was promptly signed.

Mr. Stone always felt that the signing of the original exclusive Reuter contract was a major achievement. Happy as Mr. Stone must have been about that agreement in 1893, his elation could not have equaled mine upon the signing of the contract in 1934, which gave The Associated Press its freedom to distribute its own news all over the world. I even transported myself into the belief that the signing was a supreme moment of the century in the life of The Associated Press.

Yet, curiously, I had no feeling of personal success. I did regret the years of condescending attitude Jones had assumed toward The Associated Press and toward me ever since I had first met him in

1919. However, after he had left my office, I reflected upon how unimportant the two of us were in the life of two great institutions, each of which already had existed in one form or another for nearly one hundred years.

And as to The Associated Press, I thought of how many minds, indeed, how many lives had been devoted to bringing it to the standing it attained that day when it and not the news cartel could decide upon the future of its world activities; how the twenty years I had spent intensely interested in the effort then concluded were such a

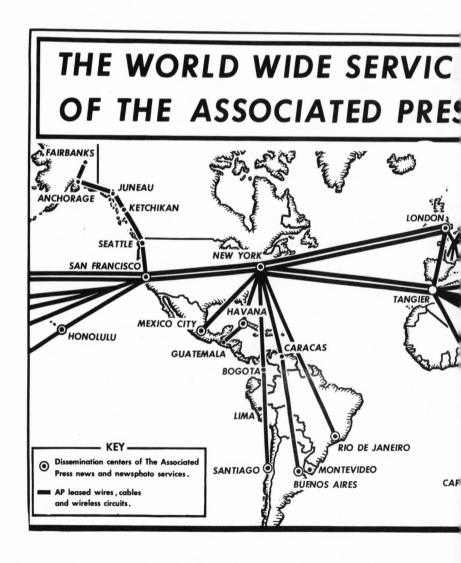

THE WORLD WIDE SERVIC
OF THE ASSOCIATED PRES

KEY

⊚ Dissemination centers of The Associated Press news and newsphoto services.

■ AP leased wires, cables and wireless circuits.

long part of my own life, but how very little twenty years amounted to in the unending life of The Associated Press. I was sure that both agencies would profit by this modernization.

They did.

The AP's release from repression in 1934 made possible its start upon a mission that it always theretofore properly should have fulfilled. Since The AP no longer had cartel restrictions, I instituted

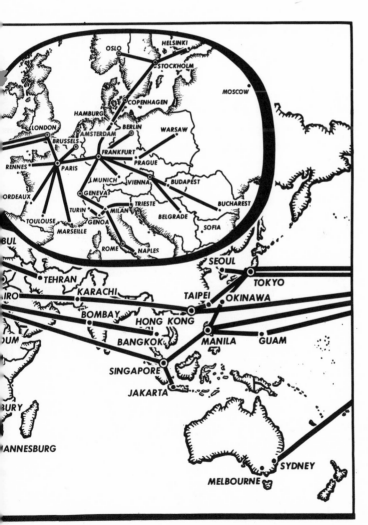

The World Wide Services of The Associated Press as of 1958.

plans for The Associated Press world service, the execution of which had been my fondest dream. They had not fully developed when World War II broke out and interposed delay. As the tide of war turned favorably toward America and its allies, however, I gave Lloyd Stratton, an assistant general manager, the opportunity to investigate the field open to the development of The Associated Press world service.

Stratton traveled thousands of miles by air to every continent in extremely perilous times. In October, 1944, he made a report to me of what his travels had pictured for the future of The Associated Press worldwise. I asked him to read it to the Board. A paragraph of the printed minutes of that important hour in the history of The Associated Press as sent to the entire membership follows:

Mr. Stratton reported his findings during his world travels in the last year and described the competitive situation facing The Associated Press at home and abroad. The general manager followed with a statement reminding the Board of the long-standing nature of the situation described, submitting comparative figures showing the income available by competitors for service development and recommending that the Board authorize the general manager to develop plans and put them into effect. The Board unanimously voted that funds not to exceed $1,000,000 annually be set aside for the purpose and that any unspent portion of the sum in any calendar year, effective with 1944, be carried over and added to the amount available for the next succeeding year.

Fortunately, we never actually needed that much money. What we did use was soon repaid. But the Board's action in appropriating the funds with the authority given it by the entire membership and, therefore, on behalf of practically all of American newspaperdom, was an historic step that made amends for the long delay previously encountered—a step in which AP newspapers always can take pride.

That is why, when the authorization was given, my mind recalled the declaration I made to members of the Board in 1914 to which I previously have referred: That since American newspapers composed the largest and most prosperous group in the world's press, they could, if they would, make The Associated Press the instrument that could by its truthful news dissemination make the whole world aware of the intellectual, ethical and material progress developed in this great country of free men.

With full authority and ample funds to proceed, I then gave to Lloyd Stratton, fifteen years my junior, the assignment that I had longed to have for myself as early as 1914 when I was thirty-four years old. Again traveling thousands of miles by air, Stratton carried out our plans to initiate delivery of AP news to the entire world. Thereafter, this service was extended each year. By 1958 it was considered one of the remarkable achievements of The Associated Press.

Robert McLean, upon his retirement from The AP presidency, said:

Under the urging of Kent Cooper, in the years between the wars the membership was extended to include newspapers in Central and South America, and in 1934 the alliances with Reuters and the European agencies with their shackling restraints were cancelled. New agreements were substituted and the supplying as well as the collecting of news was extended by The Associated Press into the remaining areas of the world. That decision and the resultant expansion stand as a monument to Kent Cooper's energy and his vision.

To this I add my own salutation to all employees who helped in this endeavor, especially to Lloyd Stratton and to Frank J. Starzel, my successor, who enthusiastically and with unusual effectiveness, directed its further expansion after my retirement.

Before World War II, the Board of Directors finally approved my recommendation that the New York headquarters be moved to a new building in Rockefeller Center that would be built and named for The Associated Press at no expense to it except as a tenant. My plea was that The Associated Press needed some dignified showmanship, an item of which could be supplied by moving into a new building in a conspicuous location. Its offices, until I got approval for the move to Rockefeller Center, were located in a loft building on Madison Avenue.

I made a statement to the employees when the move was made. Having read it now, twenty years later, it seems to have emphasized the feeling of sentiment I had about the staff and The Associated Press itself at the time, and still have. It follows:

The Associated Press Building to which the New York offices shortly are to move is a monument to its newspaper members and its employees.

Through ninety years, they jointly have striven that an accurate, unbiased chronicle of events, interestingly recorded, be available to newspaper readers.

With the occupancy of the new building, I hope I may be pardoned for expressing a sentiment to the entire staff which for want of a specific opportunity of so doing I may have suppressed too long.

I am now and for twenty-eight years have been an employee of The Associated Press. I began here after a varied experience in newspaper and news agency work. I came here and I stayed here because I saw that employee opportunity and recognition could be enlarged. The business of The Associated Press was the conduct of a news service. The stress was on the product, not on the personnel. That was true of other institutions in those days. My feeling then was and still is that the stress should be on the creation of a spirited, competent personnel, for, given the proper personnel, adequately accommodated, the news service will take care of itself.

We have gone a long way in trying to keep the stress where I feel it belongs. No one knows better than I the disappointments and discouragements. They were by no means all incurred by lack of employee understanding. But knowing that mutual co-operation between the newspaper members and The Associated Press employees was a prerequisite to proper accomplishment, and being myself employee-minded, I did what I could where it was most needed when it was needed.

But this is not an outline of all I tried to do or shall continue to try to do. I shall confine it to the matter of this new building of ours.

First, when I came to The Associated Press twenty-eight years ago, AP headquarters were in the old Western Union Building at 195 Broadway. In 1913, I selected and gained approval of the move to 51 Chambers Street—an improvement, I assure you. Next, in 1923, I recommended and gained approval to come here—383 Madison Avenue—also an improvement. Now and for the last time in what I shall have any part, we go to The Associated Press Building in Rockefeller Center. That move

The Associated Press Board of Directors (1940) in the New Associated Press Building at 50 Rockefeller Plaza—Left to right: *Paul Bellamy; George B. Longan; E. H. Butler; H. J. Grant; General Manager K.C.; Clark Howell; E. K. Gaylord; Houston Harte; J. L. Horne, Leonard K. Nicholson; Colonel Robert R. McCormick; W. H. Cowles; Joseph R. Knowland; E. Lansing Ray; Frank B. Noyes; President Robert McLean; Stuart H. Perry; Paul Patterson; John Cowles.*

means a very great deal to me. I hope it will prove to mean much to you.

The sentiment I want to express is this: There is nothing in my life that means more to me than the association I have had with those who have contributed their best to the success of The Associated Press. Twenty-five years ago I think I knew each employee in the New York office and many of those elsewhere well enough to call each by his first name. There were not so many of you then. We have been making more and more jobs available, and a lot of the old-timers have passed on. At the same time, I have been busy in other parts of the world. But still the sentiment I express remains true in spite of the fact that I have not been able to enjoy the camaraderie I once did because of conditions that rule otherwise.

Therefore, in going to this newest home, I have to take this means of saying to those who work in New York that I hope the new surroundings will be, as they were planned, conducive to your happiness and health and contentment. These new quarters will be our new business home. I hope you will like them.

To those in other bureaus, I hope this new central office will be a symbol of the distance we have traveled and a token of what I wish could be done for all of you everywhere. It is comforting to know that working conditions have been improving constantly, and I am encouraged to hope that continuing endeavor will result in still further improvement. This is an objective which never can be absent from our thoughts of the future.

Thus it can be that what you have aided in accomplishing in the past shall continue into the future; that "by The Associated Press" shall prevail as long as the rights of a free press continue to make possible an uncensored, unfettered collection and dissemination of truthful news.

26

THE GOVERNMENT
MAKES ITS CASE

A RUMBLE that later developed into a government suit to end The Associated Press "franchise" rights occurred late in 1940. It was then that Roy Howard told me about a talk he had with Thurman Arnold, assistant attorney general of the Unitied States in charge of antitrust litigation. Howard said Arnold had called on him in Washington to ask what the United Press attitude would be if the government took action to annual The Associated Press "franchise" rights. Howard answered that the United Press might be benefitted, but that even if it were, he would be opposed to Government interference in The Associated Press business because it could result in The Associated Press being declared a common carrier. In that case, as a public utility, he added, it would come under Government regulations. He told Arnold he ought to get in touch with me.

Howard's suggestion brought me my first experience with the majesty of the Government's imperially expressed demands that private business be conducted on a plane acceptable to the public prosecutor or else! I had heard that Arnold was a genius who really had studied the Sherman and Clayton antitrust acts. He invited me to have luncheon with him in his office at 1:30 P.M. one day late in January, 1941. I was there promptly. His secretary conducted me into a mammoth room, so spacious that it could impress or even frighten visitors because of its size. At two o'clock he came in the back door, which was only a few steps from the desk at the side of which I was sitting.

He asked me who I was. When I told him, he said, "Oh, yes," and started to upbraid me for operating a trust. Since he was trying to emphasize each point to his own satisfaction, he talked for twenty minutes barely stopping for breath. I was getting the "full treatment" which the defendant in a criminal court proceeding is supposed to get from the district attorney.

Then his secretary came in to express astonishment that Arnold was there. She said she would order lunch for us. Arnold said he had had his lunch. Apparently I was to get none. My feeling by then was that even if the entire Associated Press membership and I were to be criminally indicted, I was going to get that lunch I had been promised. So I spoke up to Arnold: "Well, if you don't mind, I haven't had mine." Arnold seemed displeased at having been interrupted in his dissertation, but the secretary took matters in hand and summoned a waiter. From the modest menu I selected a grapefruit, an egg sandwich and a cup of coffee.

Arnold then went on with his speech and demanded to know why The Associated Press wouldn't serve the Washington *Times-Herald*. I am not a good listener when I'm hungry and felt relieved when the waiter announced that lunch was ready in the private office in the rear of the big room where we had been sitting.

Between grapefruit squirts in my eye, he continued to threaten legal action against The Associated Press. I managed to interrupt to express a request that he postpone his threats until I ate my egg sandwich, and asked him to tell me something funny. I said I liked to hear amusing or light conversation while eating. He then relaxed and did me the courtesy to explain why he had kept me waiting a half-hour. He said he was in New Haven the day before and expected to leave there on the midnight train for Washington but that somebody, having misunderstood, bought him a ticket to go in the wrong direction. He said he didn't look at the ticket but just boarded the train.

Finding a big fellow asleep in the lower berth, he made the porter shift the fellow to the upper so he could have his lower. In the morning, he awoke to find himself not in Washington, where he expected and wanted to be, but in the South Station in Boston. He then took a plane from Boston to Washington. I commended him for his bravery in sleeping beneath the big fellow he had routed out and who must have been angry with him. He said indeed the big fellow was angry.

When he finished that, I was still drinking my coffee so I asked him to tell me another. He told me one about the biological urges of a female cat; that when he was mayor of a small town in Wyoming, a woman called up to complain about the meowing all night long of somebody's cat on her backyard fence. He asked the woman how many nights the meowing had been going on. She said for four nights. Arnold, knowing the duration of the biological urges of the female cat, assured her it would not happen the fifth night. The next morning she called him up to thank him for stopping the cat's meowing.

After lunch, we returned to the "grand salon," where he told me that The Associated Press might not have been a trust when it was small, but that it had gotten so big and impressive in size that it had no right to be exclusive. He said it ought to be as easy to get in as walking into the Union Station. Such interpolations as I could make did not lessen his unhappiness over the cutting remarks Mrs. "Cissie" Patterson, owner of the Washington *Times-Herald,* made every time he saw her. He said "Cissie" always would banter him with: "You are not afraid of General Motors or the U. S. Steel but you are afraid of The Associated Press." He said, "She makes me feel as though she thinks I have no guts, and so I am going to go for The Associated Press."

He immediately suggested a quick solution: that The Associated Press accept a consent decree at once that would permit "Cissie" to have the membership, or better still, The Associated Press could just start service to her, and he would forget the whole thing—just like that! I told him that there were a number of legal questions involved and that I would prefer that our lawyer discuss matters with him. I had not been able to do so anyhow because he did all the talking. I bade him adieu, turned and left, laughing to myself.

I don't know whether Arnold noticed my amusement as I left. If he did, he may have thought I either was laughing at him or was jauntily throwing off his threats of what he was going to do to The Associated Press. Actually, as I took the long walk from his desk to the door at the other end of the big room, I was quietly laughing at neither.

I was thinking of an amusing incident of which his long talk had reminded me. Mrs. Leslie Carter once said that the late Herbert Bayard Swope was a guest at a dinner party she attended. Swope had a fine record as a journalist, was the first Pulitzer prize-winner when employed by the New York *World,* was an intellectual, a raconteur and excelled in banter and debate.

"But," Mrs. Carter said, "until Herbert started that night, I never had realized how long even such an interesting individual could talk without stopping. We do have long speeches in some dramatic roles," she said. "There is Hamlet's soliloquy, for instance, but it does have an end. That night after dinner Herbert was in fine form—one in a circle of a dozen or so. He started to talk, and kept on talking.

"Interesting, yes, but after a while I leaned forward, caught his attention, quickly stuck out my tongue and as quickly leaned back in my chair. He looked at me questioningly a second or two while he continued talking. Then I again leaned forward, got his eye, stuck out my tongue and got a really severe look as he kept on talking. Later I did it again. He turned to me and said: 'Why are you doing that? That's the third time you have done it.'

" 'Oh,' I said, 'I was just getting in a word edgewise.' Herbert joined in the laughter. It was a happy evening."

So if Thurman Arnold did wonder that I seemed amused, if he noticed I was laughing to myself as I left, he can read this and know that my experience with him reminded me of Mrs. Carter's little story.

The matter of Government action against The Associated Press strung along until the late Marshall Field announced that he was establishing a Democratic paper in Chicago in support of President Roosevelt's New Deal. Associate Justice Robert Jackson told me three years later at a White House Correspondent's dinner that while he was attorney general he had refused to sanction Arnold's bringing any action against The Associated Press on behalf of Mrs. Patterson's Washington paper; that by the time Marshall Field wanted to get The AP service, the President had "kicked me upstairs" as an associate justice of the Supreme Court. There Jackson had to disqualify himself from considering the Government suit against The Associated Press because he had disapproved Arnold's proposal that legal action be taken on behalf of "Cissie" Patterson.

The second incident that took me to the Department of Justice occurred after Francis Biddle succeeded Jackson as attorney general. The Chicago *Sun* was not happy without The Associated Press service, which the Chicago *Tribune* had exclusively in the morning field in Chicago. Thereupon, I was told, the President sent for Biddle and said:

"We have a friend in Chicago for whom we must get The AP service. We have also got an enemy of the New Deal in Chicago who has The AP service and won't let our friend have it. Is the law such that we can make The Associated Press serve our friend?" Biddle took up the question with Arnold, who leaped at the chance and assured Biddle that the law favored the accomplishment of the President's desires. President Roosevelt said to go ahead.

Immediately thereupon, Arnold threatened The Associated Press with litigation, first with criminal action, then civil action, unless it immediately made its service available to the Chicago *Sun*. He coupled it with a demand for the admission of "Cissie" Patterson's Washington paper. Then, to give the entire membership a taste of the treatment I had gotten from Arnold and to show that the Justice Department meant business, FBI men were sent all over the country visiting AP members.

The FBI agents are gentlemen. Their regular business is to run down hardened criminals and to populate the government's Alcatraz prison in San Francisco Bay, so they expressed regret upon confronting publishers of American newspapers to discuss the application of the Chicago *Sun* for Associated Press membership.

The resentment that flared among newspaper publishers because of the visits of FBI men lost the Chicago *Sun* a lot of publisher friends. Their good will was regained, however, when Field's son, Marshall, Jr., took over as publisher of the paper a few years later. President Roosevelt admitted he had ordered the filing of the suit against The Associated Press when he was asked by a political friend, an AP member, why he had ordered the attorney general to attack The Associated Press. His reply was: "Why, I don't wish The Associated Press any bad luck; I just want to give it another 'membah!' "

In due course, being curious, and at President McLean's suggestion, I called on Attorney General Biddle after the Chicago *Sun* had failed of election to membership. He received me in his unpretentious office not too graciously, for he, too, raised his voice menacingly. As I wanted him to lower his voice, I told him I was not there to discuss the law; that I wanted to see whether a solution could be worked out to the Government's satisfaction and still leave The Associated Press in a sound position. Biddle quieted down.

The "conference" ended. There followed an exchange of letters, but my intervention in trying to avoid the suit had no other result than to make me aware of the persistent force the United States Government can apply to do a favor for a political friend.

Before the Government proceeded against The Associated Press, there were members who had asked Colonel McCormick, of the Chicago *Tribune,* to grant a waiver that would permit The Associated Press Board to elect Marshall Field's Chicago *Sun* to membership. They said they wanted him to do so to save The Associated Press an expensive law suit. He said they wanted the *Tribune* to make the sacrifice so they could still hold their "franchise" rights intact for themselves in their own cities. Therefore, to each of them, he told me, he replied that he would give a waiver for the whole Chicago territory if all AP members would likewise waive for their cities. His suggestion was not pursued.

I recalled that before Field had any idea of starting the Chicago *Sun,* Colonel McCormick had told me that he thought the position of the *Tribune* in Chicago would be benefitted if it had a competitor in the morning field, which it did not have. He said he did not like the idea of having the only morning paper in such a large city.

After the U. S. Government suit against The Associated Press was begun, I reminded McCormick of his conversation about wanting a morning paper competitor in Chicago and asked him why he did not waive. He said:

"I would have been glad to have waived had Field asked me. He never did. Instead, the President of the United States intervened with the power of his office to bring it about. Yet the grandson of a man who was an ardent supporter of my grandfather's Chicago *Tribune* in its early days could have had an AP membership if he had asked me to propose it."

Colonel McCormick could only guess why Field had not asked him. He thought it may have been that the hatred of President Roosevelt for the Chicago *Tribune* because of the latter's attacks upon the President was so deep-rooted that Field did not want to offend the President by asking a favor of Colonel McCormick lest Roosevelt would hear of it and be displeased. McCormick could think of no other reason. At any rate, McCormick said, Marshall Field never even told him he was going to start a newspaper although he had enjoyed cocktails with him in Field's home in Chicago a few days before Field's announcement that he would establish the Chicago *Sun*.

Thurman Arnold left the Government service before the prolonged legal proceedings against The Associated Press were begun in 1943. As the litigation proceeded, there were many comments by members but none as amusingly expressed as that of Charles M. Palmer, owner of the St. Joseph (Missouri) *News Press* and *Gazette*. Palmer was a charter member of The Associated Press at the time of its re-organization in New York.

In his nineties, he was saluted in the membership annual meeting for his record of continuous attendance at those functions. He was a firm believer in the idea of maintaining the "franchise" rights. He believed that without them every newspaper in America would rush into the membership, not realizing that most newspapers in America already were in the membership. When the lower courts upheld the Government contention, a poetic urge seized Palmer and he sent this to me:

> Poor old Kent with the old AP
> Has his full share of troubles,
> But what will all his troubles be
> When the New Deal its membership doubles?

With the rhyme came this note:

Dear Kent:

I presume that you are going to appeal to the Supreme Court. Which reminds me of the case of the amiable young lady who, learning that she was pregnant, rubbed her abdomen with vanishing cream. Your appeal to the Supreme Court will do just about as much good.

A Merry Christmas to you!

C.M.P.

A Supreme Court decision, which was not handed down until June, 1945, finally settled matters, with the Government the winner. By that time Roosevelt was dead, but what he had started ended with

The Associated Press by-laws being amended by court order. The AP "franchise" rights were thus annulled for all time.

With the annulment, three newspapers which promptly got membership were: the Chicago *Sun,* the Washington *Times-Herald* and William Randolph Hearst's Detroit *Times.* No other change resulted. The earth did not tremble. The heavens did not fall. No one surrendered his membership then because of the Supreme Court decision and had not by 1958, thirteen years later, even though no member any longer held a "franchise" that could keep a competitor in his own city from getting The Associated Press service. By that time the Washington *Times-Herald* had been absorbed by the Washington *Post.*

Of all the thousands in the newspaper and press association business, especially Associated Press members and Associated Press employees, I must have been the only individual who, after the Supreme Court decision, had a really firm conviction as to why The Associated Press did not start to disintegrate because of the loss of the "franchises." I assume that I was the only one who thought of that reason because not then nor since has it been mentioned.

Nevertheless, as compensation for all I had pleaded for permission to do and had done, it pleases me to believe that the reason the Supreme Court decision did not weaken The Associated Press was because of the defense I built up during thirty years against the day the Government might attack and gain annulment of the "franchise" rights.

For by the end of those thirty years, besides my constant discussions with members about AP loyalty, there had been created a new conception of value in an Associated Press membership, namely, the excellence of its news, news photos, features, Wirephoto, regional news and a score of others, all produced by a talented and spirited staff. This evaluation had taken the place of the old one about keeping a competitor out.

Most rewarding was the fact that this change had taken place so smoothly that another generation assumed it always had been what it was in its 1945 form with no reason to think of the past or of what might have been, had not the "radical" changes occurred.

Nor was there reflection by publishers after 1945 on what this Associated Press policy contributed in developing reader interest in news that brought the tremendous increase in all newspaper circulations in the second quarter-century. It was in that period that the amazing daily total figure of 55,000,000, perhaps the saturation point, was reached. Other factors played roles in gaining those circulation increases. They are not referred to here because they had no connection with creating a new basis of value for Associated Press memberships.

Although nothing was said about this new conception of the advantages of AP membership after the Government won its case, many favorable expressions regarding the novel developments in the service had been made before that 1945 decision, both verbally and in letters. One letter was particularly welcomed because it came from one who recently had acquired an AP membership for his paper. The man who wrote the letter based his appreciation of The Associated Press upon the service delivered to him—not because of any "franchise" right. Actually, that letter came to my mind a little more than a year later when Thurman Arnold first set upon me. I felt like saying to him: "Do what you want to do, Mr. Arnold. I have a sense of security for the future of The Associated Press."

The letter was from John Cowles. He and Gardner Cowles bought the Minneapolis *Star* as their entry into the Minneapolis field. The *Star* did not have an Associated Press membership but got one with its purchase of the Minneapolis *Journal.* A short while afterward, this wholly unexpected letter came to me:

September 6, 1939

Dear Kent:

It is impossible for me to exaggerate how much having the *Star-Journal,* both daily and Sunday, in The Associated Press means to me. Incidentally, although I think I quite fully appreciated the enormous value of Wirephoto right from the start, every week that passes intensifies my conviction that when you created Wirephoto you did one of the two or three biggest things that have ever been done in The Associated Press' entire history.

With warmest regards,

Sincerely,
John Cowles

There was another reflection about the result of the Government's suit. I heard no one speak of the fact that twenty years after Frank

Munsey had paid nearly $2,000,000 for a membership, he could have had it for nothing after the Court's decision. Transactions of this sort had not been uncommon.

One was that in which Captain Patterson, of the New York *Daily News,* figured. Without an AP membership, he had built a newspaper with the largest circulation in the country. But, like Munsey, he wanted an Associated Press membership in 1926 because The AP, being a co-operative, backed by most of the newspapers in the United States, would make the New York *Daily News* structurally sound.

He got it seven years after the establishment of his paper by paying $350,000 for the New York *Commercial Bulletin,* an all but unknown little trade paper with a small circulation. The Ridder brothers, Bernard, Victor and Joseph, had bought the *Commercial Bulletin* and had transferred to it their *Journal of Commerce* AP membership. They then sold the *Commercial Bulletin* with its Associated Press membership to Captain Patterson so that he could have the membership for his New York *Daily News.* Additionally, Patterson lent them $150,000, which was subsequently repaid.

The Ridder brothers are sons of the late Herman Ridder, of the New Yorker Staats Zeitung. He was one of the founders of The As-

Irvin S. Cobb (1930)—
He kept a promise.

sociated Press and a member of its Board of Directors at his death in 1915.

Financed partly in the beginning by the transaction with the *Daily News,* the Ridder brothers went on to build one of the most successful newspaper chains in the country. It reaches from coast to coast and includes fifteen newspapers.

Always with the permission of the authors, letters to me frequently became the bases of good news stories which proved of general interest when published textually. The first one was from John Bouman, in 1925, which related his sufferings in the Arctic in connection with the Amundsen rescue expedition. One of the later ones was from Irvin S. Cobb, humorist, and author of *Exit Laughing,* written two years before he died. Irvin made good on a promise to me after he wrote this book that if I survived him, and he was in his last sickness, he would prove his undying love of humor by writing me an amusing letter.

He was desperately ill in December of 1943. On the tenth of that month, in his own handwriting, he sent to me his "epistle to the Corinthians and the Paducahans." He was then too ill to receive visitors, but I asked his wife if I could publish it. She gave permission for me to do so. She declined, however, to let me have a picture taken of him at the time to go with its publication because "he just looks too sick." This is the Cobb "epistle":

Dear Kent:

Through the public prints it has been brought to my attention—as the politicians love to put it—that I am dangerously ill. Among my devoted public this report appears to have occasioned considerable anxiety. In fact, one of them wired (collect) asking for the details and the other called by long distance (charges reversed).

In reply I would say that at this writing I am doing much better than originally was expected by the accommodating and affable undertaker down the block. His interest was most touching for a while. If, as and when I get ready to depart elsewhere, I promise to keep friendly newspapers fully advised. As someone else so aptly has said: "I used to be a newspaperman myself."

I take credit for one thing. So far as the available records show, I am the only person who under similar circumstances did not wittily remark—

with or without credit to the author—"the reports of my death have been greatly exaggerated."

For those who enjoy morbid particulars, I might add that the doctors are still tapping me for impulsive little freshets of dropsy but the results of these acquatic sports and pastimes will, they believe, diminish as time passes. For a while though, they tried too hard to be cheerful, if you get what I mean. And I'm still just a trifle worried about St. Swithin's Day.

The approach of the holiday season gives me double incentive to thank all the kindly souls who have shown solicitude regarding my state of health or lack of such. As for me, I content myself with the refrain: "Merry symptoms and a tappy new year."

Gratefully
Irvin S. Cobb

A great spirit, a great humorist and a dear friend of mine for more than forty years, left this world early in 1944 when Irvin S. Cobb died.

In that fifth decade of the century and thereafter, I became aware of the accelerated pace by which death was taking Associated Press members, Associated Press employees and many other friends.

It was always a wrench to my heart to lose any one of them. But when they began marching out of this life every month or so by twos, threes and fours, I believed the path to heaven must have started to get a little crowded. Besides the scores I have previously mentioned who were my close friends and are now gone, a few more must represent all of those hundreds I cannot name. For at one time or another, I knew more or less intimately almost every member of The Associated Press, their managing editors and a great many AP employees.

Charles Harkrader, a former Associated Press member of Bristol, Virginia, once offered to "lay a bet" that I had known more newspapermen and remembered their names and faces than anyone. As counting, not "proving," how many would be impossible, I could only thank Harkrader for the compliment. But they were numerous. Best of all, so far as I know, none that I did know was my enemy.

But of those who are gone and whose names may not appear in what I am writing, these must represent them: Amon Carter and James North of Fort Worth. It was Amon who said: "Down our way we never think of The Associated Press when we want anything done about news. We just think of Kent Cooper and tell him." And there

*Amon Carter tells one to K.C. at Associated Press
luncheon in 1950, as General Eisenhower listens.*

were Donald Sterling, of the Oregon *Journal;* Grove Patterson, of the
Toledo *Blade;* John Brice, of the Atlanta *Journal.*

It was George Booth, of the Worcester *Gazette,* long an AP director, who just before he died wanted to say something to me that he
must have known would touch me deeply. He wrote that when I retired "a feeling of great loss for The Associated Press and for me personally has overcome me." Other friends were Lansing Ray, of the St.
Louis *Globe-Democrat;* Will Cowles, Sr., of the Spokane *Spokesman-
Review;* Josephus Daniels, of the Raleigh *News and Observer;* Theodore Miller, general manager of the American Telephone and Telegraph Company; Joseph Pulitzer, of the St. Louis *Post-Dispatch;*
Sevellon Brown, of the Providence *Journal;* Ed Butler, of the Buffalo
News; Governor Cox, who owned newspapers in Dayton, Springfield,
Atlanta and Miami; John Golden, renowned New York theatrical
producer.

Then there were jovial Paul Patterson, of the Baltimore *Sun;* and

*George F. Booth (1948)—
"A feeling of great loss
has overcome me."*

another *Sun* man, a musical genius and, like Paul, a wonderful pal, the inimitable Henry Mencken; to say nothing of Merlin Aylesworth, the first president of the National Broadcasting Company, whose death broke up a golf foursome composed of John N. Wheeler, Bruce Barton and myself.

Also, there were Leonard Nicholson, of the New Orleans *Times-Picayune,* and Paul Bellamy, of the Cleveland *Plain Dealer,* both members of the Board of Directors; John Stewart Bryan, owner of the Richmond *Times-Dispatch* and the *News-Leader,* a gentleman from Virginia if there ever was one; Fisher Curtis, The Associated Press treasurer; Stuart Perry, of the Adrian *Telegram,* long an AP director; O. S. Warden, of the Great Falls *Tribune,* also a former AP director; Frederick I. Thompson, of the Birmingham *Age-Herald,* a former AP director; Heinrich Mantler, of the Wolff Bureau of Berlin; J. G. Doletsky, of Tass of Moscow; Charles Houssaye, of Havas of Paris; Ogden Reid of the New York *Herald Tribune;* George B. Longan, of the Kansas *City-Star,* who, before he became an AP director as the member for the *Star,* wrote me that he very much wanted to work for The Associated Press under my direction; George Cameron, of the San Francisco *Chronicle;* Oswald Garrison Villard, of the New York *Post;* E. P. Adler, of the Davenport *Times,* also president of the Lee Syndicate; Florence D. White, of the New York *World;* Judge Bingham, of the Louisville *Courier-Journal.*

One whose depth of feeling for The Associated Press I shall never forget was W. G. Rice, of the Houghton (Michigan) *Gazette.* He was a charter member of the organization and spoke for all the charter members I was able to round up to receive special honors at the annual luncheon of 1935. And there was Grantland Rice, sports columnist beloved by all who knew him; the president of the Australian Associated Press, Sir Keith Murdoch, of the Melbourne *Herald;* J. F. B. Livesay, general manager of the Canadian Press; Brian Bell, Milo Thompson, Marion Sheen, all three valuable AP men; John H. Perry, Sr., of the Perry chain of Florida newspapers; Dr. Nicholas Murray Butler of Columbia University; Yukichi Iwanaga, of Rengo News Agency of Tokyo; Dr. Luis Mitre, of *La Nacion* of Buenos Aires; Aurelio Miro Quesada, of *El Comercio* of Lima, Peru.

I could name one hundred more who died in that fifth decade or later and many times a hundred if I could go back into the years before 1940—men who supported me in my work, and others who were staunch friends. As to those who were with me in The Associated Press as members, I was blessed with the friendship of their successors, who must know that I often think of them and those who preceded them. And if I tried to list all those who are gone, my eyes would so dim with tears that I could not see to write their names.

27

FOUR TIMES
FIFTEEN

IN CONTEMPLATION of my sixty years in news work with newspapers and press associations, I have thought that my life divided itself into four separate little dramas, each of which embraced a period of fifteen years.

The time from 1891 to 1906 covered the formative years—from newspaper carrier to establishing my own press association. In that time I came to know that whatever career I was going to make for myself, it would be in news agency work.

In the years from 1906 to 1921 I saw opportunity ahead that aroused my ambition to try to scale the heights in the work I had chosen. I seized that opportunity and hopefully proceeded to plan some radical departures for The Associated Press, to which I had decided to pledge the rest of my life.

Then came the period from 1921 to 1936, which were years of fulfillment of many of those plans, executed with a pressure that furnished the momentum necessary to overrun the barriers that the practices of an earlier day had set up.

The final period, from 1936 to 1951, was the quindecennial that heralded the end. It gave me an opportunity to observe what the fulfillment of my plans had done for The Associated Press and gave me the feeling of satisfaction for which I hoped.

With that satisfaction, time rang down the curtain in 1951 on the fourth of the little dramas and ended my working years. There is a poignancy that envelops anyone when he knows he must retire from active work, leave further ideas unpresented, and be deprived of the business associations which have made his life happy, even if, as in my case, by request of his employer he has remained active six years beyond the retirement age. However, I saw every change and improvement I had been allowed to make grow to youthful strength if not maturity.

Those that were not approved may be sanctioned in time. They were thought to be too radical then. Some day they may not be so regarded. Though much was left to do, everything that had been done was a part of me, as would have been the others had I remained to gain approval to create them, outfit them and launch them.

ments to strengthen The Associated Press and keep it even further ahead of its growing competition. However, I inevitably accepted the fact that plans yet undisclosed should fade into nothingness and that I

Had I not retired, these ideas might have produced additional ele- should be content alone for what I did accomplish.

In 1943, the Board of Directors honored me with the title of executive director, a distinction which never had been conferred upon the chief executive of The Associated Press. I continued, however, in the general managership. Though I had not been asked to train a successor, I had hoped that upon my reaching retirement age, the Board of Directors would pick my successor as general manager from among The Associated Press employees.

My hope was realized in 1948 when Frank J. Starzel was selected by the Board to succeed me in the general managership. He had been with The Associated Press nineteen years. In 1942, I placed him in charge of traffic, and named him an assistant general manager in 1943.

At the Board's request, I remained executive director of the organization until 1951. For twenty-six years I had borne responsibilities that could not be shared. In discharging those responsibilities, I received the loyal support of a truly fine group of executives, the line extending from the new general manager, the executive editor, and the assistant general managers to the chiefs of bureau throughout the world. The Associated Press was benefitted by their competence and industry. It still is!

I had wanted it this way because I had tried to build for the future, hopeful that the employees, under the leadership of one of them, would project The Associated Press into a further period of development.

What I had turned over to them was an Associated Press that its members and employees unquestionably had made supreme. It was, at mid-century, without question the world's greatest news, news photo and feature service!

Its entry into the foreign field finally had been made, not to try to domineer, but solely to co-operate with the world's press. In that way The Associated Press was dedicating itself to prove my statement previously quoted, that this country's great gift to other peoples is "true and unbiased news—the highest original moral concept ever developed in America and given the world."

An interesting challenge to the supremacy of The Associated Press came in 1958 when the first corporate change in fifty years in the news agency business occurred. It was then that the news and news photo operations of the Scripps-owned United Press Associations, and the news and news photo operations of the Hearst-owned International News Service, were combined as the United Press International. The United Press Associations and the International News Service had been created some fifty years ago by E. W. Scripps and W. R. Hearst respectively primarily to serve the large newspaper chains of each of them. The Scripps interests are in control of the new corporation. But it was announced that a Hearst-owned company holds stock in it and that the latter would have three directors on its Board.

A statement of the policy that would guide the management of the United Press International appeared in *Editor and Publisher* on June 7, 1958. It follows:

United Press International—the amalgamation of United Press and International News Service—settled down this week to the self-appointed task of developing the best world-wide news service whose house flag vaunts the profit motive of private enterprise.

Frank J. Starzel (1958)—General Manager of The Associated Press.

UPI's president, Frank H. Bartholomew . . . proclaimed an intention to produce "the best news report that newspapers have ever seen," and in so doing, to demonstrate that an agency with a profit as an incentive can do better than a co-operative that works on a cost-sharing basis.

Because The Associated Press is the co-operative referred to, that statement of the United Press International's policy is a direct challenge to every member of The Associated Press. The success or failure of this announced determination to excel will, therefore, depend upon the reaction thereto on the part of the members of the co-operative non-profit organization, because it is entirely in their control to maintain its superiority. If the members lose interest in the opportunities and responsibilities inherent in that great co-operative concept, The Associated Press will have lost the quality that gave it both life and supremacy—the position which The Associated Press deservedly has held ever since it became the first national press association and first set the high standards for press association news presentation.

Upon retiring, one sometimes leaves a record of what he has done. Others may examine it if they are curious. When the end has come, he leaves off there, and that is that. But he can think hopefully of the future if the chosen work of one of his descendants should be that to which he devoted sixty years of effort. With me that could be true because my only child mothered my namesake, whose first job was as an office boy with the New York *Sun,* then with the New York *Illustrated Daily News.*

On Election Night in 1950, he was on duty at the *Daily News.* His job was to take Associated Press and United Press copy from the teletypes for the editors. During a rest period, he wrote this letter to Charles E. Honce, now a retired Associated Press executive:

Many times when I brought in both AP and UP copy, the two editors who were reading it spiked the United Press and used The Associated Press. The AP copy was faster and more complete. Each time this was done I got a funny feeling in the pit of my stomach. Here were two of the hardest-boiled guys I ever expect to see in the newspaper business relying on The Associated Press to get them the fastest and most accurate accounts of the election. I guess I felt funny because I am the grandson of the man who has for so many years been the top man and to me the very symbol of The Associated Press. I saw the result of his many years of hard work as they were flashed onto The Associated Press teletype in the ticker room. As I carried them to the various editors, I almost felt as if I were working for him.

At seventeen years of age, he went from the New York *Daily News* into the Marines and to Korea, where his spleen and other items of his innards were shot out by a slug that went through his body, missing his heart by one-fourth of an inch. Recovering, he returned and entered Indiana University, my alma mater, which is also that of his mother, as it was of my father and mother. He majored in journalism and graduated with the idea that journalism would be his career. Without my knowledge, he sought and obtained a reportorial job with the Columbus (Indiana) *Republican* just sixty years after I left that paper to work as a reporter on the Indianapolis *Press*.

Maybe news work is in his blood. Maybe in time he will prove that it is. If not, maybe one of my other two grandsons will. Again maybe not. But if one of them does, my love of news work will be reincarnated.

As a part of the drama of that quindecennial which was the twilight of my active life, The Associated Press directors as individuals—my great and good friends—had privately given dinners, with me as their guest of honor in 1945, and again in 1950. They were thoughtfully suggested and arranged by President McLean. At the 1950 dinner they presented me with a beautiful silver plaque inscribed as follows:

To
KENT COOPER
from the members of the Board of Directors
THE ASSOCIATED PRESS
on the completion of twenty-five years as
general manager and executive director
with warm appreciation for his services and leadership
and affectionate greetings to him as a friend
his associates on the Board pay this tribute.

Seven years after Robert McLean personally selected this token for me, Benjamin M. McKelway succeeded him as AP president. McKelway was elected editor of the Washington *Star* by its Board of Directors in 1945. Frank B. Noyes was president of the Evening Star Newspaper Company at the time. If Mr. Noyes were alive, he would be proud of his protégé's election to the presidency of The Associated Press. McKelway is a great-nephew of St. Clair McKelway, the famous editor of the Brooklyn *Eagle* at the turn of the century, who, like Noyes, was an incorporator in 1900 of the present AP. Thus, the new president's feeling for the association is deeply grounded.

Naturally, because of my close association first with President Noyes

Robert McLean (1944)—
Generous in his tributes.

Benjamin M. McKelway
(1957)—Nurtured in The
Associated Press traditions.

and then with President McLean, their tributes publicly expressed shall ever be thankfully remembered. I have previously quoted what Mr. Noyes said in 1930. At the annual luncheon in 1943, Mr. McLean introduced me as a speaker with this:

We have another who has dedicated his life to The Associated Press. Mr. Noyes has just spoken of the rare genius and ability of the man who is the operating head of The Associated Press and who, by practicing what he preaches, as well as preaching what he practices, gives reality to an ideal.

Kent Cooper needs no introduction to this gathering. That we admire him and his ability and cherish both is only a part of the story. He is the inspiration, guide, counselor and friend and the driving force behind those very remarkable men flung across the seven seas whose product, blended together under his direction, is the news report of The Associated Press.

At both private dinners some remarkable tributes were paid to me and on both occasions I expressed my profound appreciation. I did not, however, at the conclusion of my active years, have an opportunity formally and publicly to thank all of The Associated Press members in a similar vein. I merely vanished without ceremony.

But if I could publicly have expressed myself to Associated Press members and employees as I do now to those who read these lines, I would have said that if they wanted to know what had motivated me in my endeavors on their behalf, it was that I did not strive to see how much good I could do for myself, but how much good I could do for them through their Associated Press.

This, then, must stand as my farewell to all Associated Press members, their managing editors, and last but not least, to all Associated Press employees.

I have the highest conception of the mission of newspapers. It was an honor to serve them for nearly sixty years. Profoundly I feel that they must prosper so that they may continue to inform the public. For that reason until my dying day I shall yearn to be instrumental in advancing their welfare.

As for the future, my thoughts rest hopefully but with humility upon one sentence referring to me which I have previously quoted from Malcolm W. Bingay's impressions of the first Associated Press Managing Editors Association meeting at French Lick in 1933:

He has implanted so firmly his ideals that a faithful staff will carry on long years after this generation has passed.

In 1958, just a quarter of a century after that French Lick meeting, Charles A. Fell, executive editor of the Birmingham (Alabama) *News,* declared:

Kent Cooper is the man who led our American journalism into a new

Sir William John Haley (1952)—
"From the Manchester Guardian
to editor of the London Times!"

era of enterprise, comprehensiveness and effectiveness. All of us owe him
a very great debt of gratitude.

Another reason for satisfaction in those last fifteen years was making the acquaintance in 1942 of William J. Haley, of the Manchester
Guardian, now Sir William John Haley, editor of the London *Times.*
He was then a member of the Reuter Board, one-half of whose directors represent the Press Association, which is made up of the British
provincial press. The other half is composed of representatives of the
London Newspaper Proprietors Association.

Haley had come to me as the Reuter Board's representative to talk
over the future relations of our two agencies. We became fast friends.
A forward-looking contract which he and I drew up was promptly
approved by the Boards of Directors of both institutions. It was more
agreeable to Reuters and replaced the one I had made with Sir Roderick Jones in 1934. Thereafter, I was able to renew friendship with
the talented Christopher Chancellor, Reuters' new general manager,
and future amicable relations between our two agencies were assured.

Chancellor's friend, Lord Rothermere, proprietor of the London
Daily Mail, is a director of Reuters. In New York in the fall of 1946,
my wife and I had a dinner for him. Afterward Arthur Hays Sulzberger, publisher of the *New York Times,* one of the guests, wrote me:

Dear Kent:

I feel that one of your friends ought to put in writing for you his memory of the compliment Lord Rothermere paid to you at the dinner at which he was the guest of you and Sally.

My memory of it is this:

You said that insofar as it was practical to do so, Reuters has been transformed from a privately owned, profit-making news agency into a practical co-operative in which most all of the British press had joined. And you complimented Lord Rothermere on this accomplishment and said you felt this had permanently brought a close tie between Reuters and The Associated Press. Lord Rothermere referred to your remarks as follows:

"Mr. Kent Cooper has paid high compliment to Reuters and the British newspaper publishers for having transformed Reuters into a truly co-operative effort patterned insofar as practical after The Associated Press of America. I want to say with emphasis that this was really an accomplishment of Mr. Kent Cooper, for it was he who showed us, not only that it ought to be done, but how to do it, and I for one feel eternally grateful to Mr. Cooper for his interest. I am sure that I speak for all of our associates of the British press who are charting new accomplishments for Reuters."

Faithfully yours,
Arthur Hays Sulzberger

Arthur H. Sulzberger (1935)—
He wrote a welcome letter.

What Rothermere said so enthusiastically that night presaged the honor that was to come to him two years later, and to me five years later. For The Associated Press Board invited Rothermere to be the guest of honor and speaker at The Associated Press centenary luncheon in April, 1948. Rothermere accepted. In his address on that occasion, at which Christopher Chancellor also was a guest of honor, he said that he had brought an invitation from the Reuters Board for me to be the guest of honor at Reuters' centenary dinner in London in the summer of 1951.

This was recognition of me from another part of the world. That it came from Reuters, with whose former managing director I had struggled for fifteen years for the right of The Associated Press to serve its own news throughout the world, brought me deep satis-

Reuter Centenary (1951)—Distinguished guests. To the left of K.C. (speaker): *Mrs. Geoffrey Fisher, wife of the Archbishop of Canterbury; Prime Minister Attlee; Lady Dumas; Viscount Rothermere; Mrs. Cooper; W. A. Hawkins, chairman of the Press Association of Great Britain; Viscountess Rothermere; Sir Anthony Eden; Sir Christopher Chancellor; Mrs. Attlee* (seated at table but not shown) *Sir Lloyd Dumas, chairman; the Archbishop of Canterbury; the late Devadas Gandhi of the Hindustan* Times, *son of the Mahatma; Herbert Morrison, British Secretary of State for Foreign Affairs; Lady Chancellor.*

faction. To be thus publicly acclaimed abroad reminded me that "a prophet is not without honor save in his own country."

As Sir Christopher Chancellor said at that dinner in July, 1951, at London's Grosvenor House, the guests included the Prime Minister, "luminaries of the British Diplomatic Corps, the Archbishop of Canterbury, the Lord Chief Justice of England and other pillars of Church and State; great names of science, the arts, letters, stage and screen; the chiefs of Britain's armed forces, leaders of industry, of banking and finance, shipping and aviation; the City of London in the person of its Lord Mayor; the City of Edinburgh in the person of its Lord Provost; leading politicians of all parties and the heads of the great government departments of England; poets, scholars, lawyers, leaders in the world of entertainment and sport; illustrious guests from overseas—from all

parts of the Commonwealth, from the United States and from other countries."

Lord Rothermere, introducing me, said in part:

> We could not have as our distinguished guest tonight a man who is held in higher esteem or respect in the world of news agency work than Mr. Kent Cooper. He has directed the fortunes of The Associated Press for many years, and he is the architect of The Associated Press as it is today.
>
> He has held to the ideals for which he has worked. Most of you will have known Mr. Kent Cooper's book, called *Barriers Down,* but Mr. Kent Cooper, throughout his life has fought for the liberty of news; and by liberty of news he means the right to collect and transmit news for the benefit of the people everywhere. . . .
>
> It is therefore wholly fitting that he should be our honored guest tonight. He is our good friend and he will always be welcome here whenever he comes [applause].

In acknowledging Lord Rothermere's generous words and in proposing the toast of "Reuters," I paid tribute to the great British news agency, its trustees, directors and to its general manager, Sir Christopher Chancellor. Sir Lloyd Dumas, of Adelaide, Australia, chairman of the Australian Associated Press and a director of Reuters, who presided at the dinner, replied to the toast. He delineated the role the new Reuters is playing in the news agency field.

Sir Christopher Chancellor, proposing the toast of "The Guests," said:

> I address my final words to the Prime Minister. Some time ago I was sitting in Mr. Kent Cooper's office in New York. Suddenly he said to me: "Tell me now—does your Government really leave you alone? Does it never try to interfere with the news you send abroad?" My answer was as follows: "I was in charge at Reuters before the present Government came into power and I have been in charge all through Mr. Attlee's premiership—never once have I known any pressure or interference with the news that Reuters send out to the world." [Applause.]
>
> I recall Mr. Cooper's manifest pleasure when I gave him this answer. Mr. Attlee feels, I believe, just as strongly as Mr. Cooper that governments—all governments—should keep their hands off the news [applause].

In responding to this toast, the Prime Minister, the Right Honorable Clement R. Attlee, concluded:

I was particularly glad to hear what Mr. Chancellor told us of his conversation with Mr. Kent Cooper. This Government has, and in the future will, leave Reuters entirely alone [applause].

The last to speak was the Archbishop of Canterbury, Dr. Geoffrey Fisher. He proposed the toast of "Our Reuter Hosts" and seemed astonished when only a dozen arose. They were the directors and trustees of Reuters who had given the dinner. The Archbishop said:

I have a very pleasant and happy task to perform: that is on behalf of the vast multitude here present to thank the gallant few for their hospitality. I say the gallant few because, as you saw just now, when the toast was that of our hosts to the guests here tonight, those who rose to do us this honor were not more than a dozen [laughter]. And it is to that gallant dozen that I now direct your attention that we may express to them the gratitude we feel for their hospitality to us here tonight. And for many other things. What shall we thank them for?

First, I am going to thank them for making me read the book *Reuters Century,* which otherwise but for the fact I was coming to this dinner tonight I should never have read [laughter]. And I am delighted to have read it. I found it of absorbing interest. I always find it greatly interesting to read about the funny pursuits of other people. And I entered a realm in that book completely unknown to me before. And when I thus entered a little way into the experiences of other people I found how they behave, I put the book down and said: "Well, that's splendid, but thank goodness I am not a newspaperman!" [laughter]. As no doubt when you read your theological books [prolonged laughter]. . . . well, I won't finish that sentence.

But as I remember my reading of *Reuters Century,* I confess that I find myself surprised and even taken aback tonight because here everything is billing and cooing between Reuters and The Associated Press of the United States. As I read the book they were bitter enemies, and Mr. Kent Cooper led the fight from the other side [laughter and applause]. Well, I am very glad to find that in one sphere of human endeavor peace has supervened.

Then, secondly, we have to thank our hosts and Reuters for the news, for the right of the people to know. And I humbly but reluctantly join in thanking them for it [laughter]. Personally I confess that I am simply appalled by the amount of the news and the speed with which it is thrown at us. Not long ago I was for four weeks on board ship going to Australia and four weeks coming back. The only news we got was from the ship's daily bulletin on typewritten sheets. I read it the first day and then I said "why?" [laughter] . . . and I never read it again [laughter]. And I then found if you didn't read the news, there was no news! [laughter]. And I suddenly realized that if nobody else read the news either, there would never be any world news, and Mr. Attlee, our Prime Minister here, could shut up shop. And we should all get on [laughter] . . . I mean that we would all be so much happier if we didn't know what everybody else was doing all over the world.

There is a queer kind of misapprehension that if you know all about everybody else you get on much better. As a matter of fact, you don't [laughter] because your instinct is that as soon as you know what the government of another nation is doing you want to tell them not to keep on doing it, and then all kinds of international friction arises. So you understand why it is with a certain reluctance that I join in gratitude to Reuters [prolonged laughter]. . . .

And then, finally, and now wholeheartedly, we all thank Reuters and salute Reuters for its integrity, a word that has been used several times here tonight. And that is a very real reason for our profound gratitude to a great institution [applause]. You cannot have integrity without freedom. It is only free men who can show themselves to be deserving of fundamental integrity. And freedom and integrity always have gone together, though freedom is always a temptation and does not necessarily mean integrity as well.

It is the triumph of Reuters that they have fought always for these two combined positions—freedom and integrity [applause]. Impartiality in reporting is not so much an intelligent virtue as a spiritual one. That is why in the office I hold I am glad to thank Reuters for this magnificent impartiality and sincerity [prolonged applause].

There was something so genuine and inspiring about this recognition of me that I wished all my friends from home had been there, as were two Associated Press directors, Harry F. Byrd, Jr., and Paul Miller, accompanied by their wives; also Mr. and Mrs. Robert U.

Brown. Mr. Brown was there as the president and editor of *Editor & Publisher,* the trade journal of American newspaperdom.

In a way I had the feeling that evening of having come home after a long, very long absence, so enthusiastically was I greeted. Perhaps my feeling arose from the depth of time because all my ancestors on both sides of my family came to America nearly 200 years ago from England and Scotland—the Ogilvies and the Greens, besides the Coopers.

None of them ever went back, but one of their descendants did, indeed. Then, too, I had been honored in the city which is the birthplace of my wife—long since an American citizen.

And so this story of some sixty years of newspaper and press association activity comes to a close leaving only a postscript to tell of my boyhood days. In finally deciding to write what I have, and in reflecting upon the support my wife got from many others to encourage me to tell of those sixty years, I recall one of the most rewarding letters I ever received. It was written some fifteen years ago by M. M. Oppegard, publisher of the Grand Forks (N.D.) *Herald,* who was an Associated Press employee until 1929. Unfortunately for me, I have only seen him casually at two or three Associated Press meetings during the last thirty years. The letter follows:

Dear KC:

I sincerely hope every publisher and editor of AP newspapers reads your report in the annual volume which I received today. Once more it demonstrated the warm affection, the real pride and comforting loyalty you have for the men and women of The AP. It should be an inspiration to The Associated Press membership to know the affairs of our great mutual undertaking are in your capable hands.

It seems to me much too little has been said about the many things I think we should all know and appreciate concerning the part KC has in this inspiring picture. True, we resolve at our state meetings in general terms, and we point with pride quite appropriately, but too few of us outside The Associated Press personnel really see the picture in its true perspective.

In your praise of the men in dangerous foreign service, as well as in less hazardous tasks on the home front, there is written between the lines the real reason why such praise is possible and why your obvious pride is justified.

I know, and all AP men know, the real reason these men and women "come through" unfailingly. It is their direct contact with the "KC spirit," something even greater than The AP spirit, though they accept them as one.

There is not one among them, I am sure, who has not in his heart a stirring desire to do you proud rather than win recognition from editors and publishers, whose knowledge of the men and scrutiny of their work can only be incidental to their own tasks.

I wish the part you have played in molding these AP men could be better known to those same editors and publishers. I realize they voice their opinion and express their satisfaction in this regard, and I do not question their sincerity. But I wish they could all have heard you say, as I did, at an AP employee meeting, that you hoped we all would have a passion for The AP that was second only to the sexual urge—and we were young!

Members and employees of The Associated Press, as well as some of the haggard gentlemen in other news-gathering organizations, know whose genius is responsible for the bettering changes so constantly made in The AP, each lending some new polish to the best news report in the world.

In the years I have known you, from the time I first really met you, down through the years that have ripened the admiration I feel for you, I have felt you had something known best to the fortunate AP employees; of The AP membership not many can have felt its full import, for only men you have guided can know it best. So far, in anything I have read, it has been inadequately told.

That brings me to the purpose of this letter. It is the suggestion that you write, not necessarily your own autobiography, though that would serve admirably, but at least a report on a third of a century in the important field of news gathering.

No one is better equipped to do it. There are so many angles that need publicity. I know, for instance, that Alexander Graham Bell—or Don Ameche—invented the telephone, but you discovered its full use.

This is no bunk; I have nothing to gain by apple-polishing. The ideas you have applied to each phase of The AP that has been your immediate job furnish a fountain of inspiration. It is true that in your book, *Barriers Down,* there is casual mention of some of the things you did, but you hardly skim the surface.

Take the matter of centralization of the AP's national set-up. You will well remember the turmoil of the old days, when each division made up its own rules, frequently in conflict; when a newspaperman had to be a good bookkeeper first; when a bureau had to fight to get anything into the service, for only a few Big Towns were thought to contain anything newsworthy.

The AP election service became a national institution and accepted as official; the financial service topped its sphere—all these things didn't just happen; somebody was pushing more than buttons to set them up.

The change in the concept of news—that maybe the thing behind it was more important than the public recital.

These are rather rambling thoughts, but you have veritable footnotes of history on which to hang your tale, and I don't mean monkeywise!

I am so enthusiastic about the idea that I will even promise to buy a copy—that is, of course, if you will autograph it.

28

POSTSCRIPT

I HAVE INTENTIONALLY left until last the brief telling of a part of my life that I have reason to cherish—my childhood. Those were the years during which I had the boon of living in the home of my high-minded, well-educated, devoted, praying father and mother and three sisters, Maud, Bertha and Beryl, who never resented the special attention given their only brother, younger than they. They probably realized he needed it!

I am sure that Father and Mother must have mutually felt more love and devotion for each other in the last decade of their short lives, when they saw the end coming, than they did when they were first married. Their mental capacities were superb. They shared the joys of reading to each other the finest English and Latin literature. Father had a photographic memory. He could write out a long speech, read it aloud three times and then recite it correctly word for word, as mother "held copy" on him.

A silver-tongued orator, a contemporary in Congress with another orator, William Jennings Bryan, Father was declared by his congressional friends to be Bryan's equal, even surpassing the Nebraskan in the sincerity of his manner. When in 1896 Bryan was first nominated for the presidency, Father's health had begun to fail. Three years later, at forty-eight years of age, he was gone. The lonely, lovely lady that she was, Mother followed him five years later.

Whatever educational and religious grounding I got in my life came more from Father and Mother than from my schooling or

Mother

Father

church. That is why I write of these precious years with appreciative reverence. In those surroundings, I was unconsciously girding myself for the future, only a few peaks of which I have briefly mentioned in this story of my working years. Having participated in a wide world of activity for more than a half-century, no single volume that I could write could tell it all. But this part of it must be told.

Two of the six winters Father was in Congress we spent in Washington. It was there that I first became acquainted with the daily *Congressional Record*. And for the benefit of all children whose parents receive it, I report finding a good use for the *Record*. Father believed in not sparing the rod. Once when I was due for punishment, he sent me to the basement to wait while he cut a switch from a magnolia tree. There I saw several old copies of the *Record* and slipped one of them inside the seat of my pants. With the first lash of

The Cooper Family (1886)—
Mother; Kent; Beryl; Bertha; Maud; Father.

the punishing switch the sound was different. So was the feeling. In fact, there was no feeling, but I howled just the same. By the fourth application of the switch, Father became suspicious of the sound, reached in and got the *Record,* whereupon he broke into laughter.

Nearly seventy years ago he regaled the cloakroom of the U. S. House of Representatives with the little story of how I had found a practical use for the *Congressional Record.*

Of all there was to do and see in Washington, I then liked riding the cable cars best. I always sat in the open front car where the motorman gripped and released the cable. Once, Father said I could take the cable car down to the Navy Yard to hear the Marine Band practice. As I ran to catch the front cable car after it had been started, my hand caught the railing but my foot missed the running board.

A bearded gentleman in uniform quickly grabbed me under both arms and easily lifted me over him to an inside seat. He was not a large man; I sat there thinking how strong he was to lift me that easily. When I got to the band practice, I realized that he was the band's conductor.

When I told Father what had happened, he said John Philip Sousa probably saved my life. I'd never heard the name. Father was grateful, took me to call on the great musician and told him I said he seemed to be very strong.

"From constantly waving my arms while conducting, perhaps," Sousa said.

They talked for a while. Referring to the band, Sousa told Father of the time General Nelson A. Miles, then head of the U. S. Army, a great general and well known as a disciplinarian, heard a Marine Band concert for the first time. Afterward, Sousa asked him what he thought of the band.

"Very good, I guess," Miles said. "But the discipline is bad. Every time you turn and face the musicians on the left, the ones on the right stop playing, and vice versa."

I recall three incidents that happened to me prior to my tenth birthday, when we were once again back in Indiana. Two of them may be thought commendable. As to the last, well, I am not *sure!*

The first was when my uncle, Howard Duffy, let me help him "keep store" evenings after supper during the pre-Christmas rush. He assigned me to the China Shop corner. My duty was to welcome a customer and hold on to him or her while I rang a small bell to

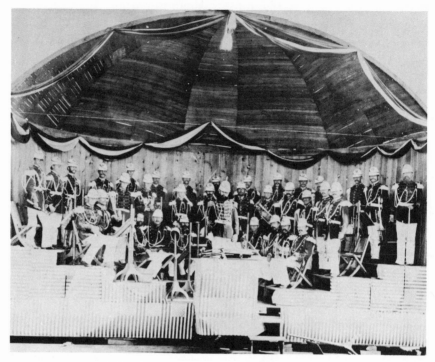

John Philip Sousa (center) *and the U.S. Marine Band
(1890)—The bearded gentleman's arms were strong.*

attract one of the grown-up clerks or my uncle, who would take over
and make the sale. On Christmas Eve, my uncle said I could have
either a dollar or I could select a piece of china. He chuckled with a
beloved uncle's satisfaction when I chose a piece of china with a $5
tag on it. I wrapped it in pink tissue paper, took it home and presented
it to my mother, saying: "This is for you. I got it with the first money
I ever earned." I shall never forget my mother's happiness.

The second was a plea that I be permitted to join the Church even
though I was not ten years of age. My sisters had joined and I was
forlorn about being barred as too young. When I pleaded, Mother
asked me why I insisted. I thought of the hymn with the words "to
wash my sins away," so I told her I wanted to be baptized to wash
my sins away. That pleased her. But still hoping to delay my baptis-
mal ceremony, she asked: "But what would you do to gain forgiveness

if you sin after you are baptized?" My answer was: "I would pray."
Why I spoke those three words at the age of nine I have no idea. I
must have gotten a little help from Divinity itself, for I uttered them,
and I was baptized.

The third incident involved something of tragedy and venegeance.
Until it happened I never knew how high a cat could jump flat-footed
in one leap. I found out because I had a pet rabbit confined in a
six-foot-high, chicken-wire pen open at the top. When I acquired the
rabbit, my cat humped its back in a plain show of angry jealousy
every time I entered the rabbit's pen to feed and pet it. I had no idea
a cat could leap over a six-foot-high netting, but as I witnessed later,
that cat could jump still higher. One morning I found the bunny
dead and rather badly chewed up. The cat looked guilty. I con-
demned him, got my shiny new hatchet, stroked the cat with apparent
affection with my left hand, put his tail over a wooden block and
whacked it off close up with one blow.

Up from the center of the rabbit's pen to the low eaves of the
one-story barn went the cat in one leap. It must have been seven
feet. The second leap took him a greater distance, not so high, but
over the top of the roof into the alley. Transmogrified as he was, he
never came back. I had neither a rabbit nor a pseudo rabbit in the
form of a cat without a tail, as I had planned.

Mother was horrified. She wrote Father, who was in Washington
attending sessions of Congress, that I was "developing a hard, cruel
disposition. He cut off his cat's tail because it killed his rabbit."
Father's reaction was one of high glee. "The boy has a sense of
justice," he wrote. Because Father saw it that way, the rest of the
family forgave me.

The Columbus (Indiana) of my boyhood was a quiet, God-fearing
community in which life flowed sweetly without any of the alarms
such as those which arise from the present-day global turmoil. Like
much of the rest of the United States, Indiana knew about the foreign
world but had little contact with it. The Middle Western belt of states,
of which she was a part, lay peacefully between the eastern seaboard
and the rough and ready West. She listened contentedly to the crackle
of the growing corn in her well-tended acres.

In the 1880's, with a population of 4,000, my native town was as
good a little place as any for a growing boy. The idea that public

Before the cat was transmogrified, it looked up at its master.

recreation facilities had to be furnished to save its youth from crime never had been heard of. We just took our fun where we found it. As gas lights gave way to electricity, the board and gravel sidewalks gave way to cement.

Those who sported the now long forgotten "ordinary," or one big wheel and one little wheel bicycles, found the cement walks smoother riding than the muddy streets. We called those bikes "head breakers" because if one of them hit a large enough rock in the road, the rider would fall forward on his head if his arms didn't save him. Later came the "safeties," the present-day bicycle with two wheels the same size. With their advent, bicycle traffic on the sidewalks presented a hazard for pedestrians, so a city ordinance—the first time I ever heard that word—put the bicycles back into the streets.

Then came the roller-skate craze. The cement sidewalks served very well except in rainy weather, at which time I would ask three or four of my pals up to the Cooper attic, which had a good strong floor in spite of the cracks between the boards. It never occurred to us that the noise of the four or five pairs of roller skates made any difference to my family down below. It was noisy to us but we didn't mind, and Mother hadn't complained. Then one day I took off my skates and went down the attic stairs to ask Mother if the boys could stay for supper.

On the second floor, where Mother was, the sound from above was deafening. I could not speak loudly enough for her to hear me. Her back was toward the door as I entered, so she didn't even see me. There she sat sewing. She was in the little rocking chair, an heirloom in which her grandmother had rocked my grandmother to sleep, and in which Mother had rocked her four children. I went around in front of her to try to make her hear me. She had a sweet smile of contentment.

When she looked up and saw I was talking to her she took wads of cotton from both ears, smiled and said: "You boys must be having a good time." I asked about the boys staying for supper and she said: "Yes, if they will go home and ask their mothers." Back went the cotton in her ears. I climbed the stairs to the attic skating rink, suddenly conscious of the terrible noise. I couldn't stand it. After that, on rainy days we used the attic only if Mother was attending a missionary society meeting.

Summers with their long days were glorious; winters with their short days were not. School was out at four P.M. and it was dark by five—not nearly enough playtime, especially for me, because I had to go several blocks each afternoon to bring Moxie, our cow, home to milk. She spent the night in our barn, and before school each day I took her back to the pasture. That all sounds very easy but it had its distractions. For the pasture was an old graveyard on East 10th Street. All the bodies were said to have been moved to the new cemetery, Garland Brook, two miles east of town, but I doubted it. That is, I doubted it when I played until after dark without having gone to get Moxie.

To get to the gate of the abandoned cemetery, I had to go up an alley that seemed awfully dark and very long, though it was only a half-block. There were barns on each side of it, but they were used only as chicken houses. The chickens, of course, were supposed to be asleep after dark, but some of them must have had insomnia, perhaps indigestion, for I found that an alarmed chicken a few feet away from a graveyard can make more eerie sounds than any spook that ever spooked!

As I ran down the dark alley, however, I was sure of one thing: I would not have to go into the abandoned graveyard to find Moxie. She always was obligingly right at the gate waiting patiently for me to open it, apparently as glad to see me as I was to see her. And no guardian assigned to protect a child could have given a greater sense of security than Moxie gave me when, after I opened the gate, she trudged along beside me back to our barn.

When I got home, I told Mother that I didn't like that graveyard pasture. She said we could not have Moxie unless we had a pasture for her, and asked me if I wanted Mr. Koehler to resume bringing us milk each day. When I thought of how Mr. Koehler drove by and merely rang a big bell, which brought Mother or my sisters out with two crocks to be filled with milk and carried back into the house, I decided I didn't want them to do that again. So Moxie and I continued back and forth in daylight and darkness to the old graveyard pasture.

As time went on, nothing happened and I forgot my fears. Mother said that Father had bought the pasture for practically nothing because no one wanted to build a house in an abandoned graveyard. Seventy years later, when I last saw it, only one venturesome home owner had built a house in one corner of it. I am sure he didn't know it once had been a graveyard!

In 1890, I spent the summer vacation with Uncle Henry Rhorer on a farm forty miles away, near Bloomington, Indiana. In a large grove 1,000 feet from his house I picked up half a dollar near a rotten log. I had no more than started to leave with my treasure when I stepped into a bumblebee nest. The bees pursued me and stung me many times. When I reached the house, my grandmother, wanting to take my mind off my wounds, comforted me with:

"One bumblebee sting means good luck. With all the stings you got, no telling what luck you'll have. Why," she asked, "don't you go back to that spot and dig? You may find a fortune."

I got a kitchen knife and went back. Carefully avoiding the side of the log where the bees' nest was, I stuck the knife in the ground and flipped up three pieces of silver. One of them was a French five-franc piece with the date of 1807; another was a five-peseta Spanish coin of 1812; the third was a Mexican five-peseta piece of 1811. My cries brought my uncle and a hired hand. They dug a hole big enough to bury an elephant. Altogether, 104 pieces of silver were found. I thought I was rich until a week later. Father came and said I must turn the money over to my uncle because it was his since it was found on his grounds.

Meanwhile, the *Courier-Journal* of Louisville, Kentucky, not far away, had sent a reporter to "interview" me and make drawings of the coins. It was the first time my name appeared in any newspaper. The reporter was a good one. Even at that age I was fascinated with what he wrote. It was about me! The reporter made the story good by posing the probability that some soldier had returned from the Mexican War, camped on the spot, buried his treasure, gotten sick and died there. I have since reflected that the reporter did a good job of making a possibility a probability.

When I returned to school that fall, I became aware that a boy in my class, instead of staying in school until four o'clock with the rest of us, was allowed to leave at three-forty-five P.M. to carry a paper route. He was let out early because he had to fold his papers before he could deliver them. I decided there and then that I had to have a newspaper route. Out of school fifteen minutes early and with a job—both were glorious to contemplate!

Not, however, until the next year, when I was eleven years old, did I get the job when the boy's family moved to another town. He sold me his route for $3. During that first week, I would leave school at three-forty-five P.M. and hurry with him to the newspaper office. He showed me how to fold the papers and did the route once with me to introduce me to his 100 customers. They were all on "the other side of the tracks." The introduction was important to him and to me. Each customer had to know I was authorized to collect the 10¢ a week every Saturday morning for the paper. I kept 3¢ of it. My first week's earnings went to pay for the route I had bought. By the second or third day, there was no longer any doubt about it. The smell of printer's ink had me, and I never recovered.

Cartoon by Kessler (1927)—"Out of school fifteen minutes early and a job—wonderful to contemplate."

During that summer vacation, I worked as a printer's devil and was paid $1 a week besides what I collected from my newspaper route. I was something of a nuisance in the composing room because I started to make suggestions to the foreman on how to improve matters. He said I really would not be initiated as a printer unless I ate some lead sawdust out of the miter box. I believed him, did it, and got a stomachache that sent me home.

The next day I was allowed to start "sticking" type, and I didn't like it. Until I had to take each letter out of the case and "stick" it, I never realized there were so many words eight to twelve letters long. I decided I would prefer being a reporter to a typesetter. Before the summer was over, I asked the editor if I could be a reporter at the $1 a week I was getting for being a printer's devil. I got the job and began to write in a style that amused the editor and brought remarks from the newspaper's readers.

Posted daily at the Columbus, Indiana, railway station, I made note of passengers who took the trains for Indianapolis, Louisville, or even nearby Franklin and Seymour. I thought it a waste of time to be forever writing that a citizen "took the train for Indianapolis" or another "left today by train for Louisville," etc. Of course, as everyone knew, in order to get to any of these places, one had to take the train, it being the only way to get there, besides walking or riding horseback. So I wrote that so and so "Indianapolized today" or "Franklined today" or "Seymoured today" or even "Louisvilled today." Others before may have verbalized names of towns and cities, but I had never heard of it being done. I thought of it as a way to speed up "sticking" type and still tell all the news there was in that kind of an item.

When I was twelve years of age, something happened that diluted my interest in newspaper work. Father bought me a second-hand violin for $5 and a 50¢ book of instructions. The bow was a new one. When I scraped it across the strings, it didn't make a sound. The next day being Sunday, I asked the church organist what could be wrong. "Put some resin on the bow," he said. On Monday I bought some resin for a nickel, and the sound came out of the "pie box." As the book of instructions had said nothing about putting resin on the bow, I decided the book wasn't worth the 50¢.

Father was a lover of country "jig" music. In Hoosierdom they were called "hoe-downs." To Father's disappointment, I never learned to play one. To Mother's disappointment, I preferred music to my homework. I liked and played Strauss' waltzes and Sousa's marches, to which the one-step was danced. As a result, with the aid of a chum who played the guitar, I soon began furnishing music for small dance parties—60¢ a night for me and 40¢ for the guitarist. From that, it was only a step to become a fiddler in the theatre orchestra, where I got $1 a night and a ticket in the parquet circle, which sometimes I gave to a girl, oftener to my friend Roy Jackson.

Wanting to emulate my piano-playing sisters, who were laboriously learning that instrument with the aid of a teacher twice a week, I took up the piano "by ear" and soon annoyed them by playing faster than they did the simple melodies they were practicing.

I also put my piano playing to a novel test. It had been easy for me and my guitar-playing friend to serenade the girls we knew. It was also very old-fashioned and therefore not novel. So I decided to put a piano on Mr. Schultz's dray for serenading. The novelty of that appealed to the piano mover, the music-loving Mr. Schultz. To anyone who has not heard the dulcet tones of a piano in the open air in a quiet little town on a summer night, I can say that he has missed a very lovely part of music that cannot be heard otherwise, even though the music be rendered amateurishly.

I got the Clevenger music store to let me have a piano to put on the Schultz dray, and at eleven o'clock I started out to serenade the town. Mr. Schultz charged $1 for the hour from eleven to twelve P.M., and Columbus got a serenade, amateurish as it was, the like of which had never been heard there before.

The next day, our town was talking about it, and Mr. Clevenger had the idea of putting an advertisement in the paper on which I was a reporter that summer. The advertisement declared that the piano used for the musical treat which awakened the townsmen the night before was from Mr. Clevenger's store. He told me he sold the piano the next day.

All of this fun serenading and theatre fiddling was dividing my interest between newspapering and music, with the latter in the ascendancy. Then I began to compose tunes. When my first little composition was played by the orchestra in Crump's Opera House in my home town, I was sure I would embark upon a musical career.

I wrote words for my music and vice versa—I never stopped to think which came first. But my invasion into musical composition began, when I was fourteen years old, with "My Village Girl." The theme of the lyric was that an ambitious small-town boy of those days had told his sweetheart to wait until he went to the big city, got rich, came back and made her his bride.

Neither the words nor the lilt of the melody pleased my dear mother. She was convinced that I would forever be the town fiddler. To me at the time, however, that was as worthy an ambition as most of the people in that small town had achieved.

But my carefree days ended when I had to face life's realities with the failing health of my father. I began to realize what he meant about responsibility when he wrote me a letter from Washington, during the last term he served in Congress, to which he had been elected as a representative. I still have the letter, written upon "House of Representatives, U.S." stationery. In the upper left-hand corner is a picture of the Capitol. The letter follows:

February 18, 1895

Master Kent Cooper,
Columbus, Indiana

My dear boy:

I have a letter from your mamma this evening and she tells me that you have been a good boy. I am so glad. I know we cannot be always good, however hard we try, but we can keep on trying.

Somehow I think more and more about you the older I get. One reason is I suppose that you are coming into man's estate and will very soon have to decide for yourself what kind of a man you will be. On the other hand, I am getting more and more to feel that it will not be long until you will have to fill my place. I want you to take up the struggle where I leave off.

You are able to keep up with your classes, and I have never had the least doubt that if you would devote your energies to your studies, you could easily be the smartest boy in your room. Your teachers have always said so. And yet you have not done well. This you can correct. If you are a true manly determined boy, you can pull up out of the hole and surprise the whole school and make me very happy. The greatest difficulty with a boy of your age is the disposition to incline to do silly things to get some silly boy or girl to laugh and to be looking about the room or playing with your books or papers wasting time and disturbing others. The mind of a boy is like a colt. It wants to kick up and run away from work. It wants to think about what may be going on outside or in some other part of the room. The mind must be "broke to work." We have to learn how to think. That's what schools are for.

Now try it. Put your hands up to your eyes, just as we put blind bridles on a foolish horse, one that wants to shy at everything, and then shut out all that is going on about you. And then think with all your mind on the lesson before you. Don't think of anything else until you know that lesson and know it well. Remember that everything in acquiring an education goes on like the building of a house. What you learn in one room makes a foundation for that which you are to build on in the next. Now if you have not understood or have forgotten or only poorly learned the work in the lower grades, you will never get a good safe building up.

I will soon be at home and then we will talk it over.

Good night.

Lovingly,

Geo W. Cooper

When Father came home a month after that letter was written, he seemed to me not to be the animated man he always had been. He had suffered defeat for re-election in the Republican congressional landslide in 1894, four months before. That hurt his pride, for he was sensitive. But worse than that, as the panic of those years impoverished the nation, he had disagreed with his friend Bryan on the latter's campaign for the "free and unlimited coinage of silver." Father knew that adoption of the Bryan policy would mean the end of the gold standard. He was, at the time, Indiana's outstanding Democrat who wanted to safeguard "sound money." Always having been a Democrat, it hurt him deeply when he decided he would have to bolt the Party.

Answering a call of his Democratic friends who believed as he did, he agreed, in spite of his failing health, to run for governor in 1896 on a Democratic sound-money platform. Though he knew he had no chance of election with a divided Democratic Party, he nevertheless felt it his duty to stump the state, and he did so with all the strength he could summon from his old-time vigor and oratorical prowess.

By the next spring, however, he was ready to follow his doctor's advice and go to New Mexico and Colorado. When he got there, he bought a pony and equipment for sleeping outdoors the whole summer long. He returned in the fall, somewhat improved. A year later, I entered the University of Indiana. By the following spring, father's condition demanded surgery. It was then discovered that tubercular germs had invaded his bone marrow. Death came in 1899 as a relief to him and to Mother, though she never felt that way about it. She alone nursed him. In a letter to my sister Bertha (then Mrs. Fenwick Fraser of Crookston, Minnesota) he wrote in part:

My darling daughter:

That we have all neglected you " 'tis true, and pity 'tis, 'tis true." Last week the girls were attending Teachers Institute, and this week they have gone to Bloomington. This leaves all the work on your mamma's hands.

I require a great deal of help. She has to dress and undress me, dress the wounds on my back, my knee and hand, and do a hundred other things for me both night and day. Very much has been said about my patience, but as a matter of fact it cannot compare with hers. She never complains. She works all day and rests on a couch by my bed at night, and on the slightest complaint or movement on my part, she is on her feet. If there shall be any special reward in heaven for patience and self abnegation she will get the highest. . . .

> Lovingly,
> Geo W. Cooper

Father was buried on Thanksgiving Day. The local paper said it was "the largest attended funeral" the little city of Columbus ever saw. His prolonged illness had driven the musical muse out of me. I earnestly wanted to be a newspaperman. The letter he wrote to John Holliday, to which I previously have referred, had opened the door of opportunity.

Wanting to make a home for me in Indianapolis, where I worked, Mother moved there and, during the next five years, she kept fading away with inoperable cancer. Her happiness was in my work. Every evening, I brought her a paper with my stories marked. When I got a by-line, I honestly believed her joy was greater than mine. She would say: "If only your father were here to see what you have done!" It was all truly great to her, but of no concern to others. She died Christmas Eve, 1904.

Kent Cooper (1958).

Some twenty-five years after Father died, and twenty years after Mother followed him, I became the executive head of The Associated Press. In contemplation then I thought of Mother's statement: "If only your father were here. . . ." and I said to myself, "If only Father and Mother were here . . . !"

More than anything I wanted them to know the goal reached by the boy who, Father so truthfully said, needed a "blind bridle" to keep him at his studies, and the same boy whose mother worried that he would be nothing more than the "town fiddler." I wanted them to know because it was those two who gave me what I needed to reach the position I attained.

That was the heritage they left me. And it was my appreciation of and love for them that gave me the urge to accomplish. I hope those who may appreciate what I did for The Associated Press will feel that my heritage served me well.

New York—1958

INDEX